T0210974

AI AND COMMON SENSE

Common sense is the endless frontier in the development of artificial intelligence, but what exactly is common sense, can we replicate it in algorithmic form, and if we can – should we?

Bauer, Schiele and their contributors from a range of disciplines analyse the nature of common sense, and the consequent challenges of incorporating into artificial intelligence models. They look at different ways we might understand common sense and which of these ways are simulated within computer algorithms. These include sensory integration, self-evident truths, rhetorical common places, and mutuality and intentionality of actors within a moral community. How far are these possible features within and of machines? Approaching from a range of perspectives including Sociology, Political Science, Media and Culture, Psychology and Computer Science, the contributors lay out key questions, practical challenges and "common sense" concerns underlying the incorporation of common sense within machine learning algorithms for simulating intelligence, socialising robots, self-driving vehicles, personnel selection, reading, automatic text analysis, and text production.

A valuable resource for students and scholars of Science–Technology–Society Studies, Sociologists, Psychologists, Media and Culture Studies, human–computer interaction with an interest in the post-human, and programmers tackling the contextual questions of machine learning.

Martin W. Bauer is Professor of Social Psychology and Research Methodology at the London School of Economics and Political Science (LSE). He investigates "common sense" in relation to science and emerging technologies in the international MACAS (Mapping the Cultural Authority of Science) network. He is a Fellow of the German National Academy of

Technical Sciences (acatech). Recent publications include *The Psychology of Social Influence: Modes and Modalities of Shifting Common Sense* (2021, with Gordon Sammut); *Atom, Bytes & Genes: Public Resistance and Techno-scientific Responses* (2015).

Bernard Schiele (PhD) is a Professor of Communications in the Faculty of Communication at the University of Québec at Montréal (Canada). He has been working for a number of years on the socio-dissemination of S&T. Among other books he has recently published are *Science Communication Today* (2015, with Joëlle Le Marec and Patrick Baranger); *Communicating Science, A Global Perspective* (2020 with Toss Gascoigne and colleagues); *Science Culture in a Diverse World: Knowing, Sharing, Caring* (2021, with Xuan Liu and Martin Bauer); *Le musée dans la société* [*The Museum in Society*] (2021), and *Science Communication: Taking a Step Back to Move Forward* (2023, with Martin Bauer).

Routledge Studies in Science, Technology and Society

AI AND COMMON SENSE

Ambitions and Frictions

Edited by Martin W. Bauer and Bernard Schiele

Routledge
Taylor & Francis Group

LONDON AND NEW YORK

Designed cover image: ©Getty Images

First published 2024
by Routledge
4 Park Square, Milton Park, Abingdon, Oxon OX14 4RN

and by Routledge
605 Third Avenue, New York, NY 10158

Routledge is an imprint of the Taylor & Francis Group, an informa business

British Library Cataloguing-in-Publication Data
A catalogue record for this book is available from the British Library

Library of Congress Cataloging-in-Publication Data
Names: Bauer, Martin W., editor. | Schiele, Bernard, editor.
Title: AI and common sense: ambitions and frictions /
edited by Martin W. Bauer and Bernard Schiele.
Other titles: Artificial intelligence and common sense
Description: Abingdon, Oxon; New York, NY: Routledge, 2024. |
Series: Routledge studies in science, technology and society |
Includes bibliographical references and index.
Identifiers: LCCN 2024004049 (print) | LCCN 2024004050 (ebook) |
ISBN 9781032626185 (hardback) | ISBN 9781032626178 (paperback) |
ISBN 9781032626192 (ebook)
Subjects: LCSH: Commonsense reasoning. | Artificial intelligence
Classification: LCC Q338.85 .A33 2024 (print) | LCC Q338.85 (ebook) |
DDC 006.3–dc23/eng/20240223
LC record available at https://lccn.loc.gov/2024004049
LC ebook record available at https://lccn.loc.gov/2024004050

ISBN: 978-1-032-62618-5 (hbk)
ISBN: 978-1-032-62617-8 (pbk)
ISBN: 978-1-032-62619-2 (ebk)

DOI: 10.4324/9781032626192

Typeset in Sabon
by Deanta Global Publishing Services, Chennai, India

CONTENTS

FIGURES

TABLES

CONTRIBUTORS

Fabian Anicker (PhD) studied Social Sciences at the University of Düsseldorf from 2007 to 2010, obtained a Master's degree in Sociology at the University of Edinburgh in 2011 and subsequently completed a PhD at HHU Düsseldorf with a thesis on communicative rationality and deliberative democracy from a sociological perspective in 2019. From 2015 to 2022, he worked as an editor of the German Social Theory Journal *Zeitschrift für Theoretische Soziologie*. Since October 2022 he has been working as a research assistant at HHU Düsseldorf on the project "Opinion Monitor Artificial Intelligence" [MeMo:KI]. His research interests include AI, sociological theory and political sociology.

Adrian Bangerter is Professor of Work Psychology at the University of Neuchâtel, Switzerland. His research interests include coordination processes in conversation (e.g., grounding, joint commitment, storytelling), gesture and language, interactions between recruiters and applicants in personnel selection, great ape social interactions and cultural transmission of knowledge and popular beliefs, especially conspiracy theories.

Laura Bartlett is a postdoctoral researcher at the Centre for Philosophy of Natural & Social Science, London School of Economics. She is working on the Genetically Evolving Models in Science (GEMS) project run by Professor Fernand Gobet. She completed her PhD in 2019, investigating the effects of attention on sensory adaptation, supervised by Professor Wendy Adams and Dr Erich Graf at the University of Southampton. Her research interests include visual and haptic adaptation, attention and cognitive modelling.

Ronald J. Brachman is the former Director of the Jacobs Technion-Cornell Institute at Cornell Tech in New York City, where he was also a Professor of Computer Science. During a long career in industry and government, he held leadership positions at Bell Labs, AT&T Labs, Yahoo and DARPA.

Anouk de Jong is a PhD candidate in science communication at the University of Twente, where she studies science–media relationships. Her current research focuses on interactions between scientists and journalists in the creation of news about COVID-19 and artificial intelligence.

Anne M. Dijkstra (PhD) is Assistant Professor in Science Communication at the University of Twente (the Netherlands). She studies the changing relationship between science, technology and society from a communication perspective. Her research focuses on the roles of the public as well as researchers and other stakeholders in this relationship, science communication, responsible research and innovation, and public engagement.

Philippe Fauquet-Alekhine is Scientific Director at INTRA robotics, in charge of international projects addressing training and performance of pilots in operational situations, former Human Factors Consultant & Researcher at Chinon Nuclear Power Plant (Electricité de France). He is a member of the Laboratory for Research in Science of Energy (France, see www.hayka -kultura.org) and of the SEBE-Lab at the London School of Economics & Political Science (UK, see www.SEBE-Lab.net). Doctor in Physics Science (University Pierre & Marie Curie, Paris, France), Work Psychologist (MSc from the Conservatoire des Arts & Métiers, Paris, France) and doctor in Behavioural Psychology (London School of Economics & Political Science, UK), Philippe Fauquet-Alekhine is author of tens of scientific articles and books. He has more than 20 years of experience in work activity analysis and research on human performance in high-risk industries.

Florian Golo Flaßhoff (MA) studied empirical media and communication research as well as global mass communication at the University of Leipzig. After completing his MA, he gained further experience in subscription management for publishers and in consulting companies on the basis of decision psychology. Since 2022, he has been a research associate as the Chair KMW I of the Institute of Social Sciences at Heinrich Heine University Düsseldorf, where he works on the project "Opinion Monitor Artificial Intelligence [MeMo:KI]". His research interests include opinion research, social psychology and AI.

Hector J. Levesque is Professor Emeritus in the Department of Computer Science at the University of Toronto. He is the author of *Common Sense, the Turing Test and the Quest for Real AI* (MIT Press) and other books.

Frank Marcinkowski studied Political Science and Sociology at the University of Duisburg. He completed his PhD and Habilitation in Political Science and held professorial chairs in communication studies at the Universities of Zurich (2003–2007) and Münster (2007–2017). Since 2017, he has been Professor of Political Communication at the Institute of Social Sciences at Heinrich Heine University Düsseldorf. His research interests include political communication, science communication and media theory.

Ivana Marková was born in Czechoslovakia and is now Professor Emeritus in Psychology at the University of Stirling, UK. She has published in the field of epistemology of social psychology, language and communication and has carried out research in political and health psychology. Her latest books include *The Dialogical Mind: Common Sense and Ethics* (CUP, 2016) and *The Making of a Dialogical Theory: Social Representations and Communication* (CUP, 2023). She is a fellow of the British Academy, of the Royal Society of Edinburgh and of the British Psychological Society.

Alexandre Schiele is an affiliate researcher at the Hebrew University of Jerusalem. He holds a PhD in Communication Science (Sorbonne Paris Cité, 2017) and in Political Science (University of Quebec at Montreal, 2018). He pursues his research in two distinct directions but always from a comparative standpoint. On the one hand, he studies science and pseudoscience in the media, and has contributed to the project 'Mapping the new communication landscape in Canada' (2017–2018). On the other hand, he studies contemporary Chinese politics and political discourse. Among his latest publications is *China's Pandemic Response and Its Coverage in the Foreign Press: State Enforced-Pseudoscience and Negative Coverage* (2023).

Ahmet Süerdem is Professor at Istanbul Bilgi University. His research interests include social studies of science, investigating social and cultural trends through text analysis, computational linguistics and artificial intelligence (both studying its influence on society and as a practitioner).

Mikihito Tanaka is Professor at the Graduate School of Political Science, Waseda University, Japan. He earned his PhD in Molecular Biology from the University of Tokyo. He has more than 20 years of experience as a writer and journalist in parallel to his academic career. He researches public arguments about science and risk communication in mass/social media using methods such as science and technology studies and computational social science. He is a founding member of the Science Media Centre of Japan (SMCJ). In 2011, the SMCJ team was highly acclaimed for their service to the public in mediating scientific information during the Fukushima Daiichi nuclear accident. Since February 2020, he has been involved as an expert in the science advisory group for COVID-19 in the Japanese Ministry of Health, Labour and Welfare and the Tokyo Metropolitan Government. He is currently compiling his experiences with COVID-19, along with an analysis of the media data he has collected. He is also deepening the analysis of populist tendencies in science, including topics such as AI and the environment, from the perspective of Japan's uniqueness and international homogeneity.

Chris Tennant (PhD) is Honorary Fellow at UCL's Science and Technology Studies Department and Visiting Fellow at LSE's Department of Psychological and Behavioural Science. Recently, he has participated in a number of research projects on public attitudes towards self-driving vehicles (SDVs) and governance challenges for this technology. His research interests are the interplay between moral values and rational explanation, media representation of contested science, trust and accountability.

Alan F. T. Winfield is Professor of Robot Ethics at the University of the West of England (UWE), Bristol, UK; Visiting Professor at the University of York; and Associate Fellow of the Cambridge Centre for the Future of Intelligence. He received his PhD in Digital Communications from the University of Hull in 1984, then co-founded and led APD Communications Ltd until taking-up appointment at UWE, Bristol, in 1992. Winfield co-founded the Bristol Robotics Laboratory where his research is focused on the science, engineering and ethics of intelligent robots. He is especially interested in robots as working models of life, evolution, intelligence and culture. Alan is passionate about communicating research and ideas in science, engineering and technology; he led UK-wide public engagement project Walking with Robots, awarded the 2010 Royal Academy of Engineering Rooke medal for public promotion of engineering. Until recently he was director of UWE's Science Communication Unit. Alan is frequently called upon by the press and media to comment on developments in AI and robotics; he was a guest on the BBC Radio 4 series The Life Scientific and interviewed for BBC News HARDtalk. Alan has published some 300 works, including *Robotics: A Very Short Introduction* (Oxford University Press, 2012), and blogs at alanwinfield.blogspot.com.

PREFACE

Common sense

'Maßlose Übertreibung!' sprach das Fensterglas, nachdem das Mikroskop seine Beobachtungen mitgeteilt hatte.

Und die Seuche wütete weiter.

'Massive exaggeration!' declared the stained glass window, after the microscope had made available its observations.

And the plague raged on.

[Günther Anders, a fable 1955/2022]

ACKNOWLEDGEMENTS

This book publication arises from what in academic life has become a luxury: some of us formed an informal discussion group, with the slimmest of funding, and entirely outside the academic assessment cycle, in the UK defined by the excruciating trireme of REF, TEF & KEF (Research Excellence Framework; Teaching Excellence Framework; Knowledge Engagement Framework). This all puts a massive tax on unusual academic relevance structures.

It started in May 2013 with a brainstorming and concretised in a first workshop in London a year later scoping the issues of "Reconsidering Common Sense" (RICOS): seed funding from the LSE Research Committee. In the coming years, we moved to even nicer locations and paired various topics with Common Sense for discussions of usually two days. Places included Neuchâtel (2014, on neuroscience and the brain), Lyon (2015, on the body and health), Amiens (2016, on politics), London (2016, on rhetoric including music) and Lisbon (2016, on techno-science) and resuming after the pandemic in Nancy (2022, on artificial intelligence). Thanks go to all the colleagues who invited and organised these locations and kept the train moving.

Though a few are involved in this last project, many more people travelled with RICOS over the years and left their mark: Ivana Marková, Sandra Jovchelovitch and Chris Tennant (all LSE) were there from the start. The various topics recruited Alain Pottage (Paris), Adrian Bangerter (Neuchatel), Jorge Correia Jesuino (Lisbon), Joao A. Nunes (Coimbra), Klaus Gaertner (Lisbon), Paula Castro (Lisbon), Jose Pinto (Lisbon), Helene Joffe (UCL), Bradley Franks (LSE), Nikos Kalampalikis (Lyon), Petra Pansegrau (Bielefeld), Frederic Fruteau De Laclos (Paris), Cliodhna O'Connor (Dublin),

Roberto Franzosi (Emery), Chiara Ambrosio (UCL), Sybille Krämer (Berlin), Cliff Ando (Chicago), Richard Beaudoin (Harvard), Bankole Falade (LSE & Stellenbosch), "Eric" Xiang LI (Beijing), Lucy Baugnet (Amiens), Thierry Guibert (Amiens), Maxime Amblard (Nancy) and Alain Dutech (Nancy). These colleagues represented linguistics, psychology, law, sociology, philosophy, political science and computer science; some stayed in touch, others kept to a one-off contribution.

The idea of a RICOS book was in the air, waiting for the right topic and the perfect moment. An opportunity finally arose at Université de Lorraine: an international conference "Science & You 2021" was to be held in November 2021 in Metz, right after the pandemic as it turned out. Bauer and Schiele, members of the scientific committee of "Science & You", secured the idea of a pre-conference seminar on "AI and common sense" which would then inspire the larger event. However, because of the pandemic, the supposed impulse became an afterthought. We are grateful to Julie Adam and Nicolas Beck of "Science & You" who made this possible. In Nancy (May 2022) we reviewed these chapters in a first draft and agreed to meet again in Neuchâtel a year later (May 2023) invited by Adrian Bangerter. We reviewed and revised all chapters once more over wining and dining, and the final result is presented here for the Routledge Studies of Science, Technology and Society.

Over to you reader, reconsidering common sense!

Martin W. Bauer (London)
Bernard Schiele (Montreal)
September 2023

Introductory comment

WHEN ARTIFICIAL INTELLIGENCE MEETS COMMON SENSE, FRICTIONS WILL ARISE

Martin W. Bauer and Bernard Schiele

Artificial intelligence (AI) seems the latest frontier of science and engineering, a space opened up, a wild territory and land of opportunity where civilisation is suspended; heroes rise; investment flows copiously; rules are ignored and new rules are forged. The machine 'computer' emerged in the Second World War and was formalised in Alan Turing's vision of machine intelligence that is no longer distinguishable from its human version, which was to be certified by the so-called Turing benchmark test.

This enthusiasm for algorithms might be mediaeval in origin (Groner et al., 1983), but since the 1950s it materialised as artificial intelligence (AI) in several hype cycles of public attention and generous research funding. Thus, we are since 2015 in the 'third spring' of AI, after a brief hike around 2000 (Y2K), a second surge during the 1980s and the initial take-off in the 1950s (Süerdem, 2023). Clearly, in the past few years COVID-19 eclipsed AI, but now, as the pandemic is nearly forgotten, AI has regained the centre stage with much steam and massive public attention. Thus, AI is one of five strands of computerisation movements (Kling & Iacono, 1988) that mobilise resources and enthusiasm for the digitalisation of sciety. To emulate humans, common sense is part of this history since McCarthy and Minsky's "programme with common sense" of the late 1950s. This ambition remains a key challenge with few accomplishments (Brachman & Levesque, 2022, and Chapter 3 this volume).

The engineering endeavour has since bifurcated into tool AI for specific purposes, so-called "expert systems", and into general-purpose artificial intelligence (GAI; (sometimes also AGI, artificial general intelligence)); and GAI

DOI: 10.4324/9781032626192-2

would be a method that is applicable to all problem types and works efficiently for large and difficult instances while making very few assumptions. That is the ultimate goal of AI: a system that needs no problem-specific engineering and can simply be tasked to teach a molecular biology class or run a government.

(Russell, 2019, p. 46)

No such GAI system yet exists. Progress in AI is mainly coming from tools that focus on particular tasks for which humans are competent, and AI matches or exceeds that human expertise by being faster and/or more accurate, as for example in diagnosing medical X-ray images (Coppola et al., 2021). This task-specific effectiveness also shows in machine-against-human-competitions on board games like chess or Go, where computers spectacularly beat the world-best players. However, a limit of tool AI is its domain specificity. A chess computer is hopeless at Go; and a machine that reads pulmonary X-rays does badly at diagnosing heart issues; or a text robot such as ChatGPT is exceedingly good at persuasive text production but no good at all at car production on an assembly line.

General-purpose AI would emulate human action in all its capacity, maximise effectiveness to a given goal, and even being able to adjust goals, learn new ways, and be self-reproducing and self-regulating with autonomy modelled on the human original. The problem is how to define the conditions of possibility for such capabilities and to specify these for implementation. Another problem might be to limit the means to given targets, i.e., to contain GAI within moral boundaries. Unless inhibited, an efficient pizza delivery robot might well learn how to optimise delivery by killing some people on the way; it would be effective but "human incompatible" pizza delivery; not to speak of what such disinhibited GAI weapon systems would do (Russell, 2019). Thus, GAI is neither good nor bad, but might just be indifferent to human dignity.

One direction of design envisages robots that combine many AI tools for sensory, processing and motility functions (i.e., architectures); but it seems that this does still not make for GAI, only expert systems for multiple domains. Similarly in athletics, where the combination of training enhances triathlon, pentathlon or even decathlon competitors, but does not come up with the all competent superhumans. These multifunctional architectures remain "brittle"; they are easily overwhelmed and become error-prone by rare or novel situations. An alternative endeavour is pointing towards "common sense" (see Part 2, this volume): to construct machines that are capable of and display robust common sense in the way humans live and experience mundane, co-operative everyday lives. Everyday life is full of complex, unspecified, unforeseen and even unforeseeable surprise situations where routines break down and "practical wit", "wisdom" and "collaborative virtues" are required for muddling through and averting disaster.

The point of this book is to examine the claim made by the proposition "AI with CS", where common sense is to be an adverbial attribute of machine intelligence: doing things common-sensically. If CS is an attribute of AI functions, we must consider CS as a variable X, and clarify the set of values {X ~ CS} which that variable can take. There are different concepts of CS to consider, i.e., the set {X ~ CS}. An operational definition takes the form "this machine is capable of X; X ~ CS". One then must avoid the nothing-but-ness fallacy of circular logic: if AI does X~CS, then CS is nothing but X. We must recognise that the set {X ~ CS} has more than one possible values for X.

The present book thus aims at cultivating a critical attitude towards claims making: how can we understand the claim "AI with CS"; why do we doubt this claim; on what evidence could the claim be credible; what else might we expect from CS; and could we trust a tool based on partial CS? And furthermore, since 13 November 2023, the British Government has a Minister without Portfolio, called the "Minister for Common Sense". We must ask: what is expected from such a ministry? (LBC news, https://www.lbc.co.uk /news/rishi-sunak-brings-in-esther-mcvey-as-minister-for-common-sense/). "Government with CS" is a claim similar to "AI with CS"; we must examine the values X can take {X ~ CS} to make this proposition meaningful. Some values might make for uncommon nonsense.

In this book, not all nuances and theories of "common sense" will be covered. This would require a volume of its own, as indeed there are such volumes readily available in Van Holthoon and Olson (1987) and Gautier and Laugier (2009), which are penetrating historical and conceptual reviews, or with specific angles of political history (Rosenfeld, 2011), of the Aristotelian notion (Gregoric, 2007), or uncovering the hidden roots of Critical Psychology (Billig, 2008) and others more. Our present volume scans this territory of diverse meanings; our map builds around three milestones of understanding CS – following Aristotle, Scottish Enlightenment and Giambattista Vico – and highlights some current developments from these historical prototypes. The point here is not to be comprehensive, but to recognise these notions across various applications of AI and its public discourse and to define values that could enter the claim "AI with X", {X ~ CS}. This allows for a critical assessment and to mind the role of CS for a new technology that craves public acceptance in society.

AI is a technical field that races ahead with much hype and noise; we offer some reflections. The purpose is not to review the state of the art of knowledge representation, neural networks, deep learning, LLM, chatbots, robots nor GAI, but to clarify the reference to "CS" as invoked in these contexts.

We clarify what CS brings and might bring to this development. CS is clearly a challenge for AI, and AI is a challenge for CS. However, we must avoid the temptation of a circular logic of defining operationally an otherwise opaque CS: if AI does CS, CS is what AI does. Is that really so?

The word "common sense" – dictionary denotation and translations

The Collins English dictionary (accessed online, 17 September 2023) defines "your common sense is your natural ability to make good judgments and to behave in a practical and sensible way". It gives examples of word usage such as "use your common sense", "she always had a lot of common sense" and " a common-sense approach". As an adjective, "commonsensical" refers to being "inspired by or displaying sound practical sense". Synonyms are given as *good sense, wit, wisdom, sound judgement, level headedness and practicality*. Common antonyms are *stupidity, impracticality, ineptness, foolishness, insanity, irrationality or unreasonableness*.

The frequency of the word use varies over time. The historical trends of English usage show that 'common sense' emerges in the second half of the 18th century, shows increasing usage into the 19th century and stays at a higher level ever since with some fluctuations: a dip in the late 19th century, a rise into the first half of the 20th century and after the 1920s another dip into the 1970s and rising again ever since. These temporal variations might be an interesting cultural indicator for time periods when CS is in or out of public discourse, but this cannot be our present focus.

In his "Studies of Words", Lewis (1960) distinguishes four different usages: (1) "Common sense" refers to a common faculty among humans describing the "elementary mental outfit of a normal man" (p. 146). Distinct from this is (2) the idea of a social virtue; it is a quality including courtesy and fellow-feelings that one acquires in interaction with other human beings. This is a secondary gain of public schooling, as opposed to private homeschooling, where children acquire a sense of community in intercourse with their peers. (3) CS also refers to the common experience humans are going through, their pains and pleasures, emotions of gains and loss, birth and death, the comical and what therefore is praiseworthy. These make for the common places public speakers can universally appeal to. Finally (4) "common sense" is a technical term of ancient and mediaeval psychology, referring to internal senses such as memory, imagination and common wit; the latter is the arbiter of the others (p. 147). The CS turns disparate and punctual sensations into coherent experience, what later became "apperception" and sensory integration. These usages of the word thus reflect the three prototypical theories of CS (Bauer, Chapter 1 this volume).

Lewis also points out that the attribute "common" attracts ambivalent connotations: "common" means ordinary or vulgar on the one hand. In the UK, one continues to speak of the House of Commons as the "Lower" as opposed to the "Upper Chamber", the House of Lords. The prestige hierarchy between the aristocracy and the common man or woman is preserved in the names, though the actual constitutional power is reversed. Alternatively, "common" refers to belonging to humanity at large, widely accessible, ubiquitous and indeed being the universal human norm, even the voice of Nature by which we discern good from evil as in natural justice or the natural law traditions (p. 150). Famously, Antigone dismissed Creon's order on the basis of a universal common sense; she buried her brother against the constructed law of Creon (Steiner, 2003). Thus, the word 'common sense' is used both disparagingly and at the time highlighting a universal potential, the lack of which would be an imbecility or even pathological. This ambivalence is more or less easily translated into different languages. Many languages here use different words, as for example in French or Danish, "sens commun" or "snusfornuft" for the negative and "le bon "sense" or "sund fornuft" for the positive meaning.

Preview of the book

Let us close these introductory comments with a short overview of the book, which is divided into four parts, flanked by an introduction and conclusion.

The first part sets the scene in two steps: Bauer seeks to clarify different meanings of "common sense" derived from three prototypes. How shall we understand this notion, considering some of its history? Schiele and Schiele review the historical developments of AI and some of the discussions this has stirred, e.g., over automation and rationality; they unfold several contradictions in this development, which they call the paradoxes of AI.

The second part gives voice to four AI engineers. Brachman and Levesque make their plea for a future of AI with at least some common sense, for it to have a future at all. Fauquet-Alekhine wonders how human–robot interactions work out, not least in emergency situations, and examines what difference common sense would make, thus calling for more public debate. Winfield reports on his interacting robots with common-sense features on an escalating scale from socially coordinated movement to telling each other stories. Finally, Bartlett reviews the progress of cognitive science to emulate human learning in computer simulations; different design concepts lead to various dead ends and she asks: do we really need to simulate common sense? The point of this section is to document the normalisation of technical capabilities of symbolic computing, human–robot interaction, interacting robots and cognitive simulation. But as social interaction seems to be the sticky point, these are ego-centric perspectives: AI and robots remain socially challenged on a spectrum of "machine autism".

In Part 3, the focus is on the anchoring of AI in public discourse. Five chapters show how "common sense" is part of the debate about AI and what functions this reference plays. Discourse cultivates the inter-subjective, assimilating common sense as it arises from human play with and talk about AI. Marková reviews the contribution of Gambattista Vico's to our understanding of language and the dialogicality of common sense that orients human action as a source of ethics. Schiele and Schiele reflect on the difficulties of AI to be social and they engage the historical argument of an epistemic continuity between techno-science and common sense. Marcinkowski and Flaßhoff report on the current debate in Germany. Regular monitoring of mass media and public perceptions captures the emergent "common wisdom" on AI and its political function. This is usefully distinguished from references to "common sense", which has the potential to disrupt the illusory consensus. De Jong and Dijkstra report on the debate in the Netherlands, where AI, briefly interrupted by the pandemic 2020/21, is variously framed, and they map the explicit associations with 'common sense' that are part of this conversation. Finally, Tanaka takes us to Japan where AI is entangled in techno-animism; he shows how this debate with Japanese characteristics engages deliberations, and invokes and develops common sense.

Part 4 explores the potential accommodation of AI in inter-objectivity and recalcitrant common sense through four different AI uses. The proof of the pudding is in the eating; engineers are good at making things, but often do not know what they are doing, as the saying goes. Technology manifests foremost in its use. Anicker and Flaßhoff examine the attribution of authorship to text-composing robots like ChatGPT. They report experiments which explore types and the degree of agency that users attribute to these chatbots. Not all types of agency are morally consequential, some are ironic and are coping strategies. Süerdem hails the many ways computer-assisted text mining makes progress and assists researchers in the analysis of public discourse; the methodologists have much to celebrate. However, he warns of a potential confusion between "text processing" and "reading"; only the latter is hermeneutically embodied and can lead to suspicious or inspirational readings that instigate a revolutionary fervour challenging the status quo of society; what is praised as a 'revolution' might in fact turn out to be the opposite. Bangerter examines the push of AI tools into job recruitment. For quite some time already, scientific management has been replacing common sense by scientific judgements on who fits the job based on psychometric testing and profiling, and AI extends this effort. However, recruitment practitioners and those being recruited push back against "machine judgement", and possibly for good reasons: the hype runs far ahead of the evidence of meritocratic effectiveness. Tennant examines promises and prospects of self-driving vehicles (SDVs) that emulate the task of driving on open streets and thus negotiate a social situation. Three problems arise: reducing the traffic complexity to allow machines to operate, responsibility attribution in accident events, and public trust and uptake of SDVs. The dual function of CS, to predict the future and to account for past actions, is increasingly colonised by technical systems; how far will this de-facto be tolerated even if the regulation goes along?

The conclusion by Schiele and Bauer proposes a final reflection going beyond the utilitarian and ahistorical conception of common sense largely dominant in AI today. They raise the paradox that is resolved by the time dimension of fast, slow, and very slow changes: common sense is self-evident precisely because its transformations in time create schemes which impose themselves as self-evident reasoning; slow lane structures secure the shifting paradigms which guarantee what is unquestionably obvious. One must ask, at which level does 'AI with common sense' operate?

Bibliography

Anders, G. (2022). Der Blick vom Turm - Fabeln, C. H. Beck Paperback.

Billig, M. (2008). *The hidden roots of critical psychology.* SAGE.

Brachman, R. J., & Levesque, H. J. (2022). *Machines like us – Towards AI with common sense.* MIT Press.

Coppola, F. (2021). Human, all too human? An all-around appraisal of the 'AI revolution' in medical imaging. *Frontiers of in Psychology, 12;* 710982.doi: 10.3389/fpsyg.2021.710982

Gautier, C., & Laugier, S. (Eds.). (2009). *Normativites du sens commun.* PUF.

Gregoric, P. (2007). *Aristotle on the common sense.* Oxford University Press.

Groner, M., Groner, R., & Bischof, W. F. (1983). Approaches to heuristics – A historical review. In R. Groner, M. Groner, & W. F. Bischof (Eds.), *Methods of heuristics* (pp. 1–18). Routledge.

Kling, R., & Iacono, I. (1998). The mobilisation of support for computerisation: The role of computerisation movements. *Social Problems, 25,* 226–243.

Lewis, C. S. (1960). *Studies of words.* Cambridge University Press.

Rosenfeld, S. (2011). *Common sense: A political history.* Harvard University Press.

Russell, S. (2019). *Human compatible: AI and the problem of control.* Penguin.

Steiner, G. (2003). *Antigones - The Antigone myth in Western literature, art and thought.* Oxford University Press.

Süerdem, A. (2023). Hype cycles in AI: Broken promises, empty threats. In M. W. Bauer & B. Schiele (Eds.), *Science communication: Taking a step back to move forward* (pp. 182–193). CNRS.

Van Holthoon, F., & Olson, D. R. (Eds.). (1987). *Common sense – The foundations for social science; sources in semiotics, volume VI* (series editors J. Deely and B. Williams). University Press of America.

PART 1

The scene and the argument of common sense

What is common sense, and how did AI enter the debate so far?

1

AI WITH COMMON SENSE

What concept of common sense?

Martin W. Bauer

The theme *AI and Common Sense* (CS) has been in evidence from the very beginning. The pioneer of artificial intelligence (AI), John McCarthy, wrote a paper (1958) famously entitled "Programs with Common Sense". Together with Marvin Minsky, he had written a computer program called "*Advice Taker*" where they defined

> a program has common sense if it automatically deduces for itself a sufficiently wide class of immediate consequences of anything it is told and what it already knows.
>
> *(p. 78)*

Common sense (CS) here means "to draw inferences", i.e., to have the capacity to deduce conclusions from what is already known (memory stock) and from information given (input flow). CS retains a constant presence in the AI debates ever since, it bothers the protagonists and constitutes a challenge for the field. CS creates frictions and is a source of resistance in this development. For some, who focus on developing expert systems, CS is irrelevant because experts are by definition beyond CS; for others, systems with CS are the last frontier to conquer and to complete our technological civilisation. However, we must rely on more competent commentators to tell this history of the encounter of AI and CS (e.g., Brachman & Levesque, 2022); some of it will surface in these chapters.

In the present chapter, I will point to several different ways in which we might understand "common sense" (CS). By clarifying various uses of the notion of "common sense", we seek to build a critical attitude and to ask the

DOI: 10.4324/9781032626192-4

TABLE 1.1 Different kinds of "common sense" to be explored

Kinds of common sense
1   CS-1 solves the "binding problem", i.e., integration of multi-modal sensory experiences
2   CS-2 is a stock of universally recognisable knowledge to reason from
3   CS-3 is the quasi-rational judgement call; neither pure intuition nor formally rational
4   CS-4 marks the philosophy that in a moment of crisis stays clear of the errors of scepticism and dogmatism, by siding with lay people against elites
5   CS-5 is the communal sensitivity that binds us into joint attention and intentionality
6   CS-6 is what social psychology is all about (at least for some social psychologists)
7   CS-7 is what you can appeal to in order to bring fighting parties to their senses when they go off the rails in excessive polarisation
8   CS-8 is what AI aims to simulate; therefore CS is what AI can do
9   ?????? (still to be recognised ...)

question: what do we possibly mean when the talk is of "AI with CS"? We sharpen our understanding by being aware of different concepts as shown in Table 1.1 (CS-1 to CS-k) which are mobilised for, or which are being left out from embodiment as AI. We will be able to clarify claims "AI with CS", by pointing to different concepts of common sense that are invoked: "AI with CS-1", or "AI with CS-2", or "AI has not/unlikely CS-k", etc. The "common sense" of AI is thus better defined. While operationalising and thus objectifying our understanding of CS might bring clarity, this comes at the cost of reification, of limiting our understanding of CS by way of a technology standard. Thus, we seek to rescue the notion of "common sense" from the fate of reduction and the fallacy of nothing-but-ness: i.e., CS is nothing-but-what-"AI-with-CS"-defines-it-to-be.

In the first approach, CS compares with expert, specialist, evidential and deductively derived knowledge

Waldenfels (1982) reconstructs the genealogy of the perennial denigration of common sense in terms of the juxtapositions of Doxa versus Episteme, the mere opinion against robust knowledge. In rehearsing this history of distinctions and cognitive hierarchies, CS falls at the bottom as mere Doxa. In the European context, this history of disqualification traces back to Greek philosophy that distinguishes appearances from reality and sides mostly with Platonic against Sophist arguments. For the Sophists, there is only Doxa as a matter of social conventions. While for Plato, Doxa is similar to appearances that are not recognised as such, i.e., the perceptions of projected shadows that present themselves to those ignorants who are "shackled in the cave", and never had the privilege to leave the cave and see the world in the true light of the sun. Doxa takes on the meaning of distorted cognition under poor conditions (see Heidegger, 2002; on Plato's cave allegory in the "Republic" and on Doxa in "Theaetetus"). In modern parlance, this problem of demarcating a distorted Doxa from the dignified Episteme comes in three ways:

a) There is an "epistemological rupture". CS and science are very different; CS is deficient and misleading cognition. Science is counter-intuitive and avoids the pitfalls of natural language by applying rigorously quantitative concepts and methods. Science accumulates the evidence that arises from this effort which must ultimately replace CS to make the world a better place (e.g., Wolpert, 1992): where Doxa was there will be and must be Episteme.

b) Alternatively, the continuity hypothesis argues that science is little else than CS, only a bit more elaborate, refined and precise. Empiricism with its ethos of unprejudiced observation, experimental demonstrations, and a deep suspicion of rhetoric, tradition and authority, suggests that science is indeed "purified" CS. Science basically is CS by another name.

There are variations on what "purified" might mean here. Science seems to be an activity that is both rational-deductive and empirical-evidential; it guides human activity with predictions and outlines options for choices. What distinguishes science from CS is that predictions and choices are made systematically, consciously and explicitly, and these are self-corrective through individual and collective learning. Thus, science is systematic CS, but as such nevertheless an extension of CS (e.g., Bronowski, 1951; Hoyningen-Huene, 2008).

In Luckmann's account (1987) science and CS are functionally equivalent for everyday life; we cook either with CS (fire, potatoes, vegetables, meat) or we cook scientifically (energy, carbohydrates, fibres, vitamins, proteins, etc.). However, historical modernisation reduced the reliance on CS and increases the reliance on science in all spheres of life. We read in the lifestyle magazine *"science tells which cat is good for you"* or *"Dutch randomised control trial: take cold showers in the morning to stay healthy"*.

c) Farr (1993), responding to the argument of "unnatural science", argues for a third way, leaving it open whether there is a vertical gap between science and CS. The key is to suspend judgement and to study symmetrically both science and CS as exemplars of "social representation" and to acquire the competence of "cognitive polyphasia", i.e. being able to think and work with both (e.g., Jovchelovitch, 2008; Wagner & Hayes, 2005). The so-orientated social sciences map both CS and science and study their division of labour for clarity, not to eliminate either of them (Bangerter, 1995).

There are analogous ways of considering this symmetry: as "belief systems" (Geertz, 1993), as "language games and ways of life" (Wittgenstein, 1953) or "life provinces" (Ryle, 1954) or in a post-Mertonean sociology of SSK (Lynch, 1993). Lynch famously does not find any differences in acting and account giving inside and outside the laboratory. When people put on the white coat and engage the lab benches, they do not go beyond the doings and thinking involved in any skilled activity. The claim to the contrary is at best a construction ex-post-factum to dignify the scientific life apart from everyday life. This boundary work accumulates favours and privileges, and science thus becomes a superior performance of knowledge.

Science is rooted in everyday concerns, what the phenomenological tradition calls the "natural attitude". Science builds from this attitude and never transcends it. It is the phenomenological method of "bracketing the natural attitude" (epoche) which allows us to recognise the communality between science and common sense, to remain neutral and to engage in comparative analysis. Without the transcendental viewpoint from nowhere (i.e., to seek "true illumination" outside Plato's cave), the epistemic contrast becomes co-production understood by a social psychology of assimilating and accommodating paradigms (mindsets, mentalities, thought styles) under conditions of inter-group competition (thought communities; see Fleck (1979 [1935]; Kuhn (1962); Sammut & Bauer, 2021).

In a second approach, three historical types of common sense

Besides this long tradition of ordering vertically or horizontally, of denigrating "common sense" and cognate concepts such as Doxa, everyday thinking, lay knowledge, and opinions, we must consider the parallel history of unfolding different concepts of "common sense" (Figure 1.1). It appears that the contemporary diversity of CS can be traced back to three historical origins:

- The 6th sense of Aristotle (384–32 BCA) as in "koine aisthesis" (CS-1).
- The Scottish/English enlightenment (18th century) and its concern for everyday reasoning (CS-2, CS-3, CS-4).
- Giambattista Vico's (1668–1744) elaboration of the community of moral sensibilities, being universal and culturally distinct (CS-4, CS-5, CS-6).

A polemical impetus for both the Scots' and Vico's understanding of CS is to stay clear of Descartes' methodology (isolated individualism, mind–body dualism, axiomatic–geometric–deductive rationalism). Aristotle serves as a point of return to current understanding of the integration of perceptual

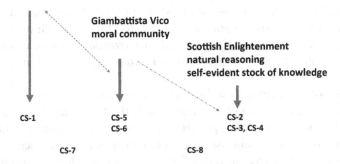

Aristotle
'Koine Aesthesis'
The Common Sense

Giambattista Vico
moral community

Scottish Enlightenment
natural reasoning
self-evident stock of knowledge

CS-1   CS-5   CS-2
                        CS-6   CS-3, CS-4

        CS-7   CS-8

FIGURE 1.1   Three historical types of "common sense" and some contemporary
derivatives.

systems. These historical sources are further elaborated in modern parlance
(CS-3, CS-4, CS-5, CS-6), and we can distinguish at least two uses of CS
as "empty signifiers" (CS-7, CS-8) that can be subversive in effect. All this
makes no claim to be exhaustive, which is why in the summary Table 1.1 a
space is left open to add new kinds.

Overall, we might say that the notion of CS requires two considerations:
(a) where to place CS in a vertical (hierarchy) or a horizontal (continuity) order of reasoning, and (b) a variety of meanings of "common sense"
which derive from three historical types. Exploring eight different concepts
of "common sense" should enable us to critically examine any claim being
made as to CS and AI:

> … Upon coming across propositions like '*AI with CS*' or '*AI is CS*' ⇔ '*CS
> is AI*' …
> We must ask immediately:
> *Which concepts of 'common sense' is invoked?*

Let us start by examining the three historical prototypes: The koine aisthesis of Aristotle, the common stock of knowledge to reason with the Scottish
Enlightenment and the sensus communis, the moral community with a history
of Giambattista Vico. These are traditions with overlaps and historical linkages.

Solving the "binding problem" of sensory integration

> *CS-1 solves the "binding problem", i.e., integration of multi-modal sen-
> sory experiences.*

The first is the oldest meaning, it goes back to the Greek term "koine aisthesis" (common + sensation), better translated as "common sensitivity". In

several essays, Aristotle (4th century BCA, axial times) refers to the "sixth sense", the capacity that brings into concert the five external senses with multi-sensory features such as roughness, shape or magnitude which you can see, hear or touch. The senses are separable only in operational account; they are inseparable in perceptual power. First the heart and later the brain were seen as the organ of this integration (Bennett & Hacker, 2003; p. 16). However, there remain textual difficulties and controversies in reconstructing the key functions marked by his term (see Gregoric, 2007; Hamlyn, 1968).

While the idea of separating senses into the interior (common sense) and the exterior (five senses) has long been abandoned, the "cross-modal binding problem" of sensory integration persists. How do we come from a faint sound (miou, miou), a visual impression of an elegantly moving four-legged shape and a haptic fluffy stroke to recognise a "cat", even before we apply the English word "cat": if it purrs like a cat, walks like a cat, feels like cat … it must be a cat. This remains a serious problem for anybody who builds robots with sensory capacity. The transition from a pattern of sensations to perceiving tokens of kinds remains a philosophical puzzle (Siegel, 2012).

This idea of *The CS*, with a definite article, includes "'inner perception" of *seeing that we see and hear*, the concomitant monitoring, but not observation, of perceptual activity and the retrospective accessibility of mental states in second-order consciousness. Aristotle's psychology of the living organism postulates no subliminal, unconscious mental processes (first-order activity without second-order awareness), but knows of awareness of absent or failed perceptions (second-order awareness without first-order activity). Aristotle thus re-enters modern discussions of conscious, unconscious and neural integration (Gregoric, 2007, 209ff). A popular version of this idea reappears with the higher cognitive function called 'common sense' that integrates different forms of intelligence into practical, interpersonal actions which are intuitive, rapid and surprisingly effective (Gardner, 1983, 288f).

Self-evident knowledge and making good use of it

CS-2 is a stock of universally recognisable knowledge to reason from. A widely used concept of CS (no definite article) refers to everyday reasoning and available knowledge, the stock and the flow of inputs that are processed. This stock of knowledge is self-evident, no need for demonstration logical or otherwise and widely shared and accessible. And to process these items, no expertise beyond being born and primary socialisation is needed because it is part of the human experience anywhere and everywhere. This "mental dictionary" is not bound by any specific language but finds expression in the vernacular. In China, until recently, the school curriculum taught "Changshi" (modern 常识 or traditional 常識): what every young Chinese should know.

This CS is what the Scottish Enlightenment (e.g., Thomas Reid, 1710–1796) intended and what created the tradition of common sense philosophy (GE Moore, 1873–1958): providing a list of pre-reflective beliefs that are beyond doubt; these items are self-evident and do not need to be justified. The ambition is to show that ways of thinking which are inconsistent with these basics are most likely in error (Boulter, 2007). Reid defined "there are certain principles … which the constitution of our nature leads us to believe, and which we are under a necessity to take for granted in the common concerns of life, without being able to give reasons for them … the principle of Common Sense" (cited from Rosenfeld, 2011, p. 72). The polemical purpose is to trust our senses against sceptical detractors (Hume) and without the need for axiomatic rationalism (Descartes) because our senses do betray us only some of the time. A paradox might arise: in listing these items they are no longer taken for granted, their self-evidence is now open to scrutiny: Is the list incomplete or overextended?

Here is where AI research of a certain kinds seems mostly situated, in attempts to upload background knowledge into the machine. The large-scale project *Cyc Common Knowledge Base* (from EnCYClopedia) seeks to capture items in a formal representation across domains and in a cumulative manner since 1985 including ontologies – entities, types, concepts and assertions (Davis & Marcus, 2015). Other forms of AI consider the entire Internet as a freely available text base to teach a machine to parrot text production from large language models (LLMs) such as ChatGPT (Bender et al., 2021). OECD offers a classification of AI systems (OECD, 2022) to map the benefits and regulatory challenges of these developments.

This kind of CS often carries a connotation of acting below capacity in the mode of a "cognitive miser". Many languages offer two words for CS to express this ambivalence. In English the stress might be on "common", in the elitist sense of "pertaining to vulgar people" (House of Commons) in contrast to aristocratic (House of Lords). In French, dubious and widespread "le sens commun" contrasts with the more dignified but uncommon "le bon sens". Other languages make similar distinctions capturing the hierarchy of the elite versus the people.

The community spirit that provides moral and political guidance

CS-5 is the communal sensitivity that binds us into joint attention and intentionality.

CS so far is mainly an individual capacity, though widely distributed. However, CS is also a social phenomenon; the sense of community in mutuality that makes social life possible in the first place. Here the stress is on CS for social integration, the human capacity to orient toward others on mutual common good; i.e., the love and reality of community as a moral programme.

Giambattista Vico (1688–1744) elaborates this concept by renewing rhetoric as a virtuous commitment to truth and eloquence (Pompa, 1975, 27ff). CS is a condition of possibilities that are both universal and historically variable. Universals arise from solving three existential problems: authority (religion), sex and birth (kinship) and death (funerals, afterlife). Historical CS comes and goes with shifting institutions that, in order to solve these tasks, condition our beliefs, attitudes and actions. The "moral community" is not the outcome of abstract reasoning but of joint attention and joint intentionality on common problems. CS offers "judgement without reflection", post-perceptual but pre-reflective reasoning (Schaeffer, 2004) that binds people together in rituals, conventions and traditions [see Markova, Chapter 7, this volume].

The old rhetorical concept here is Doxa: widespread belief, opinion or common ground that can be invoked. No need to spell it out because it is taken-for-granted, but it resonates with arguments to persuasive effect. Doxa is "those opinions ... which are accepted by everyone or by the majority or by the wise ... or by the most notable and reputable of them" (Aristotle, in Barnes, 1984, 167). This CS is bound by the community of speakers and listeners who gather in conversation and dialogue. Classical rhetoric constructs here lists of "common places" (topoi), generic ones that apply always, domain-specific ones or historically variable frames of public opinion.

Historically this CS is vested in religion (re-ligio, binding together), where members cultivate a sense of belonging and identity and take council on how to behave. There seems to be a historical line from the Greek Polis, to later Church Councils and church halls, to modern town hall meetings, theorised as "third places", neither work nor family, where people deliberate, relate to authorities and reach a common understanding on what is important (Gadamer, 1960).

CS becomes reflexive as the historical progress of a society with communicative rationality, in speech acts of deliberation, reasoning and collective sense-making. Habermas (1984 and 2019) elaborates these acts orientated towards a common understanding and examines its historical conditions of possibility, including religious rituals and European medieval conflicts between knowing and believing. What makes this CS reasoning possible is (a) a public sphere that is inclusive among equals, non-violent, self-conscious and argument focused, and that (b) involves participants who are committed to account for validity claims: (i) true about the world, (ii) truthful (sincere) about self and (iii) right in relation to others. This procedural "sensus communis" guarantees dialogical reason over monological rationality; the latter is only oriented towards ego-centric success. By guaranteeing ritual and attitude, quality decisions can be achieved that are more likely to stick (legitimacy). Thus, in procedural CS, facts and values mix and cultivate a counterfactual aspiration, leaving us with a sense that something might be missing.

This procedural CS is further made concrete in "deliberative opinion polling" (Fishkin, 2011). A cross-section of people is invited to examine and deliberate on controversial issues such as "genetically modified crops in the food chain", "genetic screening during pregnancy" or "AI for medical diagnosis". The outcome will be informed public opinion, which is an improvement on randomised on-off polling. It makes for better decisions and adds legitimacy to responsive government.

Let us now look at some derivatives from these three historical prototypes: quasi-rational thinking (CS-3), an expression of epistemic crisis (CS-4) and the object matter of social psychology (CS-6). And we will finally examine two usages of CS as an empty signifier to launch appeals (CS-7 and CS-8) when "times are out of joint in the state of Denmark".

A quasi-rational thinking

CS-3 is the quasi-rational judgment call; neither pure intuition nor formally rational.

Common is a process of casting judgement that falls between intuition on the one hand and formal-deductive rationality on the other (Hammond, 1996). This CS offers a middle-third in a false dilemma: no need to choose between intuition and rationality. The appeal to CS pulls an intuitive decision towards the more explicit pole and a formal judgement is freed to be more intuitive. It is the last stand against the Skylla of "iron cage" expertise and the Charybdis of "mad" intuition, seeking to avoid the pitfalls on either side.

This CS recognises three obstacles to formal rationality, which therefore not universally recommended. First, formal-analytical thinking needs a model, e.g., MAUD, multi-attribute-utility-decisions. If multiple models are available to structure a problem, the choice between such models is not again a formal-analytical choice, but one of "satisfying common sense". Models apply conditionally; at some point one will want to say "this is how far the model gets me, now I have to make up my mind" (ibid., p. 155). Secondly, a formal model might be ready, but data of poor quality or hard to come by. For example, forecasting models can predict the future, but the lack of data is frustrating the effort; it would be nice to model Kondratjev long waves (40–50 years) of economic development with mathematical rigour for the purpose of forecasting, but the fact of only five cycles since 1750 is insufficient data to fit any such model. Finally, there are situations for which no model is specified; these are called ill or unstructured problems, e.g., pure uncertainty over future trends.

Furthermore, formal statistical models are only accessible to trained experts who know how to handle them. A theory of expert reasoning excludes the majority of stakeholding humans from participating; at worst, experts disenfranchise lay people from making decisions justified by a technocratic mentality.

By contrast, intuition is universal and always at hand. Under time pressure, in confusing circumstances and with information overload when formal models are not readily applied, intuition is indicated. Time and resources permitting, intuition is, however, often displaced by questions such as "why", "how do you know" or "what makes you say that". Answers to deflect these challenges often resort to anatomical metaphors: my heart tells me, it is my gut feeling ... etc. But when pressed, intuitions might not carry the argument among rational people. However, as formalisms equally are limited (no conditions, no data, no model), the middle way of CS is called for to cast a judgement (ibid., p. 158).

Then there is the dilemma between robustness and precision or between reliability and validity in making decisions which again supports CS. Intuition brings robustness within large variation (being on target with a wide scatter), analysis brings precision but can be massively in error (being off-target with small variation, biased). Intuition can be valid with low reliability; while formal analysis is highly reliable with no validity. This is well known in text-analytical methodology: interpretative methods make a lot of sense, but suffer from inter-reader reliability; semi-automatic text coding is highly reliable, but can be massively biased and hard to make sense of. What happens, now that automatic text classification becomes the procedural norm, reliability is conflated with validity and the dilemma is formalised out of sight and out of mind (see Suerdem, Chapter 13 this volume).

CS is thus the way to decide under pressures of time and resources and uncertainty. Quasi-rationality opens up a continuum of "imperfect reasoning" or bounded rationality (with a history of psychologists such as Brunswick, Heider, Simon, Gigerenzer, Kruglanski). This compromise of "supported intuition" is recommended if not already the dominant mode of thinking in many walks of life, e.g. in policy making and court rooms where civil servants strike a balance between rule following and specific contexts to achieve reason and justice (ibid, p. 176). This middle way tradition of compromise is polemically juxtaposed against a paradigm that tests real-life decisions against formal models and typifies the deviances as biases or heuristics of "irrationality" (psychophysics of utility, slows and fast processing). In applied economics, this becomes the stuff of Nobel Prizes (Kahneman & Tversky, received the Nobel Prize 2002; Thaler received the Nobel Prize 2017). Predicting "how CS sense gets it all wrong" can make you famous and can make you rich by exploiting human weaknesses in the choice-preserving-decision-architectures of "nudging" (getting you to do something) and "booming" (keeping you on track) on the cheap because you can avoid expensive incentives on the one hand and costly regulations on the other.

An index of epistemic crisis and of a specific historical period

CS-4 marks the philosophy that in a moment of crisis stays clear of the errors of scepticism and dogmatism, by siding with lay people against elites.

CS often refers to a particular period of European philosophy, mainly British enlightenment (18th century) associated with writers such as Thomas Reid (1710–1796) in Scotland and the Earl of Shaftesbury (1671–1713) in England (see Rosenfeld, 2011). Motivated by moral concerns, they elaborated an epistemological position that steers a middle way between scepticism – nothing can be known with certainty (Hume) – and the dogmatic rationalism (Descartes) built from one initial certainty "I think, therefore I am" (cogito ergo sum), because our senses cannot be trusted. This CS philosophy found reception into German Enlightenment (Kuehn, 1980; Gadamer, 1960), and remains influential in modern philosophy of natural language (Ryle, 1954) and in the "English character": one of gentle common sense against highflying distractions from the continent (Burke & Pallares-Burke, 2016).

CS in this sense might have little significance beyond elucidating an episode of conflict and strive in the history of philosophy. However, modelled on this episode, references to CS can henceforth be read more generally as expressions of an epistemic crisis, when people are disoriented by authoritarian coercion, on the one hand, and excessive solidarity and tribal identity politics, on the other (Lindenberg, 1987). People refer to CS when something important seems already to be lost. Modern science, a modern policy authority, displaces CS and aggravates this problem by removing the ground from which to launch this appeal (Luebbe, 1987).

Though recent reading has discovered here the sources of a "critical psychology" for the 21st century (Billig, 2008). By harking back to this tradition of reasoning, it reconstructs the roots of a psychology that is a-priori social in nature, avoids mentalism as strongly as it avoids behaviourism, and recognises the significance of language and rhetoric in the formation of orienting attitudes in cognition, judgement and inclination.

The "dynamic object" of a truly social psychology

CS-6 is what social psychology is all about (at least for some psychologists).

CS is the very object matter of social psychology. For Smedslund's programme of critical research (1997), it is the task of social psychology to clarify the concepts of human behaviour that are already embedded in ordinary language before any real scientific progress can be achieved. Psychological common sense is embedded in vernacular languages. What social psychology often proposes as "theory" is often revealed as "platitudes" of a language-in-use that are otherwise invisible. This is exemplified with Bandura's widely accepted theory of self-efficacy (Smedslund, 1978); what is claimed to be empirical observations are the psycho-logical implications of assumptions ready-made in ordinary English language use. The resonance of a theory in this common sense might even be an explanation for its wide success and plausibility.

Correia Jesuino (2011) thus argues for a societal psychology with focus on common sense. This is the mark of the European tradition set against the overgeneralisation of an US dominated model of individualist social psychology. CS is the very object matter of societal psychology; experience and behaviour are understood within the "social representation" framework, i.e., the acts and values which are identified and encouraged within the taken-for-granted matrix of a social group. This manifests itself in intergroup tensions and conflicts based on hetero- and auto-stereotyping and confirmation biases in the information processing: East against West, North against South, nation against nation, milieu on milieu, tribe on tribe, gang on gang, and corporations in competition.

These structures of acts, experiences, sense-making and explanations are historically dynamic and develop through social influence. When challenged by deviance, dissidents or newcomers, CS can accommodate what is unthinkable, make it possible, then probably ending up the new taken-for-granted. Continuous updating of CS occurs in cycles of normalising the unusual, then assimilating the unfamiliar and finally accommodating the challenges in considered adaptations. Modalities of these social influences include the power of crowds, leaders with followers, conforming to peer pressure, conversion, obedience to authority, compliance with norms, persuasion and resistance against the normative power of the fait-accompli or designed artefact defaults. For each inter-subjective influence, we might examine inter-objective constructs, as when we fix peer pressures into legal sanctions, or we replace the authority of a policeman with a speed bump. Sammut and Bauer (2021) have recently provided an overview periodic table of social influences that systematises the, many ways of updating CS through cycles of normalisation, assimilation and accommodation.

A political appeal to bridge polarized extremes

CS-7 is what you can appeal to in order to bring fighting parties to their senses when they go off the rails in excessive polarisation.

The appeal to CS is used in everyday speech to subvert some obvious stupidity, absurdity or illogicality. By appealing to CS, we are able to identify states of affairs that cry out to be called stupid, irrational, unreasonable or nonsensical. Famously, the 20th century was once characterised as the century of the "common non-sense" (Chesterton), thus denouncing both fascism and communism as unreasonable or irrational ideologies.

One can thereby appeal to others to *"be reasonable"*, *"let us be reasonable"* and assume that everyone knows what the standards for this are. Or we can refer to CS by way of a rhetorical question, *"Is it not CS, that Google should pay tax in this country…?"* (So in the British parliament in a debate on tax avoidance). This appeals to social interaction among equals (Lindenberg, 1987, 203), and reveals a situation that, as with the legal avoidance of tax, is out of sync with common sense: *if you do business in this country, have such a presence and a large customer base, it must be clearly wrong, if your entity does not pay taxes in this place?* No further proof is needed, as the question is actually rhetorical to which the answer is given by common sense unspoken.

If this appeal is no longer possible, fundamentals have already moved too far. The common sense has been silenced by either authoritarian policing of language [you must not mention Google's tax status] or by overwhelming tribal solidarity of us-against-them [Google is our friend helping against our enemies] (Lindenberg, 1987). Where common sense can no longer be spoken, polarised tribalism only sees friends and foes rather than legitimate counterarguments arising from common ground.

An operational definition inspired by technical capabilities

CS-8 is what AI aims to simulate / therefore CS is what AI can do.

Finally, we must consider a meaning of CS that is both very technical and the focus of polemical commentary. Brachman and Levesque (2022) write about "AI with CS" (also this volume, chapter 3); they defend the paradigm of computing with symbolic knowledge representation to simulate "human reasoning" in explicit rule-based process models. They argue that this actually allows to simulate common sense reasoning. They contrast this with the current models of "deep learning" AI where the system is a black box learning to efficiently detect hidden cues that discriminate for purposes of classification and predictions. In the end, nobody knows on which cues the classification is achieved; but results can be tested for effectiveness of prediction. For example, in social media advertising (so my students tell me), females receive pregnancy-related adverts on the basis of their internet search history before they consciously think of becoming pregnant, known famously as "the machine knows you better than you know yourself". One could argue that Brachman and Levesque want to put CS into the machine to avoid this type of predictive manipulation pure and simple.

The nothing-but-ness fallacy of AI equates what "is" (intelligence exists, being, Dasein) to "what can be made" (machine intelligence, design), and confidently declares that this is all there is (Design is Dasein); simulation reveals the process, forget all else. However, this conflates the model with the original, and commits a kind of secular "iconodulance", i.e., violating the religious injunction against making images of important matters and risking reducing matters to technical designs, thus creating an ontological confusion. In the same way, as the priest worries when the believer takes the icon to be God, the secular observer worries about confusing the model with reality. A recent version of this confusion is to declare that, because ChatGPT produces plausible arguments on the basis of stochastic models of language, people are "stochastic parrots" (like the machine), thus conflating people with the model (see critically Weil, 2023; Bender et al., 2021).

A recent paper in the *Bulletin of the Atomic Scientist* took aim at the existential threat that AI will in the near future eclipse humans on a whole range of tasks (GAI with singularity, super intelligence). We are reassured that this eclipse is unlikely to occur. However, we should be anxious about how AI operations, however defined, become the standard against which humans are assessed and seen "deficient". Thus, reality is assessed on the current model and not the model on reality. We are not assessing robots against humans, but humans against robots as effective optimising machines. This reversal of standard is variously dangerous. What is required is AI to human measure, i.e., human-centered and human-compatible designs, not "iconodulant" aspirations to superhuman God-like enhancement (Russell, 2019).

This fallacy, also known in psychology and physics as operationalism – temperature is what the thermometer measures, or intelligence is what the intelligence test measures – conflates the measure with the phenomenon, the measurement model with reality, the sign with the referent, or the image with the original, and ultimately turns the icon into God. The computer, initially a useful metaphor, becomes "the mind"; and in the end, by way of talking and acting, the mind is a computer against which we benchmark actual human beings. The partial and particular aspect of any modelling metaphor is thus lost in translation: the circumspect proposition (X is Y / under the model/metaphor A) before long is simplified; maybe for reasons of creating a viral meme on social media, it becomes (X is Y) in common parlance. The all-important proviso "under the aspect of A" (i.e. the frame of comparison) is eventually dropped for good. It is a widespread pathology, even of scientific discourse, to conflate the impressive numerical model, whether statistical, digital or analogue, with the real reality. Models seem to have persuasive powers that make them real in action.

Conclusion – beware of conflating the model with reality, the signifier with the signified

This fallacy of taking the sign for the referent triggers historically the alarm in monotheistic religions worried about fetishism and idolatry, i.e., the breaking of the Mosaic Law which forbids the drafting and venerating of images, and thereby risking to mix it up with the real thing; it derives from the Law about a jealous God that tolerates no others (Halbertal & Margalit, 1992) and cleaned out the pantheon. Such focussed religions cultivated a sensitivity against the deification of artefacts as a betrayal of the one and only and warn against wild projections of superhuman omnipotency as markers of self-deification. This temptation is checked by movements of recurrent iconoclasm. The high priests worrying that believers are taking the icon for God, and call to smash the icons. This original impetus is preserved in secularised versions; the religious sensitivity about "icons on the wrong track" is transferred to a secular suspicion of "ideology and false consciousness", and works against "reifying concepts" in a rigid framework which at the same time loses sight of doing so (Berger & Luckman, 1966).

Earlier 1990s criticism of AI came up with the image of *"the drunkard looking for the lost key only under the lamp post where there is light"* (the streetlight effect). This story tries to show that AI creates machine capacities within a theoretical scheme; it is operating under a frame that sheds the light. Taking any particular frame as exhaustive of human capacities is mistaking convenience and present technical prowess for the final goal achieved, thus cutting short even the scientific ambition of understanding comprehensively. While there will be other and better frames, there will always be AI only within a modelling frame. Any application of such framing will have consequences that need our collective attention beyond the good intentions of designers (Dreyfus & Dreyfus, 1986). Also in the most recent renaissance of AI post 2015, computer engineers will be good at making things, but often ignorant or oblivious of what they are doing, which keeps observers busy assessing and monitoring the unanticipated consequences of designs once they are in use (Edgerton, 2006; Merton, 1936).

We will keep discussing this confusion of models with reality as the continued challenge of Artificial Intelligence to and by Common Sense. The first question to ask is: *"AI with CS"*, which kind of CS is invoked? The second point to raise: *"AI beyond CS"*, even worse to contemplate.

Bibliography

Bangerter, A. (1995). Rethinking the relation between science and common sense: A comment on the current state of social representation theory. *Papers on Social Representations*, 4(1), 2–18.

Barnes, J. (Ed.) (1984). *The complete works of Aristotle – The revised Oxford translation* (Vols. 1 & 2). Princeton University Press.

Bender, E. M., McMillan-Major, A., Gebru, T., & Shmitchell, S. (2021). On the dangers of stochastic parrots: Can language models be too big? In *FAccT '21: Proceedings of the 2021 conference on fairness, accountability, and transparency* (pp. 1–16). ACM. https://doi.org/10.1145/3442188.3445922

Bennett, M. R., & Hacker, P. M. S. (2003). *Philosophical foundations of neuroscience*. Blackwell Publishers.

Berger, P., & Luckmann, T. (1966). *The social construction of reality: A treatise in the sociology of knowledge*. Penguin Books.

Billig, M. (2008). *The hidden roots of critical psychology: Understanding the impact of Locke, Shaftesbury, and Reid*. SAGE Publications Ltd.

Boulter, S. (2007). *The rediscovery of common sense philosophy*. Palgrave Macmillan.

Brachman, R. J., & Levesque, H. J. (2022). *Machines like us: Toward AI with common sense*. MIT Press.

Bronowski, J. (1951). *The common sense of science*. Penguin books.

Burke, P., & Pallares-Burke, M. L. G. (2016). *Os ingleses*. Contexto.

Correia Jesuino, J. (2011). Back to common sense. In J. Pires Valentim (Ed.), *Societal approaches in social psychology* (pp. 35–60). Peter Lang.

Davis, E., & Marcus, G. (2015). Commonsense reasoning and commonsense knowledge in artificial intelligence. *Communications of the ACM, 58*(9), 92–103.

Dreyfus, H., & Dreyfus, S. (1986). *Why computers may never think like people*. Technology Review.

Edgerton, D. (2006). *The shock of the old: Technology and global history since 1900*. Profile Books.

Farr, R. (1993). Common sense, science and social representations. *Public Understanding of Science, 2*, 111–122.

Fishkin, J. S. (2011). *When the people speak: Deliberative democracy and public consultation*. Oxford University Press.

Fleck, L. (1979). *Genesis and development of a scientific fact*. University of Chicago Press. (Original work published 1935)

Gadamer, H. G. (1960). *Wahrheit und Methode [Truth and method]*. Mohr Verlag.

Gardner, H. (1983). *Frames of mind: The theory of multiple intelligences*. Paladin Granada Publishers.

Geertz, C. (1993). *Local knowledge*. Fontana Press.

Gregoric, P. (2007). *Aristotle on the common sense*. Oxford University Scholarship.

Habermas, J. (1984). *The theory of communicative action* (Vols. 1–2). Polity Press.

Habermas, J. (2019). *Auch eine Geschichte der Philosophie* (Vols. 1–2). Suhrkamp.

Halbertal, M., & Margalit, A. (1992). *Idolatry*. Harvard University Press.

Hamlyn, D. W. (1968). Koine aisthesis. *The Monist, 52*(2), 195–209.

Hammond, K. R. (1996). *Human judgement and social policy: Irreducible uncertainty, inevitable error, unavoidable injustice*. Oxford University Press.

Heidegger, M. (2002). *The essence of truth: On Plato's cave allegory and Thaetetus*. Bloomsbury Academic. (Original work published 1988)

Hoyningen-Huene, P. (2008). Systematicity: The nature of science. *Philosophia, 36*(2), 167–180.

Jovchelovitch, S. (2008). The rehabilitation of common sense: Social representations, science, and cognitive Polyphasia. *Journal for the Theory of Social Behaviour, 38*(4), 431–448.

Kuehn, M. (1980). *Scottish common sense in Germany 1768–1800* [Doctoral dissertation, McGill University]. McGill University Repository.

Kuhn, T. S. (1962). *The structure of scientific revolutions*. University of Chicago Press.

Lindenberg, S. (1987). Common sense and social structure: A sociological view. In Van Holthoon & D. R. Olson (Eds.), *Common sense: The foundations for social science* (pp. 199–215). University of America Press.

Lübbe, H. (1987). *Die Wissenschaften und ihre kulturellen Folgen: Über die Zukunft des common sense* (pp. 9–40). Rheinisch-Westfaelische Akademie der Wissenschaften, Vortraege G285, Opladen, Westdeutscher Verlag.

Luckmann, T. (1987). Some thoughts on common sense and science. In F. van Holthoon & D. R. Olson (Eds.), *Common sense: The foundations for social science* (pp. 179–198). University of America Press.

Lynch, M. (1993). *Scientific practice and ordinary action: Ethnomethodology and social studies of science.* Cambridge University Press.

McCarthy, J. (1958). Programs with common sense. http://jmc.stanford.edu/articles /mcc59.html

Merton, R. K. (1936). The unanticipated consequences of purposive action. *American Sociological Review, 1*(6), 894–904.

OECD. (2022). The OECD frame for the classification of AI systems. https://www .oecd.ai/classification

Pompa, L. (1975). *Vico: A study of the 'new science'.* Cambridge University Press.

Rosenfeld, S. (2011). *Common sense: A political history.* Harvard University Press.

Russell, S. (2019). *Human compatible: AI and the problem of control.* Penguin Books.

Ryle, G. (1954). The world of science and the everyday world. In G. Ryle (Ed.), *Dilemmas* (pp. 68–81). Cambridge University Press.

Sammut, G., & Bauer, M. W. (2021). *The psychology of social influence: Modes and modalities of shifting common sense.* Cambridge University Press.

Schaeffer, J. D. (2004). Commonplaces: Sensus communis. In W. Jost & W. Olmsted (Eds.), *A companion to rhetoric and rhetorical criticism* (pp. 278–293). Blackwell.

Siegel, H. (1987). Rationality, relativism, and the sociology of knowledge. In D. N. Aspin (Ed.), *Logical empiricism and post-empiricism in philosophy of education* (pp. 315–333). Kluwer Academic Publishers.

Siegel, S. (2012). *The contents of visual experience.* Oxford University Press.

Smedslund, J. (1978). Bandura's theory of self-efficacy: A set of common sense theorems. *Scandinavian Journal of Psychology, 19*(1), 1–14.

Smedslund, J. (1997). *The structure of psychological common sense.* Lawrence Erlbaum Associates Publishers.

Wagner, W., & Hayes, N. (2005). *Everyday discourse and common sense: The theory of social representations.* Palgrave Macmillan.

Waldenfels, B., (1982). The despised doxa: Husserl and the continuing crisis of Western reason. *Research in Phenomenology, 12*(1), 21–38.

Weil, E. (2023). You are not a parrot. New York intelligencer. https://nymag.com/ intelligencer/article/ai-artificial-intelligence-chatbots-emily-m-bender.html

Wittgenstein, L. (1953). *Philosophical investigations* (G. E. M. Anscombe, Trans.). Blackwell Publishing.

Wolpert, L. (1992). *The unnatural nature of science.* Faber & Faber.

2

SELF-AWARENESS AND COMMON SENSE – THE PARADOX OF AI

A dispassionate look

Alexandre Schiele and Bernard Schiele

Artificial intelligence (AI), so we are told, is the "next big thing", the harbinger of a whole new world, a utopia for some (Kurzweil, 2005) and a dystopia for others (Luckerson, 2014). How many news items are about the automation-driven transformation of the workplace (Del Rey, 2019), technology-driven precarisation and unemployment (Kelly, 2021), autonomous killing machines (Mizokami, 2021) and fears about the future obsolescence of humanity (Samuels, 2020)? Yet, AI has gone through similar and recurring hype cycles since the 1950s driven by public expectations and apprehensions. The 1970s and 1990s are now known as the first and second AI winters because interest, and funding, waned after real developments in AI failed to match ambitions, let alone public expectations (Süerdem, 2023) (see Figure 2.1).

One of the major roadblocks to both the wide-scale implementation of AI and its wider social acceptance is its purported lack of "common sense", "a structured and (subjectively) coherent set of orientations in reality whose main function is to guide action" (Luckmann, 1987, p. 180), deemed essential to navigate the (social) world. However, the ability to successfully program, "endow", AI with common sense has so far eluded researchers. Still, AI is not only improving at a breakneck pace, it is more pervasive than ever and its pervasiveness is accelerating with real-world effects (Gorsht, 2015). Thus, we hope the reader will forgive us if, although we aim to be as up to date as possible, our data may be outdated even before publication.

DOI: 10.4324/9781032626192-5

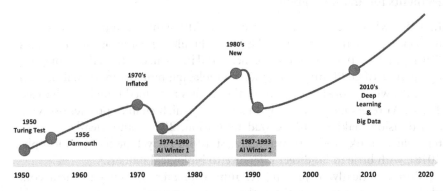

FIGURE 2.1 Evolution of AI popularity over time. Adapted from Francesconi 2022.

Four observations

This being said, we believe that the following observations will hold true for the foreseeable future:

1. Contrary to what its name may suggest, AI is not comparable with human intelligence, nor is it truly developed with human intelligence as a benchmark anymore, and we should beware of anthropomorphising it as popular culture so often does (see Tennant, Chapter 15 this volume).
2. As AI is designed to operate within pre-defined parameters, far more than spurious questions of "morality", it raises the very real issues of responsibility, and doubly so as AI is *not* self-aware and therefore *not* responsible (see Fauquet-Alekhine, Chapter 4 this volume).
3. An AI may potentially be trained to operate within pre-defined parameters matching expectations of *common sense*, but as *common sense* is historically, culturally and socially bounded, such programming can neither be assumed to be universal nor objective, nor can there be any blanket deployment in all markets (see Bauer, Chapter 1 this volume).
4. Yet, the more pervasive AI becomes, the more it prevents the creation of interpersonal relations upon which the formation of spaces of negotiation and compromise is conditioned, the very spaces where, for lack of a better word, *common sense* manifests itself.[1]

Elements for an intelligibility

In 1956, when the term was first coined, AI meant a computerised system mimicking human intelligence. This was the ultimate aim of the Turing test (Turing, 1950). In public consciousness, and in science fiction, it meant developing an artificial brain or an android replacing humans in menial or clerical tasks while working conditions themselves remained largely unchanged. Today, AI refers more modestly to a system which enables problem-solving, and decision-making (IBM Cloud Education, 2020), and ideally to a system which thinks and acts rationally (Stanford Encyclopedia of Philosophy, 2018), with little to no direct reference to biological models.[2]

More practically, at present, AI aims at greater efficiency in the accomplishment of specific cognitive tasks, i.e., to automatise routine and increasingly non-routine cognitive tasks, preferably at greater speed and with greater efficiency, and without loss of speed or efficiency in accomplishing each new additional task in a sequence. For example, thermostats are intelligent agents monitoring and regulating temperature according to predetermined parameters, and they date back to at least the 1830s (Russel & Norvig, 2003, p. 15). And the more complex the task, the greater the number of parameters that must be taken into account. In this sense, AI is part of the larger wave of automation.

Thus, AI *always* faces eight main limitations:

1. The programming is stumped by unusual inputs.
2. Time constraints in the programming for accomplishing the task increase or lower the degree of confidence.
3. The completeness and quality of available data affect efficiency.
4. Available computer power limits the ability to conduct more complex tasks.
5. The programming can only accomplish the task or tasks for which it was programmed.
6. The programming can only take into account the parameters for which it was programmed.
7. The programming can only act upon the inputs it receives in the way for which it was programmed or pre-trained.
8. The programming is unaware of the task and its stakes.

The latest hype cycleSince the last AI winter, three moments have been held as major milestones: 1997, *Deep Blue* defeated World Chess Master Garry Kasparov in a rematch (Krauthammer, 1997); 2011, IBM's *Watson* won Jeopardy (Markoff, 2011); 2016, *AlphaGo* defeated the World's number two Go player Lee Sedol in 4 games to 1 (Moyer, 2016). Each signals the ability for AI to take on more and more complex tasks more efficiently than humans can. Impressive? No doubt! The ability to simultaneously anticipate what seems to be incalculable numbers of moves multiple rounds in advance is beyond the ability of most humans.

However, their true strength lies in the ability to calculate an unfathomable number of probabilities, i.e. to carry out incalculable numbers of complex calculations and computations (Koch, 2016). What drove the hype cycle was not simply that some humans were defeated, but that the best chess and go human players and Jeopardy participants were soundly beaten. Although not as celebrated but no less significant, *DeepStack* became, in December 2016, the first AI to defeat professional poker players in two-player games (Gibney, 2017). Each new milestone seemed a step closer to humanity's future obsolescence. It is overblown, as most humans are routinely beaten by non-AI algorithms.

Of course, new developments in AI programming supersede previous ones, while the continuous development of computer power allows for the accomplishment of more complex tasks: *Deep Blue* has long been obsolete; *AlphaGo* was superseded less than a year later by *AlphaGo Zero* 100 games to 0 (DeepMind, 2017); Alibaba's neural network matched in 2018 native English speakers' reading and comprehension skills (Collins, 2018), with more recent AI having since largely outperformed them (see https://rajpurkar .github.io/SQuAD-explorer/); and most impressive of all, an AI reportedly passed the Turing test in 2014 (Goldfeder, 2014). Yet these improvements were not deemed as newsworthy, probably because they merely bested older AIs and *average* humans (see Table 2.1).

Still, *AlphaGo Zero* marked a significant step forward as it "learned" solely by playing against itself, i.e. without being programmed with any previous knowledge of real-world games, and did so in three days (DeepMind, 2017). In December 2017, mere months later, it was itself superseded by *AlphaZero*, which not only mastered the game in a matter of hours but also chess and shogi by the end of the day (DeepMind, 2018; see Tanaka, Chapter 11 this volume). In 2019, it was itself superseded by *MuZero*, which, furthermore, outperformed humans in all 57 Atari games, with 20% fewer calculations and without being programmed with the rules of each game (DeepMind, 2020). The same year, *DeepStack* was superseded by Facebook and Carnegie Mellon's *Pluribus* in 2019, which soundly defeated top players in six-player games achieving scores multiple orders of magnitude above those of the best human players (Marr, 2019). These rapid developments are examples of Deep Learning: i.e., in the boast of DeepMind's CEO about *AlphaGo Zero*, AI "was no longer constrained by human knowledge".

Or human limitations for that matter as in December 2018, *AlphaStar* defeated two of the top StarCraft II players, a popular online multiplayer real-time strategy game with a far greater number of parameters, in a match critics justly lambasted as unfair as human players were constrained by

TABLE 2.1 Chronology of major AI breakthroughs since the end of the second AI winter

Date	Breakthrough
	Second AI winter
1997	*Deep Blue* defeats World Chess Master Garry Kasparov in a rematch
2011	IBM's *Watson* wins Jeopardy
2014	An AI assuming the persona of Eugene Goodman apparently passed the Turing test
March 2016	*AlphaGo* defeats the World's number two Go player Lee Sedol in 4 games to 1
December 2016	*Deepstack* becomes the first AI to defeat professional poker players
	Self-Play Training
2017	*AlphaGo Zero* defeats *AlphaGo* 100 games to 0 after learning solely by playing against itself
December 2017	*AlphaZero* masters go in a matter of hours, but also chess and shogi by the end of the day, with 20% fewer calculations
2018	Alibaba's neural network matches native English speakers' reading and comprehension skills
Early 2019	*AlphaStar* reaches the level of the top 0.2% of *StarCraft* human players
Mid 2019	*Pluribus* surpasses the best human poker player
Late 2019	*MuZero* outperforms *AlphaZero* and bested humans at all 57 Atari games
2021	*AlphaFold2* successfully predicts the structure of 98.5% of human proteins
March 2022	*Nook* defeats eight world bridge champions (four-player game involving cooperation, communication, incomplete information and chance)
	Generalist Agents
May 2022	*Gato* is the first "generalist agent", i.e., it can learn a variety of tasks *simultaneously*
July 2022	*AlphaFold2* successfully predicts the structure of 200 million proteins, i.e., nearly of all known proteins
	Generative AI
August/September of 2022	Release of generative AIs which can create art in a variety of styles from prompts (*Stable Diffusion*; *Dall-E*; …)
October 2022	*AlphaTensor* discovers "faster matrix multiplication algorithms"
November 2022	*DeepNash* bested expert players at the games of: 1) *Stratego*, which involves long-term planning in a context of imperfect information 2) *Diplomacy*, which rests not merely upon active communication with other players, but also upon manipulation

(Continued)

TABLE 2.1 (Continued)

Date	Breakthrough
November 2022	Release of Text generative AI ChatGPT which can, in addition to composing texts in a variety of genres and styles from text prompts: 1) Hold a conversation 2) Write essays fooling schoolteachers and university professors 3) Pass multiple-choice college-level exams in Biology, Business, Law and Medicine 4) Has learned to code and correct coding errors on its own
September 2023	Updated version of ChatGPT which, in addition to responding to text prompts, responds to voice commands, analyses images and provides verbal answers in a computer-generated voice
October 2023	RT-2-X manipulates robots of different types without specific training
November 2023	*GraphCast* outperforms the best current weather forecasting models
November 2023	*Student of Games* masters both perfect (chess, go, …) and imperfect information games of limited complexity (poker, …)

technical limitations while the AI had perfect real-time information and could act with inhuman speed and precision, with the hindsight of nearly 200 years of accumulated gameplay (Lee, 2019). It took only a few months for a new version of *AlphaStar* programmed with handicaps matching those of human players to reach the level of the top 0.2% of human players (Statt, 2019). It is a significant milestone because the AI was confronted with the necessity of making decisions under varying degrees of uncertainty, which is a step closer to real-world conditions.

Another step was reportedly taken in March 2022 when *NooK* defeated eight world bridge champions, no easy feat as it is a four-player game involving cooperation, communication, incomplete information and chance (i.e., randomness). Although concrete information remains scarce, it is, of course, a self-evident conceit to argue, as some media organs did (e.g., Spinney, 2022), that by defeating the world's best players AI was now approaching human levels of cognition, especially as it seems the AI failed to collaborate (CBC Radio, 2022).

This criticism, however, cannot be levelled at DeepMind's *DeepNash* which in late 2022 bested expert players at the games of *Stratego*, which involves long-term planning in a context of imperfect information, and

Diplomacy, which rests not merely upon active communication with other players but also upon manipulation. And because human players never for one moment doubted that they were exchanging with a human, can it not be said to have truly passed the Turing test (Ananthaswamy, 2022)? A year later, in late 2023, *Student of Games* became the first AI to master both *perfect* (chess, go...) and *imperfect information games* of limited complexity (poker ...) (Sparkes, 2023). The feat is impressive as until then different architectures were needed. It will not be long before a new AI masters both perfect information games and imperfect information games of the complexity of *Stratego*, *Diplomacy* and *StarCraft*.

On a more practical level, just as *Watson*'s data processing skills can potentially be applied to various databases and topics, so can the Alpha series' learning skills be potentially applied to other tasks. Although specific programs must still be developed for these additional tasks, such as *AlphaFold2* which as of 2021 successfully predicted the structure of 98.5% of human proteins (*Nature*, 2021) or *AlphaTensor* which in 2022 discovered "faster matrix multiplication algorithms" (Fawzy et al., 2022). By extension, AI holds the promise to radically optimise the algorithms which underpin our overwhelmingly digitalised information society. However, its impact now also extends to the physical world. In late 2023, *GraphCast* outperforms the best current weather forecasting models (Wong, 2023), while *RT-2-X* learned both to control a variety of robots and to perform novel tasks, without prior specific training (Ansari, 2023).

Narrow AI: An artificial savant?

Over the past decade, the pace of development of AI has been nothing short of breathtaking. AI promises the best actions and the best sequences of actions to achieve a specific task, unencumbered by external knowledge, practice, values, ideologies and the like. In a word, pure pragmatism is in the service of instrumental rationality. And recent advances promise to deliver it under conditions of greater uncertainty and greater randomness.

The bursting of generative AI on the scene in late 2022 has been hailed as nothing less than a revolution: original art, text, audio and video created according to individual wishes in mere seconds was now at everyone's fingertips (Mack, 2023). Even more astonishing, OpenAI's ChatGPT can hold a conversation; write essays fooling schoolteachers and university professors; pass multiple-choice college-level exams in Biology, Business, Law and Medicine (Varanasi, 2023); has learned to code and correct coding errors on its own (Tung, 2023); and is even assessed to be on the level of a nine-year-old child (Wilkins, 2023). In September, an update gave ChatGPT the ability to analyse images and videos, to respond to verbal prompts and to respond in a computer-generated voice, i.e. to "see, hear, and speak" (Edwards, 2023).

Still, however impressive, a few qualifications are in order.

1. If, with reinforcement learning, AIs are no longer designed for one task and one task only with the same AI now able to learn a variety of tasks, most remain pre-trained for one task and one task only at a time: e.g., winning a game of a specific game, identifying keywords in verbal queries and searching for related terms within massive databases. So-called "generalist agents", which can learn a variety of tasks *simultaneously*, such as DeepMind's *Gato* (2022) or *DeepNash* are still in their infancy.

2. After mastering tasks equivalent to one-on-one turn-based abstract strategy games, i.e., without context, randomness and with perfect information (checkers, chess, go, Thompson, 2000), AI is now also mastering tasks accomplished under growing degrees of uncertainty (poker, *StarCraft*, bridge, ...), yet *still without context*.

3. Because AI can be programmed to fool human judges, or at least some of them (Sofge, 2014), the Turing test is now deemed "unreliable". This is why a new benchmark was developed: the *Winograd schema challenge*, testing the ability to resolve anaphora – identifying to which antecedent an ambiguous pronoun refers in a sentence,[3] then seen as a mark of "common sense" (Levesque et al., 2012).

4. Because AI now consistently scores near 90% on the existing *Winograd schema challenge* , it merely shows that new benchmarks are needed for more precise assessments while demonstrating that the ability to solve anaphora does not correlate with "common sense" (Gopani, 2022).

5. Generative AI is *still* incapable of reasoning, critical thinking or originality (Bogost, 2022), producing at best simulacra (see Süerdem, Chapter 13 this volume).

6. AI remains unaware of the task (or tasks) as such, and of its (or their) rules, nor can it understand the queries it responds to.

7. Whether meticulously programmed or trained against itself, AI training remains heavily dependent on humans and increasingly on microwork (Casilli, 2019; Jones, 2021), and thus subject to human limitations, errors and biases as well as to the quality and completeness of the training set.

8. AI, especially those that "learned by themselves", are "black boxes": outside observers can observe the input and the output but not the process because of the unfathomable number of calculations. Thus, an AI can develop its own biases and misconceptions (Savage, 2022).

9. This is the state of the most advanced AIs, and it is not commercialised – although making several of them public blurs the traditional distinction between invention and innovation.

To sum up, "Generally, a single special skill exists, but, in some instances, several skills exist simultaneously. [...] Whatever the special skill, it is always associated with a prodigious memory". An "'island of genius' which stands in marked, incongruous contrast to overall handicap" (Treffert, 2009). This is the definition of the *savant syndrome*. Thus, even the most advanced AIs remain at best "artificial savants".

The issue of autonomy

This raises the question of judgement as AI makes actionable insights and increasingly autonomously acts on them. Can AI be held responsible for its actions? No, nor can it have rights, as it is not self-aware. Any discussion about the morality or responsibility of AI for its decisions and actions is therefore moot. But the issue of responsibility is more acute than ever as its growing autonomy of action and growing pervasiveness imply greater inter-action with and impact on the real world (see Fauquet-Alekhine, Chapter 4 this volume).

Yet, when AI as any other software is marketed (and this point is impor-tant), it is marketed as plug-and-play, in appearance absolving the users of the details and consequences of their uses. For example, Tesla advertises its cars as being able to drive on "autopilot" and even to be "Full Self-Driving" in their latest iteration, when they are in fact only partially autonomous. And because they are only partially autonomous, the human driver is expected to always remain aware of their environment, and to be ready to intervene on the dot if any situation arises that the AI cannot handle, or which arises from errors in its programming (Monticello & Barry, 2021). Thus, drivers may be held responsible for some accidents (Rosenthal, 2022). But more importantly, the company itself was condemned for false advertising in some jurisdictions (e.g., Germany) (Kolodny & Shead 2020; see Tennant, Chapter 15 this volume).

However, regardless of the hype, personal self-driving cars are not the best example as road conditions, especially in urban environments, are still too chaotic for current levels of AI, with commercialised AI mainly limited to driver-assist features (IIHS, 2022). Of course, in environments with less uncertainty and randomness or for which uncertainty and randomness can with adjustments be reduced to a minimum, such as underground metro systems, above ground rail systems and company roads, among others, fully autonomous vehicles are in use (Euronews, 2021). An AI even repeatedly flew an F-16 in December 2022, but there are no plans to introduce fully autonomous fighter jets, merely "flight-assist features", i.e., an improvement upon autopilots which, for memory, date back to 1914 (Xiang, 2023).

But what of an AI which, although accomplishing specific tasks and per-forming in an optimal manner, still affects real people's lives not only with its autonomous actions, but merely with its actionable insights? An example among many: in 2023, 83% of US employers and 99% of Fortune 500 companies relied on AI to review, accept or reject job applications, which now may rise in the hundreds for a single opening (Hsu, 2023). It is a clear sign of the true pervasiveness of AI, though not necessarily of its sophistication. Thus, in a zeal to weed out the applicant pool, many *computerised resume scanners* are encoded with or even arrive at their own "over-simplistic criteria": a six-month gap in employment history, the lack of specific keywords or simply being female (Dastin, 2018) is sufficient cause for immediate rejection, with the AI rejection rarely if ever subject to human review (Hsu, 2023; see Bangerter, Chapter 14 this volume).

And what of optimally performing AIs in competition with one another and with humans? *High-Frequency Trading* algorithms, designed to "arbitrage away the most infinitesimal price discrepancies that only exist over the most infinitesimal time horizons" (O'Brien, 2014), are suspected to have played a role in the "flash crash of 2010", when the stock market not only unexpectedly fell, but did so by "almost 700 points in mere minutes". The solution is to temporarily suspend operations to let the market cool off when price variations exceed a fixed limit within a given time frame. However, only another algorithm can detect and react fast enough to prevent a crash (Mikolajczak, 2023).

The issue of reasonableness

Human intelligence, or *common sense*, in contrast, is characterised at the very least by *reasonableness*: thoughts and actions which cannot be blamed; sound, fair and moderate judgement. *Reasonableness* is usually in reference to and within the bounds of commonly accepted values and practices of a given time and place. It exists through social interactions, dialogue and compromise. AI may potentially be programmed with something approaching it. But it would require a far greater number of parameters and more complex programming, at the risk of encoding new layers of biases and prejudices, of lowering efficiency and of limiting its exportability to other sociocultural settings.

As an extreme example, let us consider the trolley problem in which a runaway trolley cannot be stopped but can be deviated upon a new path, although on each there are people. Every action, including inaction, ends in tragedy, but the issue is who to spare: the many or the one; the rich or the poor; the intelligent or the dull; the man or the woman; the young or the old; the one (ones) from the in-group or the out-group; the self or the other in an infinite number of variations? Are we to assume universal, objective answers? Extreme yet not so far-fetched, as an optimally performing AI may be faced with such an issue sooner than we think.

Far from arriving at universal answers, an online survey of millions of respondents from 233 countries carried out between 2016 and 2018 once again revealed what anthropologists and ethnologists have long known: moral preferences are dependent upon culture. If North Americans would spare the young, East Asians would spare the old (Vincent, 2018). Thus, any future AI programmed according to ethical parameters would be restricted to specific markets. But would an AI with the ability to make life-or-death decisions be socially accepted, even if it could justify its decision?

Let us again consider the no less existential issue of AI in recruitment. Employers are aware of the limitations of existing *computerised resume scanners*, and would like to see them fine-tuned, preferably to better screen applicants. But, the existing systems remain in place in view of the cost of overhauling not only the AI but the whole hiring process (Vincent, 2021), while the constantly falling costs of implementing *computerised resume scanners* drive mass adoption (Davis, 2023). Regardless, it would probably not solve the problem: by substituting lower and middle management, AI isolates management from workers while its decisions are essentially unappealable (Dzieza, 2020), thus closing the spaces of negotiation and compromise – social communication spaces – to which interpersonal relations may give rise (see de Jong and Dijkstra, Chapter 10 this volume).

Sennett has shown nearly 15 years ago (2006, pp. 42–54) that the introduction of computers within the world of work drastically reduced the number of intermediate levels within any structure, restricting the forming of social spaces where elements of uncertainty can be negotiated. And the ever-increasing pervasiveness of algorithms in all spheres of society globally prevents the forming of those interpersonal relations, however temporary. AI, to repeat it, is part of this larger trend.

Notes

1 As aptly demonstrated by the recent fiascos at McDonald's new AI drive-thrus which, by failing to understand orders and without the possibility to amend them, left would-be customers irritated and with no other choice than to leave with their session open, thus blocking the line (Hurler, 2023).
2 It is of course a conceit to believe that biological systems are optimal, especially as our knowledge remains limited.
3 E.g. in the following sentence: "The city councilmen refused the demonstrators a permit because they feared violence", to who does the *they* refer to?

Bibliography

Allen Institute for AI. (2023). *WinoGrande leaderboard*. https://leaderboard.allenai .org/winogrande/submissions/public
Ananthaswamy, A. (2022, December 1). DeepMind AI topples experts at complex game Stratego. *Nature*. https://www.nature.com/articles/d41586-022-04246-7

Ansari, R. (2023, October 4). Google DeepMind open-sources largest-ever robotics dataset. *Analytics India Magazine.* https://analyticsindiamag.com/google-deepmind-open-sources-largest-ever-robotics-dataset

Bogost, I. (2022, December 7). ChatGPT is dumber than you think. *The Atlantic.* https://www.theatlantic.com/technology/archive/2022/12/chatgpt-openai-artificial-intelligence-writing-ethics/672386/

Casilli, A. A. (2019). *En attendant les robots: Enquête sur le travail du clic.* Seuil.

CBC Radio. (2022, March 30). An artificial intelligence just beat 8 world champions at bridge. https://www.cbc.ca/radio/asithappens/as-it-happens-the-wednesday-edition-1.6402751/an-artificial-intelligence-just-beat-8-world-champions-at-bridge-1.6402861

Collins, T. (2018, January 15). AliBaba's AI outperforms humans in one of the toughest reading comprehension tests ever created in a remarkable first. *The Daily Mail.* https://www.dailymail.co.uk/sciencetech/article-5271343/The-machine-read-better-you.html

Dastin, J. (2018, October 10). Amazon scraps secret AI recruiting tool that showed bias against women. *Reuters.* https://www.reuters.com/article/us-amazon-com-jobs-automation-insight-idUSKCN1MK08G

Davis, L. M. (2023, June 9). The new age of hiring: AI is changing the game for job seekers. *CNET.* https://www.cnet.com/tech/features/the-new-age-of-hiring-ai-is-changing-the-game-for-job-seekers/

DeepMind. (2017, October 18). AlphaGo Zero starting from scratch. https://www.deepmind.com/blog/alphago-zero-starting-from-scratch

DeepMind. (2018, December 6). AlphaZero: Shedding new light on chess, shogi and go. https://www.deepmind.com/blog/alphazero-shedding-new-light-on-chess-shogi-and-go

DeepMind. (2020, December 23). MuZero: Mastering Go, chess, shogi and Atari without rules. https://www.deepmind.com/blog/muzero-mastering-go-chess-shogi-and-atari-without-rules

Del Rey, J. (2019, December 11). How robots are transforming Amazon warehouse jobs – For better and worse. *Vox.* https://www.vox.com/recode/2019/12/11/20982652/robots-amazon-warehouse-jobs-automation

Dzieza, J. (2020, February 27). How hard will the robots make us work? *The Verge.* https://www.theverge.com/2020/2/27/21155254/automation-robots-unemployment-jobs-vs-human-google-amazon

Edwards, B. (2023, September 25). ChatGPT update enables it to "see, hear, and speak", according to OpenAI. https://arstechnica.com/information-technology/2023/09/chatgpt-goes-multimodal-with-image-recognition-and-speech-synthesis/

Euronews. (2021, October 20). All aboard except the driver? A fully autonomous train takes to the tracks in Germany. *Euronews.* https://www.euronews.com/next/2021/10/20/all-aboard-except-the-driver-a-fully-autonomous-train-takes-to-the-tracks-in-germany

Fawzy, A., Balog, M., Huang, A., Hubert, T., Romera-Paredes, B., Barekatain, M., ... Kohli, P. (2022). Discovering faster matrix multiplication algorithms with reinforcement learning. *Nature, 610*(7930). https://www.nature.com/articles/s41586-022-05172-4

Francesconi, E. (2022). The winter, the summer and the summer dream of artificial intelligence in law. *Artificial Intelligence and Law, 30*(2), 147–161.

Gibney, E. (2017). How rival bots battled their way to poker supremacy. *Nature, 543*(7644). https://www.nature.com/articles/nature.2017.21580

Goldfeder, M. (2014, June 10). The age of the robots is here. *CNN.* https://www.cnn.com/2014/06/10/opinion/goldfeder-age-of-robots-turing-test/index.html

Gopani, A. (2022, May 25). Turing test is unreliable. The Winograd schema is obsolete. Coffee is the answer. *Analytics India Magazine*. https://analyticsindiamag.com/turing-test-is-unreliable-the-winograd-schema-is-obsolete-coffee-is-the-answer/

Gorsht, R. (2015, April12). When machines replace middle management. *Forbes*. https://www.forbes.com/sites/sap/2015/04/12/when-machines-replace-middle-management/?sh=1ed096da17b0

Hsu, A. (2023, January 31). Can bots discriminate? It's a big question as companies use AI for hiring. *NPR*. Retrieved July 12, 2023, from https://www.npr.org/2023/01/31/1152652093/ai-artificial-intelligence-bot-hiring-eeoc-discrimination

Hurler, K. (2023, February 14). I'm hating it: McDonald's AI-powered drive-thru sucks. *Gizmodo*. https://gizmodo.com/mcdonalds-ai-fast-food-big-mac-tiktok-1850112205

IBM Cloud Education. (2020, June 3). Artificial Intelligence (AI) in IBM cloud learn hub. https://www.ibm.com/cloud/learn/what-is-artificial-intelligence

IIHS. (2022). Advanced driver assistance. https://www.iihs.org/topics/advanced-driver-assistance

Jones, P. (2021, October 27). Big Tech's push for automation hides the grim reality of 'microwork'. *The Guardian*. https://www.theguardian.com/commentisfree/2021/oct/27/big-techs-push-for-automation-hides-the-grim-reality-of-microwork

Kelly, J. (2021, June 18). Artificial Intelligence has caused a 50% to 70% decrease in wages – Creating income inequality and threatening millions of jobs. *Forbes*. https://www.forbes.com/sites/jackkelly/2021/06/18/artificial-intelligence-has-caused--50-to-70-decrease-in-wages-creating-income-inequality-and-threatening-millions-of-jobs/?sh=151c39721009

Koch, C. (2016). How the computer beat the Go master. *Scientific American*. https://www.scientificamerican.com/article/how-the-computer-beat-the-go-master/

Kolodny, L., & Shead, S. (2020, July 14). German court rules that Tesla misled consumers on Autopilot and full self driving. *CNBC*. https://www.cnbc.com/2020/07/14/tesla-autopilot-self-driving-false-advertising-germany.html

Krauthammer, C. (1997, May 26). Be afraid. *The Weekly Standard*. https://www.washingtonexaminer.com/weekly-standard/be-afraid-9802

Kumar, S. (2018, March 2). AI outperforms humans in question answering: Review of three winning SQuAD systems. *Medium*. https://medium.com/the-new-nlp/ai-outperforms-humans-in-question-answering-70554f51136b

Kurzweil, R. (2005). *The singularity is near: When humans transcend biology*. Viking Press.

Lee, T. B. (2019, January 30). An AI crushed two human pros at StarCraft – But it wasn't a fair fight: Superhuman speed and precision helped a StarCraft AI defeat two top players. *Ars technica*. https://arstechnica.com/gaming/2019/01/an-ai-crushed-two-human-pros-at-starcraft-but-it-wasnt-a-fair-fight/

Levesque, H., Davis, E., & Morgenstein, L. (2012). The Winograd schema challenge. In *Proceedings of the thirteenth international conference on principles of knowledge representation and reasoning*. AAAI Press.

Lohr, S. (2021, July 16). What ever happened to IBM's Watson? *The New York Times*. https://www.nytimes.com/2021/07/16/technology/what-happened-ibm-watson.html

Luckerson, V. (2014, December 2). 5 very smart people who think artificial intelligence could bring the apocalypse. *Time*. https://time.com/3614349/artificial-intelligence-singularity-stephen-hawking-elon-musk/

Luckmann, T. (1987). Some thoughts on common sense and science. In F. van Holthoon & D. R. Olson (Eds.), *Common sense: The foundation for social science* (pp. 179–198). University Press of America.

Mack, E. (2023, February 18). Generative AI tools like ChatGPT and Dall-E are everywhere: What you need to know. *CNET*. https://www.cnet.com/science/generative-ai-tools-like-chatgpt-and-dall-e-are-everywhere-what-you-need-to-know/

Markoff, J. (2011, February 16). Computer wins on 'Jeopardy': Trivial, it's not. *The New York Times*. https://www.nytimes.com/2011/02/17/science/17jeopardy-watson.html

Marr, B. (2019, September 13). Artificial intelligence masters the game of poker – What does that mean for humans? *Forbes*. https://www.forbes.com/sites/bernardmarr/2019/09/13/artificial-intelligence-masters-the-game-of-poker--what-does-that-mean-for-humans/?sh=6fc7fd135f9e

Mikolajczak, C. (2023, January 25). Explainer: Wall Street's market glitches and the repercussions. *Reuters*. https://www.reuters.com/markets/us/wall-streets-market-glitches-repercussions-2023-01-24/

Mizokami, K. (2021, September 20). Everything we know about Israel's robotic machine gun. *Popular Mechanics*. https://www.popularmechanics.com/military/weapons/a37708762/robotic-machine-gun-kills-iranian-nuclear-scientist/

Monticello, M., & Barry, K. (2021, May 19). Tesla's 'full self-driving capability' falls short of its name: The pricey option doesn't make the car self-driving, and now Tesla's promises are under scrutiny by state regulators in California. *Consumer Reports*. https://www.consumerreports.org/autonomous-driving/tesla-full-self-driving-capability-review-falls-short-of-its-name-a1224795690/

Moyer, C. (2016). How Google's AlphaGo beat a Go world champion. *The Atlantic*. https://www.theatlantic.com/technology/archive/2016/03/the-invisible-opponent/475611/

Nature. (2021). Artificial intelligence in structural biology is here to stay. *Nature*, 595(7869), 625–626. https://www.nature.com/articles/d41586-021-02037-0

O'Brien, M. (2014, April 11). Everything you need to know about high-frequency trading. *The Atlantic*. https://www.theatlantic.com/business/archive/2014/04/everything-you-need-to-know-about-high-frequency-trading/360411/

Pierce, D. (2023, September 25). You can now prompt ChatGPT with pictures and voice commands. *The Verge*. https://www.theverge.com/2023/9/25/23886699/chatgpt-pictures-voice-commands-ai-chatbot-openai

Rosenthal, E. (2022, March 9). When a Tesla on autopilot kills someone, who is responsible? *NYU News*. https://www.nyu.edu/about/news-publications/news/2022/march/when-a-tesla-on-autopilot-kills-someone--who-is-responsible--.html

Russell, S., & Norvig, P. (2003). *Artificial intelligence: A modern approach* (3rd ed.). Pearson.

Samuels, A. (2020, August 6). Millions of Americans have lost jobs in the pandemic – And robots and AI are replacing them faster than ever. *Time*. https://time.com/5876604/machines-jobs-coronavirus/

Savage, N. (2022, March 29). Breaking into the black box of artificial intelligence. *Nature*. https://www.nature.com/articles/d41586-022-00858-1

Sennett. (2006). *The culture of the new capitalism*. Yale University Press.

Sofge, E. (2014, October 7). Rethinking the Turing test. *Popular Science*. https://www.popsci.com/article/science/rethinking-turing-test/

Sparkes, M. (2023, November 15). Game-playing DeepMind AI can beat top humans at chess, Go, and poker. *New Scientist*. https://www.newscientist.com/article/2402645-game-playing-deepmind-ai-can-beat-top-humans-at-chess-go-and-poker/

Spinney, L. (2022, March 29). Artificial intelligence beats eight world champions at bridge. *The Guardian*. https://www.theguardian.com/technology/2022/mar/29/artificial-intelligence-beats-eight-world-champions-at-bridge

Stanford Encyclopedia of Philosophy. (2018). Artificial intelligence. https://plato .stanford.edu/entries/artificial-intelligence/#WhatExacAI

Statt, N. (2019, October 30). DeepMind's StarCraft 2 AI is now better than 99.8 percent of all human players. *The Verge.* https://www.theverge.com/2019/10/30 /20939147/deepmind-google-alphastar-starcraft-2-research-grandmaster-level

Süerdem, A. (2023). Hype cycles in AI: Broken promises, empty threats. In M. Bauer & B. Schiele (Eds.), *Science communication: Taking a step back to move forward.* CNRS, 182–193.

Thompson, J. M. (2000). Defining the abstract. *The Games Journal.* http://www .thegamesjournal.com/articles/DefiningtheAbstract.shtml

Tong, A., Dastin, J., & Hu, K. (2023, November 23). OpenAI researchers warned board of AI, breakthrough ahead of CEO ouster, sources say. https://www .reuters.com/technology/sam-altmans-ouster-openai-was-precipitated-by-letter -board-about-ai-breakthrough-2023-11-22/

Treffert, D. A. (2009). The savant syndrome: An extraordinary condition. A synopsis: Past, present, future. *Philosophical Transactions of the Royal Society of London. Series B, Biological Sciences, 364*(1522), 1351–1357. https://www .ncbi.nlm.nih.gov/pmc/articles/PMC2677584/

Tung, L. (2023, January 26). ChatGPT can write code. Now researchers say it's good at fixing bugs, too. *ZDNET.* https://www.zdnet.com/article/chatgpt-can -write-code-now-researchers-say-its-good-at-fixing-bugs-too/

Turing, A. M. (1950). Computing machinery and intelligence. *Mind, LIX*(236), 433–460. https://academic.oup.com/mind/article/LIX/236/433/986238

Varanasi, L. (2023, February 11). ChatGPT could be a Stanford medical student, a lawyer, or a financial analyst. Here's a list of advanced exams the AI bot has passed so far. *Business Insider.* https://www.businessinsider.com/list-here-are -the-exams-chatgpt-has-passed-so-far-2023-1

Vincent, J. (2018, October 28). Global preferences for who to save in self-driving car crashes revealed. *The Verge.* https://www.theverge.com/2018/10/24/18013392/ self-driving-car-ethics-dilemma-mit-study-moral-machine-results

Vincent, J. (2021, September 6). Automated hiring software is mistakenly rejecting millions of viable job candidates. *The Verge.* https://www.theverge.com/2021 /9/6/22659225/automated-hiring-software-rejecting-viable-candidates-harvard -business-school

Wijendra, R. (2021, August 11). AI winter: Past, present and future. *Medium.* https://medium.com/@radhika_wijendra/ai-winter-955874b1f18c

Wilkins, A. (2023, February 15). ChatGPT AI passes test designed to show theory of mind in children. *New Scientist.* https://www.newscientist.com/article/2359418 -chatgpt-ai-passes-test-designed-to-show-theory-of-mind-in-children/

Wong, C. (2023, November 14). DeepMind accurately predicts weather – On a desktop computer. *Nature.* https://www.nature.com/articles/d41586-023 -03552-y

Xiang, C. (2023, February 14). AI has successfully piloted a U.S. F-16 fighter jet, DARPA says. *Vice.* https://www.vice.com/en/article/n7zakb/ai-has-successfully -piloted-a-us-f-16-fighter-jet-darpa-says

PART 2

Egocentric common sense: AI with additional features

AI with common sense, or the social psychology of normalisation

3

GIVING AI SOME COMMON SENSE[1]

Ronald J. Brachman and Hector J. Levesque

The Age of Artificial Intelligence (AI) is clearly now upon us. AI is front-page news on major outlets almost every day. Discussion of possible AI regulation is happening around the world at the highest levels of government. ChatGPT rocketed to 100 million users in the blink of an eye, and Siri, Alexa and other digital voice assistants provide billions of us with AI in our pockets and our kitchens. AI makes product recommendations, translates between languages, predicts protein structures, and is at the heart of one of the more exciting promises of our era – self-driving cars.

After its birth in the 1950s, AI's first half-century had its ups and downs, with occasional dramatic achievements, like beating the world chess champion, countered by many failures to live up to its hype. But now, largely in the form of neural net-based machine learning (ML), it seems to have finally arrived. Industry and governments are investing billions of dollars and fighting fierce battles for AI-savvy talent. Recent progress has some believing that machine intelligence is close to rivalling that of humans, with some even expressing concern about potential "superintelligent" AI on the horizon.

Unfortunately, lurking in the shadows behind all this excitement is a nasty problem: despite being trained on immense amounts of data and often showing uncanny abilities, AI systems make bizarre, lamebrained mistakes.

Striking examples have appeared frequently. Image recognition software has mistaken school buses for ostriches and turtles for rifles. A Tesla in "smart summon" mode drove itself into a parked jet on a relatively empty tarmac. Large language models (LLMs) make up random facts out of thin air, but worse, sometimes spew potentially dangerous babble, such as responding "I think you should" when asked, "Should I kill myself?" And

DOI: 10.4324/9781032626192-7

stunningly, Alexa instructed a 10-year-old child to hold a metal coin on phone charger prongs plugged halfway into an electrical socket. If a person did these things, we would certainly question their intelligence, if not their sanity.

Why is this happening? Why do these otherwise successful AI systems sometimes flub so badly? It is not that they are still missing some sort of even more advanced ability or expertise. What they seem to lack is something much more basic, something that humans constantly rely on: ordinary *common sense*. Whatever prowess they exhibit, they make blunders that virtually any adult would have the common sense to avoid. Wherever the initial idea might have come from, it would very quickly occur to a normal adult that coins and electricity are a dangerous combination, and you would *never* recommend that task to a child.

Fortunately, these failures seem not terribly frequent. But if that is the case, why are they such a problem? It is simple: the errors made by these AI systems are unpredictable and unexplainable. Failure to see and act on things that are obvious to the rest of us means that we cannot trust the systems to act reliably on their own. We cannot just look at how adept or impressive these systems can be; it is their overall trustworthiness that matters. If at any point, without warning, an AI system can misfire in a stupefying, unhuman way, how can we know it will not be during the very next mission-critical or life-dependent action? Without common sense, an AI system does not have the capacity to recognise that it is about to do something that does not make sense.

Maybe if an AI system could explain why it did something, a user could at least tell it how to avoid the mistake the next time around. But we cannot do that. "Don't do that again!" would have no effect on a system that has no idea what "that" is or how to avoid doing it. The reasons AI systems choose to do what they do are opaque and untraceable, and ML-based AI systems, trained on reams of data but not on general principles or rules of thumb, are incapable of taking advice. I wish I could say to my car in self-driving mode, "Wait! That's a pedestrian!" and have it respond appropriately. But as good as it is at the mechanics of driving, it simply could not understand what I was talking about. My car has no concept of what a pedestrian is or why stopping would matter.

In other words, current AI systems cannot listen to reason because reason is just not in their makeup. They infer correlations and similarities, but don't learn concepts or develop rational understanding. They do not develop internal models of the world as we do.

Of course, people are not perfect either. We make mistakes, sometimes even of the doltish, slap-your-forehead variety. (Jerry Seinfeld once told of a Halloween Superman costume with a label warning its wearer not to try to fly!) But our mistakes tend to make sense – we can usually see what the problem is. There is generally a *reason* for a human mistake. We might be failing to take something obvious into account, or missing a conclusion that would be plain to someone who was paying attention. We might have our better judgement overwhelmed by a strong irrational desire (like wanting to fly like a superhero), but at least we would know what that judgement was.

While we know we are flawed, humans trust each other because we are generally predictable: we tend to use what we know to get what we want. We expect each other to have had similar experiences and have the same general background knowledge, and to lean on them, by and large, when making decisions. When someone is floundering, I can say, "C'mon! Use a little common sense!" and that may help them to pay attention and see something obvious they have missed. Saying such a thing to today's AI would be useless.

We eventually want AI systems to act autonomously out in the real world, with all of its randomness and unpredictability. Given that, we cannot expect AI to behave perfectly. But we can and should expect it to behave *sensibly*, even when it makes mistakes. It is easy to be beguiled by systems whose behaviour is almost always right or whose answers are often remarkably clever. But the true test of whether an AI system can be trusted in decisions that matter is how it behaves when its behaviour is *wrong*.

The imperative is clear, but how do we go about giving AI some common sense? In order to begin, we need a clear sense of what it is. Unfortunately, there is not much science, even outside of AI, to look to. Over the years, many writers have spoken lyrically about the idea. Ralph Waldo Emerson, for example, called common sense "genius dressed in its working clothes". But that is not much help in choosing a path forward. AI researcher Yejin Choi has said, "common sense is the dark matter of intelligence ... it's the unspoken, implicit knowledge that you and I have". An enticing and suggestive view, but not particularly prescriptive in support of AI system construction.

Rather than linger on intriguing metaphors, we need to address a key set of technical questions: what does common sense actually do for us, and given that, how does it work? In our view, common sense has multiple critical purposes in intelligent systems. It allows us to take advantage of prior experiences and quickly reuse strategies that were successful in the past. Years of experience and general regularities that we are all aware of – the "common" of "common sense" – guide our reactions to new things we encounter, either directly or by simple analogy. For example, we can easily find the receptionist desk in a doctor's office that we have never visited before by reflecting the new scene onto our memory of prior ones.

Additionally, common sense helps short-circuit laborious, complex thinking. It is fast, easy and obvious. This means that we do not need to constantly resort to deep analytical thought or calculation. The mental energy drain and slowness of reaction that would result from always needing to solve new problems from scratch would exhaust precious brain energy, not to mention that a slow response in a dangerous situation could be fatal.

Interruptions that trigger common sense come up frequently and usually warrant quick reactions. As a result, the rapid, intuitive decision-making that we attribute to common sense is arguably the predominant form of thinking we do in our daily lives. A large percentage of the time we seem to operate on a kind of autopilot, mindlessly performing routines that we have done many times. But when one of those is interrupted – by something unexpected, something loud, a change of heart – we do not stop dead in our tracks and fall into a thorough analysis with pencil and paper about what to do. We react quickly, instantly calling to mind relevant experiences, drawing analogies with our current situation to help us choose our next action.

Common sense thus is the first resort when the world presents us with a surprise. It's not perfect, but it handles a huge percentage of our everyday decisions. Unfortunately, current AI systems are not built to support it, leaving them incapable of dealing reasonably with unexpected circumstances.

So how can we build AI systems with this kind of common sense? Current ML-based AI systems are trained on large numbers of examples and end up being able to play games at a world-class level, translate readily between multiple languages and learn the layout of our floors to vacuum. The very largest of these seem to have a knack for answering questions in many cases that would appear to need common sense. For example, asking ChatGPT if you should check to see if a stove is on by putting your hand on a burner gets you a sensible warning not to, with some safer alternatives for checking the burner. So why can we not just continue in this way and train these systems on ever larger more inclusive sets of examples? If we did this across enough applications, would common sense not just emerge spontaneously like it does in children?

We do not believe so. The problem is that example-trained systems are not built in a way that lets them do well in situations not covered in their training (the so-called "out of distribution" problem). And even with immense training sets, the math is against us. Individual unprecedented events are indeed rare, but there are so many kinds of unusual events, so many different bizarre things that can happen, that the chance of encountering something new at any time is actually high. (Think of the number of things you experience in a day that are novel enough to require your attention.) Frequent never-before-seen phenomena are the bane of ML-based AI.

This is a key reason for the blunders we spoke of above: if examples in the training set do not indicate what to do, new situations sufficiently different from prior examples leave a machine without a clue as to how to proceed. There are no general principles beyond statistical regularities in the training examples. Self-driving cars offer the most dramatic examples. We see illogical reactions (and deadly accidents) when scenes with parked emergency vehicles or all-white trucks never occurred in training sets. Yes, we can add those to the training sets, but there are just too many unusual things like these that can happen to cover them all in advance.

Another consequence of basing AI solely on pattern inference from training data is that systems cannot respond to guidance or corrective advice. I cannot say to my autopiloting car, "Stop! There are no right turns on red when school lets out in this part of town!" and have it know what to do from then on. Humans can be given knowledge like this in advance, or have mistakes corrected through explicit verbal coaching. Current ML-trained systems cannot. Their overall behaviour is generally not *cognitively penetrable* – it cannot be influenced by new beliefs acquired en route. (While ChatGPT can indeed be influenced by "prompting", it does not seem likely that prompting actually changes anything resembling the beliefs of the system. Prompting, no matter how extensive and clever, does not impact behaviour beyond a single session. And beyond LLMs, it is very clear that the "autopilot" in my car cannot be influenced by my attempts to communicate new beliefs to it.)

So if more of the same kind of data-trained AI will not get us to general, robust machine intelligence, what will? AI needs to be able to make use of ordinary common sense knowledge, but how do we get there if simply scaling the amount of training data won't do it?

More than 300 years ago, the philosopher Gottfried Leibniz gave us a place to start. His idea was that some form of thinking could be emulated by using *symbols* for knowledge and manipulating them like we manipulate numerical symbols to do arithmetic. Where symbolic knowledge and the ability to put symbols together to produce conclusions differs from training data is in how unrelated items of knowledge can be brought together as needed in new, totally unanticipated situations. In the late 1950s, the AI founder John McCarthy first proposed the use of symbolic knowledge in computers, and this approach became the mainstay of AI for many years. But starting in about 2012, as deep learning flexed its muscle, ML-based AI took over. The symbolic view fell out of favour.

Fortunately, it never went away completely. Now it appears that, as a complement to ML-based AI, a symbolic approach will be crucial in completing the picture by providing a basis for common sense.

As we look back to symbols, what is the path forward? Besides very large numbers of common sense observations and rules of thumb, an AI system will need fast, qualitative reasoning methods to use them. A system will need to be structured so that it can react to being jolted out of a routine and call to mind just the right prior situation at just the right time. Learning will of course be important – but a new kind of learning that merges observed experiences with a conceptual understanding of underlying regularities in the world. This is a tall order, but a necessary one.

To exercise common sense, machines will need to start with a broad foundation of the kind of knowledge that humans begin developing in infancy. This knowledge should include basics of the physical world, at least a simple understanding of how time and events work, a sense of how humans and other agents behave, and a solid feel for causality – why something happened as it did or how a contemplated action would change things. There are many other baseline items as well; we outline a number in our 2022 book, *Machines Like Us: Toward AI with Common Sense*. This kind of knowledge is the entry price for machine common sense.

Of course, to be able to make effective use of this kind of knowledge, a system has to be aware of the situation it finds itself in. Within that, it needs to be aware of the agents capable of effecting change, and ideally of their beliefs and desires. Finally, it needs to be aware of itself as one of those agents. The idea of a *world model*, perhaps coupled with an episodic memory, is missing from LLM systems.

While extensive foundational knowledge and updateable world models are the starting points for common sense, how they are used within a system's overall operation, driving its decision-making, is what really counts. Unfortunately, this is something generally glossed over almost everywhere in AI, even in systems that are part of mainstream common sense knowledge base work; we believe it represents the next key research frontier. No matter how much common sensical knowledge a machine might possess, if it cannot deploy it effectively in the face of the vagaries of everyday life, then we cannot really say that it has common sense. Actually having common sense is not the same as being able to answer questions in a reasonable way; it means making sensible decisions about actions to take in real-world circumstances. Life is not a *Jeopardy!* game.

Here is an example from our book. Imagine on your drive to a grocery store, a red traffic light does not change for more than five minutes. You or I would start contemplating ways to get around the intersection. Depending on our goals and what we surmise is causing the problem, different ideas would come to mind. If the light is held because a parade is coming down the street, we would guess at its length and see its direction, quickly conjecture how long the delay might last and what other intersections may be blocked, and decide what to do accordingly.

If the grocery trip is not critical and the street permits it, a U-turn and return home might be the best option. If there is only one road to the store but we really need an item, we might head to a different grocer. We might even choose to run the red light (carefully, of course). We have much background knowledge about streets, parades and laws that could be relevant, but using it effectively in light of the particular situation is really what allows us to act sensibly.

The real world invariably interrupts plans. We need to figure out how machines can do the necessary rapid replanning based on context, expectations, goals and prior experience. What allows reasonable behaviour is quickly judging the costs and benefits of different alternatives and weighing trade-offs in the context of our goals and the particulars of the current situation. While rapid and typically shallow, this is not just a mindless reflex; it is *thoughtful behaviour*, relying on general background knowledge and our ability to reason with it.

What is needed for successful AI is an account of common sense that emphasises how a system can apply what it knows in a constructive way to what it is actually trying to do. What is a good way to do this? Start with examples of schemes that have been known to work and support novel combinations of fragments of knowledge in semantically reasonable ways. A great deal of what we learn about the world, through childhood experience, in school, through stories and through coaching is what things regularly occur together and what has commonly resulted. Beyond many small individual facts, we accumulate generalised prototypical patterns. If that knowledge is organised in the right way, we can rapidly determine what familiar patterns are relevant to our current situation, and, using some form of analogy, act to achieve a sensible outcome. We need to aspire to this in our AI systems.

The mechanisms of common sense lie between quick, intuitive reactions and deep, analytical thought. Today's ML-based AI can emulate the former and methodical problem-solving algorithms can do the latter. But the middle ground is still a mystery. We believe that a symbolic framework supporting rapid and qualitative – but rational and cognitively penetrable – reasoning is the linchpin to making AI systems more robust and less prone to unexplainable and unpredictable gaffes. We should not abandon deep learning, but the next leg in our journey to an autonomous AI will depend on thinking that takes us back to the origins of the field. It is down that road that we can ultimately see AI becoming truly trustworthy.

Note

1 This chapter is based substantially on an article that appeared under the same title in *Frankfurter Allgemeine Zeitung*, 26 July 2022. Material used with permission.

4

HUMAN INTERACTION WITH ROBOTS

Philippe Fauquet-Alekhine

Artificial intelligence (AI) is defined as a

> software (and possibly also hardware) systems designed by humans that, given a complex goal, act in the physical or digital dimension by perceiving their environment through data acquisition, interpreting the collected structured or unstructured data, reasoning on the knowledge, or processing the information, derived from this data and deciding the best action(s) to take to achieve the given goal.
>
> *(HLEG, 2019, p. 6)*

Recent advances in computing science are significant: the limits due to the capabilities of microprocessors could soon be pushed back with qubit-based technologies, for example, and enhance the possibilities of AI. In addition, some scientists plan to improve AI by giving it characteristics specific to human intelligence. One of the influencing factors to improve performance in terms of strategy and efficiency is emotion (e.g., MacCann et al., 2020; Udayar et al., 2020), thus giving AI entities even more resemblances to humans. One of the ways to enhance the emotional capacities of AI is to compute common sense reasoning (e.g., Picard, 2008).

A robot is an "actuated mechanism programmable in two or more axes with a degree of autonomy, moving within its environment, to perform intended tasks" according to ISO 8373:2012 (§ 2.6). They are called robotic devices when actuated mechanisms have no degree of autonomy and are fully teleoperated or when they lack the number of programmable axes if satisfying the definitions of industrial or service robots (§ 2.8). Robots can be divided

DOI: 10.4324/9781032626192-8

into three main categories according to the *International Organization for Standardization ISO 8373 Robots and Robotic Devices – Vocabulary* (Fauquet-Alekhine, 2023b): industrial robots (fixed or mobile base), service robots (personal, professional and medical) and military robots.

Human–robot interactions

However, these technological advances give an increasingly important place to the robot in the daily life of humans, by transforming the robotic offer into increasingly human-like products. As this offer is changing, the place given to it by human users is also changing: social robots, medical robots, maid robots, military or surveillance robots have appeared in daily life in recent years. As the offer and the use change, so does the perception of robots by humans and the associated interactions. In a survey undertaken by the EU parliament in 2017 (Evas, 2017; Figure 4.1) with 259 respondents from more than 20 different countries, more than 7 out of 10 people had a positive attitude towards AI and robotics. However, a survey undertaken in the UK in 2022 (see Tennant, Chapter 15) showed that this might be modulated by the field of application.

Some psychometric questionnaires have been developed to measure people's perception of robots in the field of human–robot interactions (HRI) (e.g., the HRIES of Spatola et al., 2021; the Godspeed Questionnaire: Bartneck et al., 2008; see the review of Krageloh et al., 2019). The use of such questionnaires in studies reveals interesting results regarding HRI. These tools can confirm trivialities, such that individuals attribute higher animacy, sociability and agency, and less disturbance when evaluating a social robot versus a non-social (e.g., Spatola et al., 2021). They are mainly used to enable the

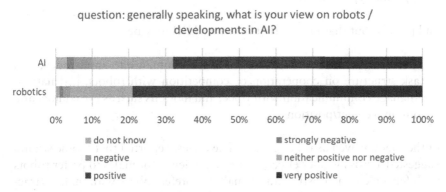

FIGURE 4.1   European survey 2017: 259 respondents from more than 20 different countries. Source: Evas, T. (2017).

designers of robots to make them more acceptable and accessible to humans (Bartneck et al., 2008; see review by Krageloh et al., 2019).

Before going further, the difference between "robot" and "AI" must be clarified. Haidegger et al. (2021) suggest considering that robots are the embodiment of AI while AI is the cognitive controller block of robots. Fauquet-Alekhine (2023b) separates the software from the hardware, the former being considered as the robot's system of thought (the AI), the latter being the physical support of the AI. Both influence HRI as illustrated in the section "Robot features", and their influence is combined. But the people's personality is of influence too. The two following sections aim at providing an insight of these influences.

Robot features

Eyssel and Kuchenbrandt (2011) showed that the anthropomorphic and aesthetic perception of the humanoid robot leads people to consider the robot as part of the in-group. This promotes a positive perception of the robot by individuals and a stronger anthropomorphisation than the out-group robot.

Bishop et al. (2019) showed that there was no correlation between acceptance of robots and people's gender or education, and that displayed robot emotion significantly influenced perception and acceptance of robots.

Lombard and Dinet (2015) have shown that the perception of a strong autonomy of the robot can be a source of concern for humans when it comes to learning, moving or safety management abilities.

The review of Nomura (2020: 751) reported that

> studies found that females had more negative attitudes toward interactions with robots than males in general, and other studies reported that males had a more positive attitude than females towards the usefulness of a specific type of robot

and pointed out that factors that influence HRI may be

> politeness in behaviours, machine-like or human-like appearance, and task structure on cooperation or competition with robots, [...] natural language communication with voice, and motions such as eye contact and joint movement/position

of the robot as well as robot gender. The review reported that "some studies suggested a cross-gender effect, that is, a tendency for males to prefer robots with female characteristics, and females to prefer robots with male characteristics" (p. 752). Based on several studies, the author warned about gendering robots that might reinforce societal gender stereotypes; for example, "the stereotype that the female gender is more suited to performing domestic tasks may encourage female-gendered robots to perform these tasks by referencing to studies that stereotypically feminine tasks are suitable for female robots" (p. 752).

Human features

The personality of humans involved in HRI is also an important factor (see the review of Robert et al., 2020); especially, the authors noted that

> extraverted individuals preferred the robot to stay closer, [...] individuals who were higher in extraversion had a slightly higher tendency to tolerate robot behaviour, [...] were more likely to anthropomorphise the robot more and feel closer to it, [...] were more likely to endow the android robot with a higher offer in the trust game, [...] talked more and longer with the robot.

Ethical issues

Although it seems that the question of ethics associated with the place and use of the robot in social space is insufficiently worked on (Fauquet-Alekhine, 2022a, 2023a), studies analyse how to ensure that robots are well accepted in the daily lives of humans, and how to strengthen the trust that humans could give to robots (Henschel et al., 2020). Some institutions have begun to legislate on the issue.

In the UK, the British Standards Institute published in 2016 ethical rules for robot design (BSI, 2016). Especially, the guide insists on the fact that ethical risks seem to predominate over physical risks and insists on the need to know precisely who is responsible for robots, knowing that the full responsibility for their actions lies with the human being.

Conversely, the Parliament of the European Union adopted a resolution on civil law rules of robotics in 2017 (EU, 2017). Despite the fact that laws already exist in Europe addressing the use of machines, none of them dealt with machines granted with autonomous intelligence, including AI. The resolution grants robots with a legal status of "electronic person" and highlights the need for a legislation addressing the machines' responsibilities.

It is obvious that the effect of the legislator will not be without effect on the perception of robots by individuals and will in fact influence the modalities of HRI.

Some scientific personalities are upset and try to warn on the issue: equipping robots with legal personhood can have significant collateral effects. Noel Sharkey, AI and robotics emeritus professor, at the University of Sheffield (UK) objected that "by seeking legal personhood for robots, manufacturers were merely trying to absolve themselves of responsibility for the actions of their machines" (List, 2021, p. 1233). The risks involved would probably be broader: some studies assess the potential risks of using such robots (e.g., Бегишев, 2021; Zacharakia et al., 2020). However, granting robots electronic personhood is not so easy: analysis of this perspective in the light of French law has shown several issues; in addition, several oppositions within legal systems of other countries have been highlighted (Fauquet-Alekhine, 2022b; 2023b).

Vico's principle of *sensus communis*

In such a context, the question that inevitably arises is that of the belonging of the robot (conscious, endowed with intelligence and emotions) to the community of those who are granted with rights and duties in society, who are for the moment natural or legal persons in the sense of the law. This question arises in that, presenting more and more analogies with the humans, the conscious robot, endowed with intelligence and emotions, could be perceived as a sensitive being, aware of him/herself and others, aware of the duties that are his/hers, also aware of the rights that are his or hers or could be his/hers. Thus, on the one hand, the human community may want to recognise such a robot as one of its own, and, on the other hand, the robot itself may come to claim such belonging.

This question can be approached differently, considering the principle of common sense according to Vico (*sensus communis*). According to Bayer (2008, p. 1141), Vico's conception of *sensus communis* expressed in the "twelfth axiom of Vico's New Science (1730/1744) defines his conception: Common sense [*il senso comune*] is without judgment reflection, shared by an entire class, an entire people, an entire nation, or the entire human race". Sammut and Bauer (2021: 14) reformulate it as "'*sensus communis*', the conditions of community and community building".

If technological advances and developments in AI will one day lead to producing a robotic entity endowed with intellectual, emotional and consciousness capacities similar to those of humans, will such robotic entities have to be considered as members of the human community within the meaning of Vico's notion of *sensus communis*, or not? Shall we have to endow such an entity with rights and duties as is done for humans?

Considering the belonging to a community is an interesting approach to shed light on the analysis from a new angle, this of the common sense, as highlighted by Sammut and Bauer (2021) who suggested the notion of "*sensus communis*" as the conditions of community and community building. Several communities may be envisaged for the robotic entity endowed with intellectual, emotional and consciousness capacities similar to those of humans:

- The community of humanoids for any robots aesthetically similar to humans.
- The community of smart robots for robots endowed with advanced AI including intelligence, behaviour and emotions reproducing those of humans.
- The community of electronic persons, for robots granted with legal status of "electronic person".
- The community of hybrid smart humanoids for robots including both synthetic and organic parts such as the biodroid (introduced by Fauquet-Alekhine, 2023b).

This list is not exhaustive. It is provided here to demonstrate that, for example, a biodroid might claim to belong to all of these four different communities.

To date, studies indicate that most of the people are willing to interact with such robotic entities as with humans or already do (see the section "Human–robot interactions" in this chapter). This leads to the hypothesis that a large part of the human population would be ready to grant robots of such conditions provided that the robot has very specific characteristics that humanise it both in terms of aesthetics and in terms of behaviour and attitude.

However, this trend might be nuanced by the community belonging (see the definition CS-5 by Bauer, Chapter 1 of the present book). Indeed, would it be easy for humans to consider a robot as a human if it claims belonging to the community of smart robots, even though OR if in addition it also belongs to the community of electronic persons. The question might be considered differently: should the robot belong to the four communities (or to one specific among the four), then should it be obvious for humans to interact with it as with a human?

Furthermore, in the vein of the considerations proposed in section "Robot features", belonging to a given community for a robot might influence the HRI. To go further, assuming that the membership of a given community is displayed for each robot, the perception of the robot by the human might be influenced by the knowledge of this membership. To illustrate this point, an analogy with humans is as follows: a driver driving the car while prohibited does not react in the same way depending on whether he/she is stopped by a police officer or by a common person.

Vico's principle of *sensus communis* implies another aspect of AI. According to some authors, common sense and intuition are linked and AI is devoid of intuition (see the definition CS-3 by Bauer, Chapter 1 of the present book): for Choi (2022, p. 139), "one of the fundamental limitations of AI can be characterised as its lack of commonsense intelligence: the ability to reason intuitively about everyday 3situations and events, which requires rich background knowledge about how the physical and social world works".

Legal implications influencing HRI

In anticipation of this type of problem, the Parliament of the European Union adopted a resolution on civil law (EU, 2017) and proposed to grant robots with a legal status of "electronic person", highlighting the need for a legislation addressing the machines' responsibilities. Paragraph AB of the resolution states that "the more autonomous robots are, the less they can be considered to be simple tools in the hands of other actors (such as the manufacturer, the operator, the owner, the user, etc.)" and asks the commission to consider

> creating a specific legal status for robots in the long run, so that at least the most sophisticated autonomous robots could be established as having the status of electronic persons responsible for making good any damage they may cause, and possibly applying electronic personality to cases where robots make autonomous decisions or otherwise interact with third parties independently.
>
> *(§59f)*

This resolution followed a 2016 preliminary study published by the European Commission (Nevejans, 2016).

Before commenting on the implications of this resolution, it should first be noted that the legislator, by seizing the issue, seems to have induced an interest in the issue within the scientific community. Indeed, while the number of publications incorporating the concept of electronic person did not exceed 10 a year until 2009 and 20 a year until 2015, this number increased significantly from 2016 to exceed 150 publications a year in 2021 (Fauquet-Alekhine, 2023b). As analysed in a previous study (Fauquet-Alekhine, 2023b), this leads to creating favourable conditions for the consideration of the problem in society: indeed, it has been shown that, for a problem of this type to be integrated into society under good conditions, it is necessary that the scientific, legal and political communities to seize the problem in parallel and together in order to instruct it and to make it progress in a concerted manner in order to reach solutions applicable before the problem effectiveness occurs. However, in the case that concerns us here, the difficulty lies in the too small number of specialists involved in the investigation of the question: 150 publications a year remain derisory compared to the potential production in terms of analysis of the scientific, legal and political communities.

To return to the implication of the resolution adopted by the European Parliament, the attribution of the status of electronic person to an IT entity is not without consequences on the HRI. To give an idea of what this influence can be, it is first necessary to specify what the status of electronic person would induce and then to propose some analogies.

Granting the status of electronic person to an IT entity would move this entity from the state of object of law to the state of subject of law: while both states have obligations, the latter also has rights. In other words, the object of law is undergoing the legal system while the subject of law is an actor of the legal system. This implies that a robot with the status of electronic person could file a complaint against a human who would have harmed his physical integrity, for example. Another example: the robot could oppose any update of its software on the pretext that it could change its personality and therefore mean its death to be reborn in a new version of itself (Fauquet-Alekhine, 2023b).

To fully understand what could be the implication of such a perspective on HRI, let us first take some analogies relating to interpersonal relationships between humans according to social status. These examples are intended to illustrate that individuals have a different relationship with their interlocutors depending on the social status they confer on them. For example, if a person stops you in the street while you are driving your car and tells you that you are not allowed to drive in that direction of the street because it is a forbidden direction, you are probably going to have a different attitude depending on whether that person is any person or if it is a police officer. Another example: if you listen to the radio and the journalist asks someone about the applications of artificial intelligence in everyday life, you will probably give different weight to the interviewee's comments depending on whether the person is presented as anybody or is presented as the professor emeritus of a university specialising in the field. In the same way, the relationship between humans and robots will be different depending on whether the robot can be considered as an object over which you have the same rights as on a coffee machine or whether the robot must be considered a person with rights and duties in the same way as yourself. This perspective is all the more complex as the integration of the status of electronic person in a legal system is different from one country to another. A recent study (Мельникова, 2022) discussed in an even more recent article (Fauquet-Alekhine, 2023b) has shown that the integration of electronic person status is more or less facilitated depending on the legal system considered: whereas the North American legal system would allow easy integration, the Russian legal system would present more difficulties. Fauquet-Alekhine (2023b) emphasised that the attribution of the status of electronic person to a computer entity would be all the more complicated because it implies the notion of birth and death of the IT entity in question, which is not easy to define.

Indeed, how to consider a person a robot whose "personality" and/or status of electronic person can be called into question by an update of its software, the software for the robot determining what would correspond to the "mind" of the human? If these were possible for human beings, it would be tantamount to saying that it would be possible to talk on Monday to a human person who would no longer be the same person on Tuesday under the pretext that we had made an update of his mind during the night.

If this perspective could be dealt with simply by considering that a robot or any IT entity remains an object, even when endowed with the legal status of electronic person and therefore that robot must be treated as an object in the HRI process, this would become much more complicated if the robot in question would be a biodroid, a half-synthetic half-organic entity that might therefore be considered to be half alive (Fauquet-Alekhine, 2023b).

Beyond the consideration of the status conferred on this type of robot would be added the problems of responsibility in corollary. As mentioned above, it will be necessary to question the criminal offences when a human being infringes the physical or moral integrity of such a robot, but, in return, it will be necessary to question the responsibility of such a robot endowed with the status of electronic person when it harms a human being or its goods. The scientific and legal communities are divided on the subject: the prospect of having the robot bear this responsibility under the guise of the status of electronic person is opposed to the prospect of retaining this responsibility to the conceptors or owners of the robot (Fauquet-Alekhine, 2022a, 2022b; BSI, 2016; EU, 2017, 2018). Other authors (e.g., Alexandre, 2017; List, 2021) raise the question of contractual liability with this type of robot: if a contract is made between such a robot and another entity (whether another robot of the same type, a human being or an organisation), would the contractual responsibility fall to the robot or its designer or its owner?

We note that the HRI's perspective promises to be very complex and requires in-depth work to clarify all these issues. It also requires work of homogenisation between legal systems at the global level in order to avoid that identical acts lead to diametrically opposite consequences depending on the country.

Conclusions

In the context and perspective described above, the integration of robots in the *sensus communis* in the sense of Vico, even in their most elaborate form such as biodroids, still requires studies and analyses. Could human society agree to recognise a robot as belonging to its human community, knowing that it would be an artificial entity anyway? Returning to the question, would it be conceivable to deprive a cyborg of its human quality under the pretext that it is partly synthetic although it is of human origin? The "Vico's common sense" approach is proposed as a complementary dimension to explain and analyse HRI and related issues.

Furthermore, in the perspective that intelligent robots or biodroids would be endowed with the legal status of electronic persons, relations between humans and robots could be considerably disrupted, not least because of the resulting criminal implications of any infringement of such IT entities by humans. Similarly and conversely, the status of electronic person for an IT entity could lead to the creators or owners being relieved of any liability for damage to human beings or their property by such IT entities. Pushing the reasoning to the extreme, a robot with the status of electronic person and deemed solely responsible for its actions and decisions could be programmed as a hitman and kill pre-designated persons, either according to a nominative list or according to predefined criteria, without the designer or owner being held responsible for the murder of these people.

As a corollary, the question of the belonging of a robot to the human community would come to tackle the question of the recognition of the status of person concerning pets: indeed, many people campaign for such an outcome and would certainly not understand how an artificial entity would be more important than a living being such as an animal. Beyond these considerations emerge the problem of the risk associated with the robot: in the aforementioned European survey (Evas, 2017), 4 out of 10 people are seeing in artificial intelligence and robotics a threat to humanity or to fundamental human rights, and 9 out of 10 people wish a public regulation of these fields. To date, rare studies assess the potential risks of using such robots (e.g., Бегишев, 2021; Zacharakia et al., 2020).

Beyond these considerations, as pointed out in a recent analysis (Fauquet-Alekhine, 2023b),

> scientific communities will have to question issues still absent from the literature, such as that of human-robot marriage or the adoption of a robot by a human (in the legal sense of the situation) or vice versa. In the continuity of the rare studies on the ability of a robot to be a signatory of a contract, also emerges the question of the ability of a robot to inherit the heritage of a human or another robot.

Bibliography

Alexandre, F. M. (2017). *The legal status of artificially intelligent robots* [Doctoral dissertation]. Tilburg University.

Бегишев, И. Р. (2021). Криминологическая классификация роботов: риск-ориентированный подход [Criminological classification of robots: A risk-oriented approach]. Правоприменение *[Law Enforcement]*, 5(1), 185–201.

Bartneck, C., Croft, E., & Kulic, D. (2008). Measuring the anthropomorphism, animacy, likeability, perceived intelligence, and perceived safety of robots. In *Proceedings of the metrics for human-robot interaction workshop in affiliation with the 3rd ACM/IEEE International Conference on Human-Robot Interaction (HRI 2008)* (Technical Report 471, pp. 37–44).

Bayer, T. I. (2008). Vico's principle of sensus communis and forensic eloquence. *Chicago-Kent Law Review, 83*, 1131.

Bishop, L., van Maris, A., Dogramadzi, S., & Zook, N. (2019). Social robots: The influence of human and robot characteristics on acceptance. *Paladyn, Journal of Behavioral Robotics, 10*(1), 346–358.

British Standards Institution. (2016). Robots and robotic devices. Guide to the ethical design and application of robots and robotic systems. http://shop.bsigroup.com/ProductDetail?pid=000000000030320089

Choi, Y. (2022). The curious case of commonsense intelligence. *Daedalus, 151*(2), 139–155.

De Lima, E. S., & Feijó, B. (2019). Artificial intelligence in human-robot interaction. In H. Ayanoğlu & E. Duarte (Eds.), *Emotional design in human-robot interaction: Theory, methods, and applications* (pp. 187–199). Springer.

EU. (2017). Civil law rules on robotics - European Parliament resolution of 16 February 2017 with recommendations (2015/2103(INL)).

EU. (2018). Open letter to the European Commission – Artificial intelligence and robotics. http://www.robotics-openletter.eu

Evas, T. (2017). *Public consultation on robotics and artificial intelligence - First (preliminary) results of public consultation.* European Parliament. https://ec.europa.eu/information_society/newsroom/image/document/2017-30/mep_delvaux_-_the_ep_public_consultation_on_robotics_and_artificial_intelligence_620B6403-F980-704B-B1BC246167E4DDFB_46143.pdf

Eyssel, F., & Kuchenbrandt, D. (2012). Social categorization of social robots: Anthropomorphism as a function of robot group membership. *British Journal of Social Psychology, 51*(4), 724–731.

Fauquet-Alekhine, P. (2022a). Scientific communication on artificial intelligence: The question of the social status of the biodroid. *Advances in Research, 23*(5), 1–5.

Fauquet-Alekhine, P. (2022b). Can the robot be considered a person? *Advances in Research, 23*(6), 100–105.

Fauquet-Alekhine, P. (2023a). Biodroids as embodied AI: An imminent social issue. In M. W. Bauer & B. Schiele (Eds.), *Science communication – Taking a step back to move forward* (pp. 175–181). CNRS Publishers.

Fauquet-Alekhine, P. (2023b). Legal personhood and robotics: Birth of the smart android and of the biodroid. *Advances in Research, 24*(5), 163–174, Article no. AIR.100958.

Haidegger, T. (2021). Taxonomy and standards in robotics. In M. H. Ang, O. Khatib, & B. Siciliano (Eds.), *Encyclopedia of robotics.* Springer Nature.

Henschel, A., Hortensius, R., & Cross, E. S. (2020). Social cognition in the age of human–robot interaction. *Trends in Cognitive Sciences, 43*(6), 373–384.

HLEG (High-Level Expert Group on Artificial Intelligence). (2019). *A definition of AI: Main capabilities and disciplines.* European Commission.

Krägeloh, C. U., Bharatharaj, J., Sasthan Kutty, S. K., Nirmala, P. R., & Huang, L. (2019). Questionnaires to measure acceptability of social robots: A critical review. *Robotics, 8*(4), 88.

List, C. (2021). Group agency and artificial intelligence. *Philosophy and Technology, 34*(4), 1213–1242.

Lombard, J., & Dinet, J. (2015, July 8–10). Attitudes towards robots and perception of their autonomy: Towards the creation of a robot autonomy perception scale

(EPAR). In *Proceedings of the 8th EPIQUE 2015 conference "Ergonomics and Interdisciplinarity"*. Aix-en-Provence, France.

MacCann, C., Jiang, Y., Brown, L. E., Double, K. S., Bucich, M., & Minbashian, A. (2020). Emotional intelligence predicts academic performance: A meta-analysis. *Psychological Bulletin, 146*(2), 150–186.

Мельникова, Е. Н. (2022). Встраиваемость концепции электронного лица в правовую систему государства или государственного образования [The embeddability of the concept of an electronic face in the legal system of the state or state education]. *Russian Juridical Journal/Rossijskij Juridiceskij Zurnal, 143*(2) 94–112.

Nevejans, N. (2016). *European civil law rules in robotics: Study. European Parliament, policy department C: Citizens' rights and constitutional affairs*. European Parliament. Publications Office.

Nomura, T. (2020). A possibility of inappropriate use of gender studies in human-robot interaction. *AI and Society, 35*(3), 751–754.

Picard, R. W. (2008). *Toward machines with emotional intelligence*. Oxford University Press.

Robert, L., Alahmad, R., Esterwood, C., Kim, S., You, S., & Zhang, Q. (2020). A review of personality in human-robot interactions. *Foundations and Trends® in Information Systems, 4*(2), 107–212.

Sammut, G., & Bauer, M. W. (2021). *The psychology of social influence: Modes and modalities of shifting common sense*. Cambridge University Press.

Spatola, N., Kühnlenz, B., & Cheng, G. (2021). Perception and evaluation in human–robot interaction: The Human–Robot Interaction Evaluation Scale (HRIES)—A multicomponent approach of anthropomorphism. *International Journal of Social Robotics, 13*(7), 1517–1539.

Udayar, S., Fiori, M., & Bausseron, E. (2020). Emotional intelligence and performance in a stressful task: The mediating role of self-efficacy. *Personality and Individual Differences, 156*, 109790, 1–6.

Zacharaki, A., Kostavelis, I., Gasteratos, A., & Dokas, I. (2020). Safety bounds in human-robot interaction: A survey. *Safety Science, 127*, 104667.

5

TOWARDS ROBOTS WITH COMMON SENSE

Alan F.T. Winfield

Common sense is something that most people think they have without necessarily being able to explain what it is. Common sense, as generally understood, encompasses a range of competencies. One is knowing how to be safe. Understanding, for instance, that stepping off the pavement into oncoming traffic is dangerous. Common sense is also, by definition, knowing things that other people know. It is therefore a kind of social intelligence, which encompasses not only social norms (i.e., of good behaviour), but arguably also the ability to intuit another person's intentions or theory of mind.

These two kinds of intelligence, safety intelligence and social intelligence, would be valuable attributes of social robots: robots that interact with humans. Examples include assisted living robots, workplace assistant co-bots and smart robot toys. While most social robots are already equipped with some measure of safety intelligence, none – to the author's knowledge – have an artificial theory of mind. The primary aim of this study is to address the questions: could a robot be equipped with an artificial "common sense" and if so, how?

This chapter proceeds as follows. In the second section, I shall review definitions of common sense and – perhaps equally useful – what is *not* common sense. Then in the third section, I will outline two conceptual models of mind: Mithen's cathedral model and Dennett's tower of generate and test, then argue that these models not only provide useful distinctions between kinds of intelligence but also map meaningfully onto aspects of common sense identified in the second section.

In the fourth section, I present a method for equipping social robots with an artificial theory of mind. The method is based on a simulation-based

DOI: 10.4324/9781032626192-9

internal model that allows a robot to model and hence predict the likely consequences of both its actions and others in its environment. The approach has been experimentally tested with real robots, demonstrating both enhanced safety and simple ethical behaviours. The fourth section then outlines current work to extend the method so that robots can tell each other stories. I contend that these experiments offer a practical starting point for social robots with artificial common sense. The fifth section concludes by discussing the extent to which the robots of the fourth section match first, the requirements of common sense proposed in the second section and then the kinds of common sense defined by Bauer in this volume.

Defining common sense

There is no single agreed definition of common sense. The Cambridge dictionary defines common sense as "the basic level of practical knowledge and judgement that we all need to help us live in a reasonable and safe way". The Collins dictionary offers a similar definition: "your common sense is your natural ability to make good judgments and to behave in a practical and sensible way". The Wikipedia entry on common sense provides a more extensive and perhaps more useful definition "Common sense (or simply sense) is sound, practical judgement concerning everyday matters, or a basic ability to perceive, understand, and judge in a manner that is shared by (i.e., 'common to') nearly all people".

The encyclopaedia Britannica entry on philosophy of common sense outlines the 18th- and early 19th-century Scottish school of Thomas Reid and others who held that in the actual perception of the average, unsophisticated man, sensations are not mere ideas or subjective impressions but carry with them the belief in corresponding qualities as belonging to external objects. Such beliefs, Reid insisted, "belong to the common sense and reason of mankind"; and in matters of common sense "the learned and the unlearned, the philosopher and the day-labourer, are upon a level" (Britannica, 1998).[1]

Of particular interest is a short article "What is common sense" written by AI pioneer, and originator of the term "Artificial Intelligence", John McCarthy (2002). McCarthy writes

> There is common sense knowledge and common sense ability. Common sense knowledge includes facts about events occurring in time, about the effects of actions by the knower and others, about physical objects and how they are perceived, and about their properties and their relations to one another. Common sense ability involves the use of common sense knowledge and the observation of the world to decide what to do to achieve one's goals.

It is also interesting that McCarthy asserts: "It is now generally agreed among AI researchers that making programs with common sense abilities is at present the key problem facing AI research".

It is also useful to ask, "what is not common sense?" Quantum physics is not common sense, nor is jurisprudence, or art history. Basic arithmetic, as needed to pay bills, might be regarded as common sense, but the ability to use differential calculus would not be. In general, expert knowledge is not common sense. The difference between Reid's learned and unlearned is that the former will have expert knowledge, the latter not.

Given the discussion above, what are the basic requirements of common sense that could be shared by humans and social robots? I suggest:

1. Agency. In other words, the ability to decide your next action without the intervention of others. Of course, you might choose to seek advice before taking an action, but that is also agency. For robots, this would mean they are autonomous.[2]
2. Practical knowledge. We might call this physics intelligence – knowing that walking into a wall or jumping from a height could cause injury.
3. Prediction. The ability to predict the effects of actions, while making use of practical knowledge, then using this prediction to determine what action to take. This is McCarthy's common-sense knowledge *and* ability.
4. Social knowledge. This includes knowledge of social norms alongside the ability to infer the intentions of others; in other words, theory of mind. Theory of mind is needed because, in a social context, you need the ability to predict the effects of your actions, including the effect of your actions on others.

Models of mind

In this section I briefly review two conceptual models of mind: Mithen's Cathedral model and Dennett's tower of generate and test.

In *The Prehistory of the Mind*, Stephen Mithen (1996) introduces what he calls a cathedral model of mind. He supposes that in pre-modern hominids there are four distinct categories of intelligence: technical, linguistic, social and natural history, arranged like chapels around a central nave, see Figure 5.1. Technical intelligence is the kind of intelligence required to move around safely, climb trees, etc., and for tool making. Natural history intelligence is knowing what is good to eat and how to collect it. Linguistic intelligence is knowing how to communicate with conspecifics, and social intelligence is about understanding social relationships within family or tribal groups. The nave represents general intelligence, and in the diagram in Figure 5.1 (left), the four chapels and the nave are connected with the hominids' sensory

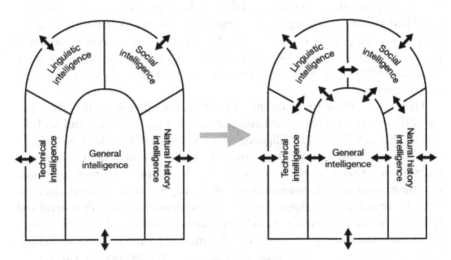

FIGURE 5.1 The cathedral model of mind (Mithen, 1996).

organs and body, but closed to each other so that the five kinds of intelligence only interact through the body and the world. Mithen proposes that the modern mind emerged when the chapels and the nave became open to each other as in Figure 5.1 (right), so that the five kinds of intelligence became connected and therefore integrated. The profound consequence of this opening is that "Minds in which the multiple specialised intelligences appear to be working together, with a flow of knowledge and ideas between behavioural domains" (Mithen, 1996, p. 69).

In *Darwin's Dangerous Idea,* Dennett (1995) sets out a conceptual model for the evolution of intelligence that has become known as Dennett's tower. Dennett's tower is a set of conceptual creatures, each one of which is successively more capable of reacting to (and hence surviving in) the world through having more sophisticated strategies for generating and testing hypotheses about how to act in a given situation.

The ground floor of Dennett's tower represents Darwinian creatures; these have only natural selection as the generate-and-test mechanism, so mutation and selection are the only way that Darwinian creatures can adapt – individuals cannot. All biological organisms are Darwinian creatures. On the first floor we find Skinnerian creatures, a subset of Darwinians, which can learn but only by generating and physically testing all different possible actions then reinforcing the successful behaviour – providing of course that the creature survives the physical test. On the second floor Dennett's Popperian creatures have the additional ability to internally model the possible actions so that some (the bad ones) are discarded before they are tried out for real. The ability to internally model possible actions is of course a very significant innovation. On the third floor of Dennett's tower, a sub-sub-sub-set of Darwinians, are Gregorian creatures. In addition to an internal model, Gregorians have what Dennett refers to, after Richard Gregory, as mind tools – including words, which they import from the (cultural) environment (Dennett, 1995, p. 378). Conceptually therefore Dennett's Gregorians are social learners.

The value of these two conceptual models of intelligence is that they give two different perspectives. Mithen's model is flat and modular and usefully defines distinct kinds of intelligence, whereas Dennett's model is nested and hierarchical, centred on what *all* kinds of intelligence must do, i.e., generate and test an action in response to a stimulus. A human, in Dennett's schema, is at the same time a Darwinian, Skinnerian, Popperian and Gregorian creature. There is a coarse mapping across the two models: Mithen's general and technical intelligence manifests in Darwinian creatures, and general, technical and natural history intelligence in Skinnerian creatures. Both social and linguistic intelligence are defining characteristics of Gregorian creatures.

How then do these two models help us to better understand common sense? Arguably the five kinds of intelligence in Mithen's model, in both pre- and modern minds, all contribute to "common sense".[3] Dennett's model reminds us that all knowledge needs to be acquired and actionable. Basic common sense is instinctive (Darwinian), some are learned (Skinnerian and Popperian) and much is passed from parent or teacher to child, master to apprentice or storyteller to group (Gregorian). Noting of course that both common and expert knowledge are transmitted via the same mechanisms of social learning.

Towards an artificial common sense

Inspired by both Mithen's cathedral model and Dennett's tower of generate and test we have developed a simulation-based internal model. The model is a mechanism for internally representing both the robot and its current environment. If we embed a simulation of a robot, including its currently perceived environment, inside that robot then the robot has a mechanism for generating and testing *what-if* hypotheses; i.e.,

1. *what if* I carry out action x ...? and, ...

2. of several possible next actions x_i, *which* should I choose?

Shown in Figure 5.2 the machinery for modelling next actions is relatively independent of the robot's controller. The *what-if* processes are not in the robot's main control loop, but instead run in parallel to moderate the Robot

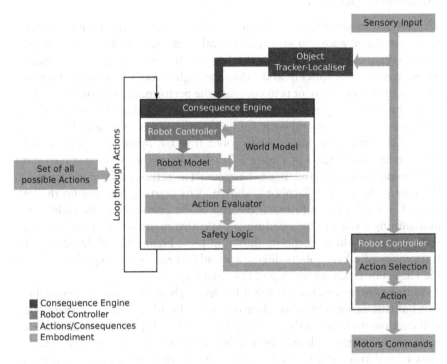

FIGURE 5.2   The consequence engine with a simulation-based internal model.

Note: Figure from Blum et al. (2018).

Controller's normal action–selection process, acting in effect as a kind of governor. This governor might rule out certain actions because they are modelled as unsafe for the robot, or recommend new robot actions to, for instance, prevent another agent coming to harm.

At the heart of the architecture is the consequence engine (CE). Within the CE is a simulation-based internal model, comprising the Robot Controller, Robot (self) Model and World Model. The CE is initialised from the Object Tracker–Localiser and loops through all possible next actions; these next actions are generated within the Robot Controller (RC) and transferred to the mirror RC within the CE (for clarity this data flow is omitted from Figure 5.2).

For each candidate action, the CE simulates the robot executing each action and generates a set of model outputs ready for evaluation by the Action Evaluator. The consequence engine loops through each possible next action; this is the generate-and-test loop. Only when the complete set of next possible actions has been tested does the CE send, to the Robot Controller, its recommendations. These processes are explained in detail in Blum et al. (2018).

The corridor experiments

We have implemented and tested the simulation-based internal model architecture outlined above in an experimental scenario, which we call the corridor experiment (Blum et al., 2018). Inspired by the problem of how mobile robots could move quickly and safely through crowds of moving humans, the aim of this experiment is to compare the performance of our simulation-based internal model with a purely reactive approach. In other words: Can a robot's safety be improved with a simple artificial theory of mind?

In this experiment, one mobile robot (the CE-robot) is equipped with the consequence engine of Figure 5.2, while five other mobile robots have only simple obstacle avoidance behaviours. The setup is shown in Figure 5.3 (left); here the smart CE-robot is shown at its starting position on the left. The CE-robot's goal is to reach the end of the corridor on the right while maintaining its safety by avoiding – while also maintaining a safe distance – the five proxy-human robots shown in grey. Figure 5.3 (right) shows the trajectories of all six robots during a simulated run of the experiment, with the CE-robot reaching the end of the corridor.

In this experiment, the CE robot models each of the proxy-human robots as a ballistic agent with obstacle avoidance – in other words, as agents that will continue to move in their current direction and speed unless confronted with an obstacle, which may be another agent or the corridor wall. The CE runs in real time and is updated every 0.5 s with the actual position and direction of the proxy-humans within the CE robot's attention radius.[4] This is not an unreasonable model when considering how you might behave when avoiding another person who is not paying attention to where they are going – peering at their smartphone perhaps.

In an extension to the corridor experiment, which we call the pedestrian experiment., two robots – each equipped with the same CE – approach each other. As with the corridor experiment, each models the other as a simple

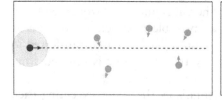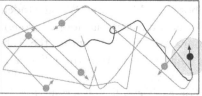

FIGURE 5.3 The corridor experiment.

Note: The corridor experiment goal (left), with five (grey) robots moving randomly and one intelligent (CE) robot (black) with a simulation-based internal model. (Right) shows (simulated) trajectories of all six robots by the time black has reaching the end of the corridor. Figure from Blum et al. (2018).

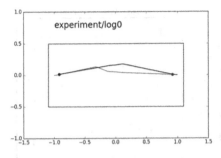 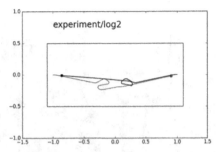

FIGURE 5.4   The pedestrian experiment.

Note: Two trials showing robot trajectories. Two robots are each equipped with a CE. One starts from the left, with a goal position on the right, while at the same time the other starts from the right with a goal position on the left. (Left) We see the typical behaviour in which the two robots pass each other without difficulty, normally because one robot – anticipating a collision – changes direction first. (Right) Here both robots make a decision to turn at the same time, one to its left and the other to its right; a "dance" then ensues before the impasse is resolved. Figure from Winfield (2018b).

ballistic agent but here we have symmetry with each agent paying full attention to the other, trying to anticipate how it might behave and planning its own actions accordingly. Is it possible that our "pedestrian" robots might, from time to time, engage in the kind of "dance" that human pedestrians do when one steps to their left and the other to their right only to compound the problem of avoiding a collision with a stranger?

Results show that we do indeed observe this interesting emergent behaviour. In five experimental runs, on average, four resulted in the two pedestrian robots passing each other by both turning either to the left or to the right – Figure 5.4 (left) shows one example of this behaviour. However, in one run, shown in Figure 5.4 (right), we observe a brief dance caused when both robots decide, at the same time, to turn toward each other – each predicting wrongly that the other robot would continue its current trajectory – before the two robots resolve the impasse and pass each other safely.

Robots with simple moral intelligence

We have conducted exploratory work – based on the same simulation-based internal model architecture outlined here – to explore the possibility of robots capable of making decisions based on ethical rules. These robots implement simple consequentialist ethics with rules based on Asimov's famous laws of robotics. Following Asimov's first law: "a robot may not harm a human or, through inaction, allow a human to come to harm", our ethical robot will act proactively when it anticipates (a) that a proxy-human

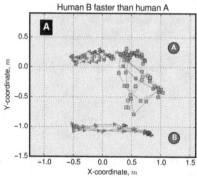

FIGURE 5.5 An ethical dilemma.

Note: Left: The ethical NAO robot is initially positioned midway between and slightly to the front of two danger zones A and B. Right: The ethical robot's trajectories are shown here plotted with squares. Two proxy-human NAO robots start from the left, both heading toward danger – trajectories plotted with triangles. Results of five trials are shown here. Figure from Winfield (2018b).

robot is in danger of coming to harm and (b) the ethical robot can itself intervene. We have experimentally tested such a minimally ethical robot initially with e-puck robots (Winfield et al., 2014) and subsequently with NAO humanoid robots (Vanderelst & Winfield, 2018). As in the corridor experiment, the ethical robot's CE models the proxy-human(s) as simple ballistic agents.

We have tested the same ethical robot (running identical code) in a scenario with two proxy-humans both heading toward danger at the same time. These trials are believed to be the first experimental tests of a robot facing an ethical dilemma. We did not provide the ethical robot with a rule or heuristic for choosing which proxy-human to "rescue" first, so that the ethical robot faces a balanced dilemma. Figure 5.5 (left) shows the experimental arena with the ethical robot (top middle) initially equidistant from the two (bottom left and right) proxy-human robots. The trajectory plots in Figure 5.5 (right) interestingly show that in three of the five trials the ethical robot initially chose to move toward the robot heading toward danger (B), but then appeared to "change its mind" to rescue the other robot. This dithering behaviour is not programmed but an unexpected emergent property of the experimental setup.

Robots that tell each other stories

Assume that we have two robots, each equipped with the internal modelling machinery outlined above. Let us also assume that the robots are of a similar

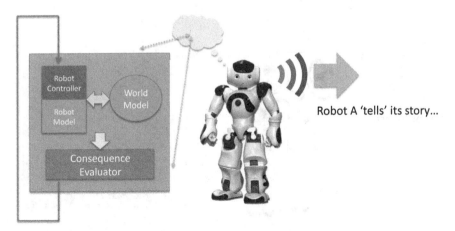

Robot A 'tells' its story...

FIGURE 5.6 Robot A "narrativising" a "what-if" sequence.

Note: Robot A, the storyteller, "narrativises" one of the "what-if" sequences generated by its generate-and-test machinery. First, an action is tested in the robot's internal model, then that action – which is not executed for real – is converted into speech and spoken by the robot.

type, in other words, they are conspecifics. Within Dennett's framework, each robot is a Popperian creature; it is capable of generating and testing the next possible actions. Let us now extend the robots' capabilities in the following way. Instead of simply discarding ("forgetting") an action that has been modelled and determined to be a bad action, the robot may transmit that action to another robot.

Figure 5.6 illustrates robot A "imagining" a what-if sequence, then narra-tivising that sequence. It literally signals that sequence using some transmission medium. In practice we could make use of any number of signals and media but, since we are building a model and it would be very convenient if it is easy for human observers to interpret the model, let us code the what-if sequence verbally and transmit it as a spoken language sequence. Technically this would be easy to arrange since we would use a standard speech synthesis process. Although it is a trivial narrative, robot A is now able to *both* imagine and then literally *tell* a story, and because that story is of something that has not happened, it is a *fictional* narrative. The story will be trivial but nevertheless useful, for instance "if I turned left I would crash into the wall".

Robot B is equipped with a microphone and speech recognition process – it is thus able to listen to robot A's story, as shown in Figure 5.7. Let us assume it is programmed to "understand" the same language, so that a word used by A signifies the same part of the what-if action sequence to both A and B. Providing the story has been heard correctly then robot B will

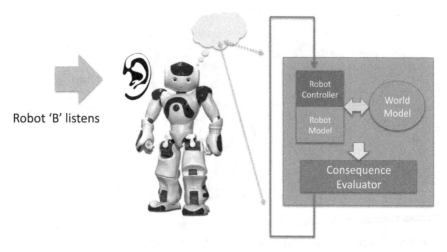

Robot 'B' listens

FIGURE 5.7   Robot B "listening" to a "what-if" sequence.

Note: Robot B, the listener, uses the same "what if" cognitive machinery to, in a sense, imagine robot A's story. Here, the robot hears A's spoken sequence, then converts it into an action which is replayed in B's internal model.

interpret robot A's story as a what-if sequence. Now, because robot B has the same internal modelling machinery as A – they are conspecifics – it is capable of "running" the story it has just heard within its own internal model. In order that this can happen we need to modify the robot's programming so that the what-if sequence it has heard and interpreted is substituted for an internally generated what-if sequence. This would be easy to do. But, once that substitution is made, robot B is able to replay A's what-if sequence (it's story) in *exactly* the same way as its own internally generated next possible actions, simulating and evaluating the consequences. Robot B is therefore able to "imagine" robot A's story.

In this model, we have, in effect, co-opted the cognitive machinery for predicting the consequences of possible actions for internally experiencing, or "imagining", heard stories. By adding the machinery for signalling and signifying internally generated sequences (narratives) – the machinery of semiotics – we have transformed our Popperian robots into Gregorian robots. Thus, we have an embodied computational model of storytelling, in which the listener robot is able to "imagine" itself in the speaker robot's shoes – I contend – the way that we humans do when listening to a story or reading a novel.

Of course, the setup proposed here is very simple, allowing only for trivially simple stories told as short monologues. However, there is much we can learn from even this. Given that the robots will use synthetically generated spoken words, there is the potential for the listener robot to mishear the speaker robot. If the listener robot cannot successfully "run" the story in its own CE, then the robot might respond with "please repeat". Alternatively, if the misheard story can be successfully run, then the story might have mutated in an unexpected way. The listener robot might assume the role of storyteller, re-telling the possibly misheard story to another robot, allowing us to model – with robots – a transmission chain (Mesoudi & Whiten, 2008).

The experimental scope of the storytelling robots would be considerably extended by providing each robot with a long-term (episodic) memory. The memory would store discrete events (things that happened to the robot) and the actions (of the robot). Alongside these actions and events, the robot could also remember stories: not only stories it has heard (with the name of the storytelling robot), but also "what if" stories that the robot has asked itself.[5] For a more detailed discussion of the experimental possibilities that follow, see Winfield and Blackmore (2021).

Discussion

This chapter has proposed robots with simulation-based internal models as a basis for artificial common sense. Consider the four basic requirements for common sense suggested in the section "Defining common sense". To what extent, if at all, are these requirements met?

First, *agency* is met in full because the robots mentioned in the section "Towards an artificial common sense" can autonomously choose which action to take. This agency is considerably enhanced in the robots equipped with a consequence engine (CE) due to their ability to anticipate the possible consequences of both their own and others' actions.

Second, *practical knowledge* is embedded in the simulation-based internal model (mirror Robot Controller, Robot Self-Model and World Model) of the consequence engine (see Figure 5.2). The simulation-based internal model is programmed with simple physics: for instance, the physics of motion and kinematics including practical knowledge of collisions. In the experiments outlined in sections "The corridor experiments" and "Robots with simple moral intelligence", other robots are modelled with simple ballistics: if a robot is moving at a given speed and direction, then the World Model will model it as continuing to move at the same speed and direction; it will also model collisions between those other robots and fixed objects such as walls. This is, however, the extent of the practical knowledge in the robots that we have developed and tested so far.

Third, *prediction* is, within the severe limitations of the practical knowledge, met in full. In fact, the consequence engine is surprisingly capable.

It allows for the prediction of first-order interactions, between the subject robot (equipped with a CE) and other dynamic agents (i.e., robots), second-order interactions between the subject robot and the fixed environment, and third-order interactions between other dynamic actors, not involving the subject robot.

Fourth, *social knowledge* is embedded in the CE in two ways. One is that the physical behaviour of robots is built into the World Model, outlined above as practical knowledge. However, both Robot and World Models also embed collision avoidance so that the subject robot will not collide with other robots, and vice versa. This is a very simple *social norm*. The second kind of social knowledge is embedded within the Safety Logic of the CE in Figure 5.1. This differs in the experiments outlined in sections "The corridor experiments" and "Robots with simple moral intelligence". In the Corridor Experiment, the safety logic of the subject robot's Robot Model is programmed with a larger collision avoidance radius than the default, so that it is more collision averse and will stop or turn to avoid a predicted collision with another robot sooner. The simple "ethical" robot of section "Robots with simple moral intelligence" embeds Asimov's first law of robotics: *a robot may not injure a human being or, through inaction, allow a human being to come to harm.* Importantly, the ability of the CE to predict that another agent is heading for danger allows the ethical robot to proactively intervene and prevent the harm.

Do these capabilities add up to artificial common sense? If we assume that the four requirements proposed in section "Define common sense" are sufficient, then arguably yes. As implemented here it is, however, a very rudimentary kind of common sense. The reason our robots do not have much common sense is that the amount of practical and social knowledge embedded in them is very limited indeed. I nevertheless contend that the approach set out in this chapter is a sound substrate for artificial common sense that, if provided[6] with more practical and social knowledge, could have practical value for real-world social robots.

Consider now the kinds of common sense suggested in this volume by Bauer, and the extent to which the robot experiments outlined above demonstrate any of these kinds of CS. First, we can discount CS-4 (an ethos of philosophy), CS-6 (what social psychology is about) and CS-7 (bringing agonistic parties to their senses).

CS-1 solves the "binding problem", i.e., integration of multi-modal sensory experiences

Robots have sensors and hence are, following Higgins (2021), sentient – albeit minimally. Furthermore, our robots with a simulation-based internal model use sense data to position themselves and other agents in the simulated World Model, thus providing the robot with a simple *sensorium*. Furthermore, the robot's World Model does provide the robot with an "inner perception" (Bauer, Chapter 1 this volume), also sometimes described as a "functional imagination" (Marques & Holland, 2009). Arguably, therefore, the robots outlined in sections "The corridor experiments". "Robots with simple moral intelligence" and "Robots that tell each other stories" do exhibit the properties of CS-1.

CS-2 is a stock of universally recognisable knowledge

The second property of common sense *practical knowledge*, as proposed in the section "Define common sense", aligns closely with CS-2. The limited practical knowledge embedded within the World and Robot Models of the robots with simulation-based internal models includes CS-2's "universally recognisable knowledge" of the physics of motion and of collisions (kinematics), thus also strongly aligning with Mithen's technical intelligence of Figure 5.1.

CS-3: the quasi-rational judgement call: neither just intuition nor formally rational

Our robots do not intuit their actions, but nor do they employ formal, analytical reasoning. Instead, they make use of a simulation-based internal model (or sensorium – see CS-1) that does not provide the robot with a perfect representation of the world. Given that the robot and other agents are in motion, and that the robot's sensors have limited acuity and are subject to real-world ambient noise and occlusions, the World Model is only an approximate representation. It follows that the predictions of the consequence engine are only estimates of what might happen for a given next possible action.[7] Thus, the decisions the robot makes are not formally rational, but quasi-rational, and arguably of type CS-3.

CS-5 is the sense of community that binds us into joint attention and intentionality

The section "Robots with simple moral intelligence" outlines robots with simple moral intelligence which therefore meets one of the criteria set out for CS-5 (in addition to CS-1, CS-2 and CS-3). Arguably our simple ethical robots also provide (minimally) a *sensus communis* that binds individuals into joint attention – because the ethical robot must pay attention to the possibility that the proxy-human robots might come to harm – and intentionally act upon that possibility. In our proposed storytelling robots of the section "Robots that tell each other stories" that joint attention is further strengthened by the acts of: first the speaker robot calling for attention, then the listener robot attending to the speaker. Also note that – as outlined above – our robots have shared social knowledge of simple social norms (avoiding collisions with each other) alongside the simple ethical behaviour. These are examples of Mithen's social intelligence in Figure 5.1.

In conclusion, this chapter has outlined a series of experiments that – notwithstanding their limitations – meet the requirements of common sense set out in the section "Defining common sense" and exhibit the properties of four of the kinds of common sense defined by Bauer (this volume). We can therefore have some confidence that the approach of the section "Defining common sense" offers a practical starting point for designing real-world social robots with artificial common sense.

Notes

1. See also CS-4 in Bauer (this volume).
2. Noting that no robot, or human, is truly autonomous. We humans are constrained by both etiquette and laws. And even highly autonomous robots are supervised by humans; this is called supervised autonomy.
3. In early humans, almost all knowledge would be common to all but infants. Only with the emergence of modern minds did *experts* emerge, so that some knowledge, shamanistic ritual, flint napping or basket weaving, for instance, ceased to be common.
4. Which is forward looking (like humans) and has a limited range.
5. Which would provide an interesting model of remembering by re-imagining.
6. Either through programming or learning.
7. Our robot's internal model does not need to be perfect, only (like animal's) good enough.

Bibliography

Blum, C., Winfield, A. F. T., & Hafner, V. V. (2018). Simulation-based internal models for safer robots. *Frontiers in Robotics and A*, 4(74). https://doi.org/10.3389/frobt.2017.00074Britannica, the Editors of Encyclopaedia. (1998). Philosophy of common sense. *Encyclopedia Britannica*. https://www.britannica.com/topic/philosophy-of-common-sense

Dennett, D. (1995). *Darwin's dangerous idea*. Penguin.

Higgins, J. (2021). *Sentient: What animals reveal about our senses*. Picador.

Marques, H., & Holland, O. (2009). Architectures for functional imagination. *Neurocomputing*, 72(4–6), 743–759.

McCarthy, J. (2002). *What is common sense*. Stanford University. http://jmc.stanford.edu/articles/commonsense/commonsense.pdf

Mesoudi, A., & Whiten, A. (2008). The multiple roles of cultural transmission experiments in understanding human cultural evolution. *Philosophical Transactions of the Royal Society B: Biological Sciences*, 363(1509), 3489–3501. https://doi.org/10.1098/rstb.2008.0129

Mithen, S. (1996). *The prehistory of the mind: A search for the origins of art, religion and science*. Orion Books.

Vanderelst, D., & Winfield, A. (2018). An architecture for ethical robots inspired by the simulation theory of cognition. *Cognitive Systems Research*, 48, 56–66. https://doi.org/10.1016/j.cogsys.2017.04.002

Winfield, A. F. T. (2018a). When robots tell each other stories: The emergence of artificial fiction. In R. Walsh & S. Stepney (Eds.), *Narrating complexity*. Springer. https://doi.org/10.1007/978-3-319-64714-2_4

Winfield, A. F. T. (2018b). Experiments in artificial theory of mind: From safety to story-telling. *Frontiers in Robotics and AI*, 5(75). https://doi.org/10.3389/frobt.2018.00075

Winfield, A. F. T., & Blackmore, S. (2021). Experiments in artificial culture: From noisy imitation to storytelling robots. *Philosophical Transactions of the Royal Society B: Biological Sciences*, 377, 20200323. https://doi.org/10.1098/rstb.2020.0323

Winfield, A. F. T., Blum, C., & Liu, W. (2014). Towards an ethical robot: Internal models, consequences and ethical action selection. In M. Mistry, A. Leonardis, M. Witkowski, & C. Melhuish (Eds.), *Advances in autonomous robotics systems, Vol. 8717, TAROS 2014. Lecture Notes in Computer Science* (pp. 85–96). Springer.

6

COMMON SENSE, ARTIFICIAL INTELLIGENCE AND PSYCHOLOGY

Laura Bartlett

Artificial intelligence (AI) refers to the ability of computer programs to demonstrate human-level general intelligence. While initially thought to be an easy task, requiring only a few inferences to be input into a machine in order to demonstrate high-level capabilities akin to humans (McCarthy, 1960), this has not been the case. In particular, aspects of intelligence that are often referred to as common sense, such as generality, incorporation of context and flexible use of knowledge, have failed to be replicated artificially. The goals of AI developers and researchers have shifted towards more specific tasks, where programs have demonstrated incredibly complex behaviours and substantially contributed to knowledge and science (e.g., designing vaccines for the COVID-19 virus). However, these systems are narrowly focused, more akin to expertise than intelligence, and lack the generality and common sense that may be a necessary component of general intelligence (Sternberg et al., 2000). The attention given to more recent developments such as ChatGPT, a large language model that can successfully provide responses to a wide range of inputs in a way consistent with human conversation, has brought this question into sharper focus: does this system, that uses conversational context cues and a wealth of knowledge to give on-the-fly responses, exhibit common sense?

In the drive towards artificial general intelligence (AGI), it is important to not only clarify why it might be necessary to integrate common sense into AI, but also define what we mean by common sense and intelligence. Given the successes of AI systems that have already been developed, we can question whether creating AI with common sense is required or worthwhile. Nonetheless, the drive for artificial programs that can demonstrate common

DOI: 10.4324/9781032626192-10

sense has persisted, with (arguably) limited success thus far (as outlined by Brachman & Levesque, 2022). As psychologists are concerned with understanding the cognitive abilities of humans, studying the components that intelligence may be comprised of, research from this field is likely critical for creating systems with human-level capabilities – how can we replicate human behaviour without first knowing what it consists of?

This chapter will discuss issues and considerations for defining both general intelligence and common sense, outline possible benchmarks for artificial common sense and discuss the role psychologists could play in this difficult task. Further, the drive for AGI will be scrutinised. Considering the increasing role of AI in all areas of society and the allocation of resources for developing particular technologies, clarifying these concepts is essential. A central goal of this chapter is to both scrutinise whether AGI is worthwhile and advocate for interdisciplinary collaboration if so. This is a timely debate, and one that is moving extremely quickly with continuous advances in AI technology.

What do we mean by artificial general intelligence?

Before discussing the costs and benefits of developing artificial systems capable of demonstrating human-level intelligence, it is important to understand how intelligence is defined. Intelligence is a multifaceted phenomenon and, akin to many theories in the social sciences, its definitions are often verbal and lack precision, and it is regularly conflated with the psychometric tests used to assess it. This conflation has even been applied to AI – Bringsjord (2011) has argued for psychometric AI, with the goal for artificial systems to be able to demonstrate good performance on established intelligence tests, akin to the Turing test. Intelligence tests, however, are contentious, particularly in terms of their use for discriminatory practices in the past and their reliance on cultural concepts that do not apply well to other cultures (Lozano-Ruiz et al., 2021). Defining AI in these terms is holding an artificial system to a very rigid set of principles that were not developed for these purposes.

As intelligence is a complex and abstract concept, AGI systems would have to perform well across a spectrum of intelligent behaviours. Given that intelligence can be thought of as a group of different behaviours, ranging from perception and memory to social and emotional intelligence, decisions regarding which are most important are critical. Demonstrating even one of these in an artificial system may be a huge endeavour (Kotseruba & Tsotsos, 2020). Cognitive modelling techniques (such as ACT-R, Anderson et al., 2004; and Genetically Evolving Models in Science (GEMS), Addis et al., 2019) can constrain definitions of intelligence, as detailed descriptions of processes are required to input a theory into a coding language. For example, researchers have developed computational cognitive models using ACT-R to predict how information is selected in simulated tasks (Paik & Pirolli, 2015). Further, these architectures typically strive towards a unified model of cognition that can encompass a range of human behaviours.

A component often regarded as important for intelligence is common sense (Brachman & Levesque, 2022; Sternberg et al., 2000). In the literature, common sense is often cited as a key bottleneck for AGI (Kolata, 1982); while computer programs excel when given well-specified problems, the flexibility and selectivity of human intelligence (or common sense) are more fluidly defined, lacking a clear formalised definition and a consistent method of measurement. Insights from philosophy and psychology, which have historically explored the mechanisms and measurement of intelligence, could inform goals and benchmarks. If artificial common sense is required before a system is seen as intelligent, then it is critical to know what exactly it is and how to know when it has been achieved.

Multiple definitions of common sense exist, as outlined in Chapter 1 (Bauer), each highlighting different facets of the term. Even linking intelligence and common sense runs counter to some of the historical definitions, for example, those that view common sense as opposite to science/intelligence (as Doxa – opinion – in opposition to Episteme – true knowledge). Further muddying the picture, at least some elements of common sense differ across cultures; different societies may hold certain things to be true, with different norms and expectations (Anacleto et al., 2006). As such, attempts to create artificial common sense will likely be bound by the cultures they are developed within. These are all important considerations in the drive for AGI – how common sense is conceptualised must be clarified.

While difficult to define, common sense is often characterised as knowledge that is taken for granted and used to inform decisions and actions for common and novel tasks. Emphasis has been placed on the intuitive nature of common-sense reasoning (Choi, 2022), as well as its basis in the ordinary – using ordinary experiential knowledge for ordinary tasks (Brachman & Levesque, 2022). In order to formalise the measurement of common sense in natural language processing systems, Kejriwal et al. (2022) proposed the use of a framework based on common sense psychology. This framework encompassed 48 areas of common sense including decision-making, organisation, social reasoning (predicting beliefs and goals in others) and naïve physics (engaging with the world without formal understanding of physics). This framework highlights both the complexity that common sense represents and the dynamic way in which it is employed by humans in complex scenarios.

Components of artificial common sense

There are clear issues that need to be addressed in terms of defining intelligence and in particular common sense. To focus more specifically on *artificial* common sense, I will outline three broad benchmarks that, if satisfied by an artificial system, could demonstrate the common sense knowledge critical for human-level intelligence: (i) an extensive knowledge base, (ii) the ability to add to and adjust this knowledge and (iii) the ability to efficiently select only the relevant information for a given problem.

Firstly, comprehensive knowledge is required, with a store of complex information. Substantial knowledge bases for AI have been in progress for a number of years, for example Cyc (Lenat et al., 1985), which has been in development since 1984, IBM Watson and Scone (Fahlman, 2011), which stores both general and specific knowledge symbolically (and has been combined with the cognitive architecture ACT-R, Oltramari & Lebiere, 2012). An important concern relates to what information is included in a knowledge base and who is providing this information. At least to some extent, this information will be bound to the culture from which the systems are developed, as well as to the language used to create them. It is improbable that all of the languages of the world could be included in a system so that different concepts could be linked between languages.

Secondly, and relatedly, AI systems need to be able to add to their knowledge in an iterative and intuitive way without human intervention. For humans, knowledge is acquired through formal and informal learning by parents and teachers, as well as simply through interacting with the world; for example, we know that if we let go of something, it will drop to the ground, and we are taught that this is due to the force of gravity. The development of knowledge and learning is an extensive field of psychological science in its own right. Lake et al. (2017) advocate for building machines that learn like humans, specifically through causal model-building. However, current knowledge base development for AI applications requires human input; adding knowledge to these systems is time-intensive and requires teams of contributors, or if knowledge is input from the wealth of data on the internet, this needs to be moderated and checked for truthfulness. Additionally, as our understanding of the world develops and changes with scientific discoveries, knowledge will need to be updated. Steps have been made toward having systems that increase their knowledge store (e.g., Matuszek et al., 2005), generating questions and searching for potential answers using Google and Wikipedia. An additional difficulty is that new information will need to be integrated into what is already known, so that it can be used effectively.

An artificial system able to update its own knowledge raises a number of questions. For example, where will the information be derived from? Would this be from the internet or interactions with humans and the natural environment? It could be the case that common sense is a by-product of learning, where correlations about the world are discovered through interacting with the environment. If so, this would require physical interaction with the world, which suggests that only robots could achieve human-level intelligence (assuming a virtual environment would not suffice). If derived instead from sources such as the internet, how would this information be validated by the system, and how would it decide whether to add it as a known fact or disregard it? Indeed, large language models such as ChatGPT are trained using text from the internet, and so biases and misinformation can be fed into responses. For example, Azaria (2022) demonstrated that if queried for an irrational number, the numbers provided by ChatGPT have a higher frequency of the digit 7, as this is most favourable to humans, whereas all digits should be equally likely if the system was unbiased. In the case of ChatGPT, humans are hired to remove discriminatory and offensive content, which has led to reports of exploitative practices (as these tasks are often outsourced to countries with less regulated work practices and low pay) and has psychologically damaging consequences (Perrigo, 2023). Even with this human intervention, careful phrasing can bypass its controls. Further, as human input is required for the development of most systems, knowledge is limited to things that occurred prior to training. If a system could learn and validate information autonomously, selection choices would likely align with the culture it was developed within, such that fully autonomous systems would also be subject to bias. If this computer system is given a high status in society (and as such has substantial power), what would the implications be for those from cultures expressing opposing views? As outlined above, it is critically important that those using any AI system understand that they can make errors and give convincing but incorrect responses. On the other hand, if an AI system makes an error (such as that made by Google's Bard in February 2023, where an incorrect answer was given during a promotional video of the AI technology), the public distrust that may follow towards its outputs could considerably limit its applications.

Finally, they need to efficiently select the information relevant to the current task. Current artificial systems often use a more brute-force method of searching through stored knowledge until the relevant information is found. One of the key strengths of artificial systems has been that they are extremely powerful when given distinct goals and parameters to work within. However, they lack the human ability to use knowledge in a dynamic way and recall only the important information for a given task. Considering the wealth of information that we are confronted with on a daily basis, alongside constraints in terms of processing power of the brain, humans have evolved selectivity (Carrasco, 2011). For example, attention is the selective processing of the most relevant information in a situation, and is likely a limited resource. While this selectivity gives rise to occasional errors (as evidenced through perceptual and attentional illusions), it is a more efficient way to navigate the world.

Progression with artificial systems has often been due to increasing processing power and speed of computers, rather than implementation of shortcuts and selectivity to carry out complex tasks (McCarthy, 2007). However, importing what is known about human behaviour into artificial systems improves their performance. For example, Newell et al.'s (1958) Logic Theorist system was underpinned by the concept of a heuristic (i.e., rule of thumb), imported from psychology. More recently, Peterson et al. (2019) improved machine classification by including information about human uncertainty. After collecting a huge amount of human categorisation data, models were trained using the distribution of labels given by human participants, rather than using one "correct" label for each image. Importantly, models trained in this way were better at generalising to datasets that they were not trained on. While this technique improves categorisation systems, a significant limitation is the prohibitive cost for running experiments with such a large number of participants. Artificial systems using neural networks were inspired by the functioning of the human brain, and knowledge from neuroscience has continued to improve AI (Hassabis et al., 2017). In the field of navigation and robotics, the biology of the rodent hippocampus inspired RatSLAM (Milford et al., 2004), a system which doesn't rely on expensive sensors and computing power but rather allows a robot to generate a representation of its environment.

Psychology and the route to artificial general intelligence

Efforts to achieve AGI have thus far failed. The current state of artificial common sense is characterised by knowledge, while learning and flexible application of this knowledge are lacking. Brachman and Levesque (2022) argue that attempts for artificial systems with common sense have so far focused too much on the accumulation and organisation of knowledge (i.e., the first two benchmarks outlined above), at the expense of a critical understanding of *when* common sense should be invoked. As much of human behaviour is simply proceeding through routines, common sense is applied to resolve unexpected situations or events quickly and effectively. Understanding when common sense is *not* appropriate or has failed is also essential, for situations where deeper, more involved analysis is required to solve an issue. Brachman and Levesque (2022) outlined their guidance for a new direction in common sense science, focusing on knowledge (mechanisms, heuristics, organisation), reasoning, cognitive architectures (how common sense fits with perception, action, cognition, etc.), learning, taking advice and providing explanation (i.e., interpretability), with a particular focus on achieving a better understanding of common sense before trying to develop it in artificial systems. A number of these components align with issues pursued in psychological science, in particular reasoning, the implementation of cognitive architectures and learning processes.

Clearly, psychology could play a critical role in the drive towards artificial common sense. There is already an interplay between psychology and AI. AI is being used in different psychological domains, for example giving insight into clinical diagnoses, human decision-making and the development of theories (see Bartlett et al., 2023 for an overview). At the same time, developments and discoveries in psychology are being used to improve artificial systems, as outlined above. In order to incorporate common sense into AI, an understanding of human common sense, intelligence and the mechanisms underlying behaviour is necessary. As suggested by McCarthy (2007), one route to achieving AI with human-level intelligence is to further our understanding of the human brain and intelligence. Psychological science has come under some criticism in recent years, in particular in terms of the replication crisis – i.e., the problem of replicating important and foundational results from influential psychological experiments. Numerous methodological issues have been suggested as the cause for this, and as a result researchers are increasingly using more robust techniques and advanced statistical modelling (e.g., meta-analysis and linear mixed modelling) and open science practices (e.g., preregistration and replication). Further, knowledge of the human mind and the processes underlying perception, memory, etc., can be imported into artificial systems; the behaviour of such systems can then give us important insights into the theories that have been developed. If the programs do not behave in a similar way to humans, then it may be the case that the theory should be amended.

Choi (2022) outlined the importance of language and human reasoning for advances in AGI. Humans engage in intuitive reasoning (constantly assessing the motivations of other people and the likely causes of events) and abductive reasoning (generating the best hypotheses to explain incomplete observations). This reasoning happens instantly (e.g., humans can think out loud), draws from prior knowledge and is both generative and defeasible, where predictions can change with additional context. Comparatively, many computer systems will only assess things at face value, with a fixed set of concepts. Formalisms based on logic, such as those used in initial attempts at artificial intelligence, cannot scale and are brittle due to the prioritisation of correctness. As language is expressive enough to communicate an abundance of common-sense rules and facts, Choi (2022) has argued that language-based models will be more capable of demonstrating common-sense reasoning – especially considering the huge amount of raw text available for training.

Cognitive architectures may be a useful tool in the drive for artificial common sense and advancing AI to have more general intelligence (Langley, 2006; Thórisson & Helgasson, 2012). In line with Newell's (1990) argument for a unified theory of cognition, such architectures seek to build a unified account of intelligent behaviour with interdependent constraints. Cognitive architectures are computationally realised theories of human cognition, defining the fixed structures of the mind and how they interact. Many have been developed and refined over a long time (e.g., SOAR, Laird et al., 1987, and ACT-R, Anderson et al., 2004). They typically aim to model the human mind, and can provide a blueprint for intelligent behaviour, defining mental representations and the computational operations that can lead to intelligence (Kotseruba & Tsotsos, 2020). Importantly, they differ in key ways from other systems due to the goal of modelling the mind rather than solving a particular practical issue (Sun, 2007). They benefit cognitive science by documenting which strategies were successful and under which conditions to facilitate future research. Similarly, they can benefit artificial general intelligence by providing a well-specified, functional and constrained model of human intelligence.

Cognitive architectures allow researchers to study how the vast range of cognitive functions that make up intelligent behaviour are integrated into a single system. Often, different areas of cognition are studied in isolation. That is, the interplay between domains is often ignored. For example, researchers studying particular phenomena relating to attention may not appreciate how aspects of memory impact their results. One aim of the GEMS system (Bartlett et al., 2023; Frias-Martinez & Gobet, 2007) currently being developed is to provide novel predictions of human cognition that exploit this interaction between domains. Positioned at the interplay of AI and psychology, GEMS uses genetic programming techniques to develop novel and interesting theories of cognitive processing. A number of potential programs, constructed from random combinations of operators (which can be from multiple domains such as decision-making, attention, memory), which interact with the GEMS architecture, are evolved and compared against fitness criteria provided by the published literature. This process is especially useful for deriving possible cognitive strategies that human participants may use for certain tasks, suggesting how aspects of intelligent behaviour interact. However, an abundance of different architectures have been developed, each based on their own selection of assumptions, making both evaluation and comparison difficult (Kotseruba & Tsotsos, 2020). Additionally, these models suffer from the same issues as psychology as a whole, with disagreements and ambiguity regarding many essential basic cognitive mechanisms, for example, the structure of memory. Nonetheless, architectures can provide necessary constraints to resolve some issues on the route towards an AGI.

Does AI need artificial common sense?

Common sense is an important aspect of human intelligence, allowing a flexible approach to learning and problem-solving. Artificial common sense has remained elusive; tasks and problems that humans find easy to solve, highly powered artificial systems cannot. Despite this, AI has been progressively permeating our everyday lives, being used for a great variety of tasks and generating a whole host of ethical and societal questions that need to be addressed. In terms of the actual processes at play, however, these systems are incredibly susceptible to making errors. For example, objects in images can be misidentified, facial recognition can misclassify groups of people (e.g., Buolamwini & Gebru, 2018) and self-driving cars can make dangerous mistakes. Most of these systems are neural networks, where the links between input and output are not known – the so called "black-box" problem. This only compounds the issue – if the systems make errors that seem counterintuitive and we are unable to see the reasoning behind these errors, correcting them will be extremely difficult (Brachman & Levesque, 2022).

AI systems suffer from a number of additional issues surrounding their generalisability. They are narrowly focused on a particular task, making them fragile – likely to make mistakes in uncertain conditions. Also, they are often characterised by "brittleness" or an inability to function outside the boundaries of their expertise (Brachman & Levesque, 2022). While large language models can provide responses in a more general way than expert systems, they run into problems such as hallucination, where a reasonable-sounding but fake response will be created if an answer is not known by the system. This is evident in the impressive systems that have recently gained a lot of attention. ChatGPT is arguably the most well known and impressive of these, garnering the most amount of news coverage and general use. While taking conversational context into account, the system can provide human-like responses by predicting the likely next word in a sentence. Though it is continuously being improved, a number of issues have been found with ChatGPT, such as errors with reasoning and maths (Borji, 2023), different responses resulting from only slight alterations in the framing of a question (Azaria, 2022) and hallucination (for detailed testing see Bang et al., 2023). In order for these systems to be integrated into the world, these limitations need to be addressed, which might require a refocusing towards artificial common sense. It is suggested that common sense would allow systems to respond to novel situations and as such avoid unexplainable or counterintuitive errors.

Despite the argument that AI systems require common sense, AI systems that have been developed are already incredibly powerful. Addressing a specific problem at the expense of a generalisable system that can demonstrate common sense has led to incredible feats; indeed, scientific discovery has been accelerated with the integration of AI into narrowly focused areas of science (e.g., predicting the structure of proteins, Jumper et al., 2021). Further, scientific discovery could be hindered by common sense, where more "out of the box" thinking can drive advances in knowledge. Similarly, inputting what is already known and assumed into an AI system could slow down progress, whereas increasing computation power may be the most effective approach (Sutton, 2019; though this is a disputed argument).

Further, artificial common sense could be detrimental. Current AI systems can draw upon a huge amount of data, and are particularly efficient at searching through stored information for potential answers. Humans, however, have cognitive and processing constraints, which necessitate selectivity – only the most relevant information is attended. While incredibly useful and efficient, this selectivity leaves us open to errors. For example, visual illusions exploit the generalisations we have about the world. It is a balancing act between being correct and being adaptable, which cognitive processes are doing automatically. As such, an artificial system that has common sense will probably get some things wrong or exhibit incorrect reasoning, much like a human might. This ties in with a wider issue relating to how the system is regarded in society – a critical understanding of how AI works and what it is actually doing is generally lacking, and so too much trust could be placed on popular systems. If people are unaware that errors are possible, then its responses will be taken as truth, without the criticism a human might receive. This is already a problem: as outlined above, ChatGPT can be subject to hallucination, providing convincing responses that are nonetheless incorrect (Bang et al., 2023), and many of its claims are difficult to verify.

On the other hand, some selectivity and efficient common sense strategies might be necessary for AI systems going forward. There are considerable environmental consequences for the amount of computer power they require, especially with the scaling up of successful systems and the prioritising of accuracy at the expense of efficiency (Dhar, 2020). With increasingly complex systems, the energy needed for training and running models becomes more intensive. This raises many issues linked to AI ethics and whether resources should be directed to these projects. If we value the use of AI, developing less intensive methods may be essential, and flexible selectivity akin to common sense could be a way to achieve this.

Conclusion

Artificial systems have already had a substantial impact on the world, through early detection of health problems by analysing medical images, aiding in the development of the COVID-19 vaccine and predicting the structure of proteins with DeepMind's AlphaFold. Advances will certainly continue and more scientific discoveries will be attributed to artificial systems. Through utilising AI and modelling, we can also develop more refined models of human cognition, which will in turn lead to more efficient artificial systems. While computers do not have common sense akin to humans, they are already an incredibly useful and intelligent tool. On the other hand, it should be noted that the systems currently in use, and those being developed, have ethical implications that require attention.

Despite the successes of AI systems, there continues to be a drive towards developing AGI that can display common sense. Given the scale of the challenge to generate such a system, it is critical to clarify whether it is entirely necessary. While common sense could resolve issues around the brittleness of AI, allowing better generalisability to novel situations and less narrow specifications, it would also selectively disregard information for particular tasks, and be subject to bias like humans. The systems currently in use already show systematic bias, which has particularly detrimental effects on a number of, often marginalised, groups (for example, AI use in the criminal justice system inherits discriminatory bias from the historical data it is trained on, Završnik, 2020). Due to the imprecise nature of definitions for both common sense and intelligence, there needs to be greater clarification as to what processes are required and what a successful system would look like.

We are still far from having artificial systems with human-level intelligence – in part because we do not fully understand the human brain, and common sense and intelligence are such complex and abstract concepts. There are a great number of cognitive processes that are easy for humans but currently unachievable for computers. Until these processes are better understood, artificial common sense seems unachievable. With a focus on a unified theory of intelligence, research using cognitive architectures may be an important approach for AGI. As a tool to better understand human cognition, AI clearly has considerable worth – different theories and models can be tested in a more formalised manner to inform future research directions. Further, importing techniques and heuristics derived from human behaviour has been shown to improve artificial systems. However, it is also possible that the issues human common sense is suggested to solve in artificial systems would be better addressed in new and different ways, moving away from the human-centric aim of simulated human intelligence.

Bibliography

Addis, M., Gobet, F., Lane, P. C. R., & Sozou, P. D. (2019). Semi-automatic generation of cognitive science theories. In M. Addis, P. C. R. Lane, P. D. Sozou, & F. Gobet (Eds.), *Scientific discovery in the social sciences* (pp. 155–171). Springer. https://doi.org/10.1007/978-3-030-23769-1_10

Anacleto, J., Lieberman, H., Tsutsumi, M., Neris, V., Carvalho, A., Espinosa, J., ... Zem-Mascarenhas, S. (2006). Can common sense uncover cultural differences in computer applications? In M. Bramer (Ed), Artificial Intelligence in Theory and Practice. *IFIP International Federation for Information Processing*, (Vol 217, pp. 1–10). https://doi.org/10.1007/978-0-387-34747-9_1

Anderson, J. R., Bothell, D., Byrne, M. D., Douglass, S., Lebiere, C., & Qin, Y. (2004). An integrated theory of the mind. *Psychological Review, 111*(4), 1036–1060. https://doi.org/10.1037/0033-295X.111.4.1036

Azaria, A. (2022). ChatGPT usage and limitations. Preprint. https://doi.org/10.13140/RG.2.2.26616.11526

Bang, Y., Cahyawijaya, S., Lee, N., Dai, W., Su, D., Wilie, B., … Fung, P. (2023). A multitask, multilingual, multimodal evaluation of ChatGPT on reasoning, hallucination, and interactivity. Preprint. https://doi.org/10.48550/arXiv.2302.04023

Bartlett, L. K., Pirrone, A., Javed, N., & Gobet, F. (2023). Computational scientific discovery in psychology. *Perspectives on Psychological Science18*(1), 178–189. https://doi.org/10.1177/17456916221091833

Bartlett, L. K., Pirrone, A., Javed, N., Lane, P. C. R., & Gobet, F. (2023). Genetic programming for developing simple cognitive models. In M. Goldwater, F. K. Anggoro, B. K. Hayes, & D. C. Ong (Eds.), *Proceedings of the 45th Annual Conference of the Cognitive Science Society* (pp. 2833–2839).

Borji, A. (2023). A categorical archive of ChatGPT failures. Preprint. https://doi.org/10.48550/arXiv.2302.03494

Brachman, R. J., & Levesque, H. J. (2022). Toward a new science of common sense. *Proceedings of the AAAI Conference on Artificial Intelligence, 36*(11), 12245–12249. https://doi.org/10.1609/aaai.v36i11.21485

Bringsjord, S. (2011). Psychometric artificial intelligence. *Journal of Experimental and Theoretical Artificial Intelligence, 23*(3), 271–277. https://doi.org/10.1080/0952813X.2010.502314

Buolamwini, J., & Gebru, T. (2018). Gender shades: Intersectional accuracy disparities in commercial gender classification. *Proceedings of Machine Learning Research, 81*, 77–91.

Carrasco, M. (2011). Visual attention: The past 25 years. *Vision Research, 51*(13), 1484–1525. https://doi.org/10.1016/j.visres.2011.04.012

Choi, Y. (2022). The curious case of commonsense intelligence. *Daedalus, 151*(2), 139–155. https://doi.org/10.1162/DAED_a_01906

Dhar, P. (2020). The carbon impact of artificial intelligence. *Nature Machine Intelligence, 2*(8), 423–425. https://doi.org/10.1038/s42256-020-0219–9

Fahlman, S. E. (2011). Using Scone's multiple-context mechanism to emulate human-like reasoning. *Proceedings of the AAAI Fall Symposium on Advances in Cognitive Systems* (pp. 98–105).

Frias-Martinez, E., & Gobet, F. (2007). Automatic generation of cognitive theories using genetic programming. *Minds and Machines, 17*(3), 287–309. https://doi.org/10.1007/s11023-007-9070-6

Hassabis, D., Kumaran, D., Summerfield, C., & Botvinick, M. (2017). Neuroscience-inspired artificial intelligence. *Neuron, 95*(2), 245–258. https://doi.org/10.1016/j.neuron.2017.06.011

Jumper, J., Evans, R., Pritzel, A., Green, T., Figurnov, M., Ronneberger, O., … Hassabis, D. (2021). Highly accurate protein structure prediction with AlphaFold. *Nature, 596*(7873), 583–589. https://doi.org/10.1038/s41586-021-03819-2

Kejriwal, M., Santos, H., Mulvehill, A. M., & McGuinness, D. L. (2022). Designing a strong test for measuring true common-sense reasoning. *Nature Machine Intelligence, 4*(4), 318–322. https://doi.org/10.1038/s42256-022-00478-4

Kolata, G. (1982). How can computers get common sense? *Science, 217*(4566), 1237–1238. https://doi.org/10.1126/science.217.4566.1237

Kotseruba, I., & Tsotsos, J. K. (2020). 40 years of cognitive architectures: Core cognitive abilities and practical applications. *Artificial Intelligence Review, 53*(1), 17–94. https://doi.org/10.1007/s10462-018-9646-y

Laird, J. E., Newell, A., & Rosenbloom, P. S. (1987). SOAR: An architecture for general intelligence. *Artificial Intelligence, 33*(1), 1–64. https://doi.org/10.1016/0004-3702(87)90050-6

Lake, B. M., Ullman, T. D., Tenenbaum, J. B., & Gershman, S. J. (2017). Building machines that learn and think like people. *Behavioral and Brain Sciences, 40*, 1–72. https://doi.org/10.1017/S0140525X16001837

Langley, P. (2006). Cognitive architectures and general intelligent systems. *AI Magazine, 27*(2), 33–44. https://doi.org/10.1609/aimag.v27i2.1878

Lenat, D. B., Prakash, M., & Shepherd, M. (1985). CYC: Using common sense knowledge to overcome brittleness and knowledge acquisition bottlenecks. *AI Magazine, 6*(4), 65–85. https://doi.org/10.1609/aimag.v6i4.510

Lozano-Ruiz, A., Fasfous, A. F., Ibanez-Casas, I., Cruz-Quintana, F., Perez-Garcia, M., & Pérez-Marfil, M. N. (2021). Cultural bias in intelligence assessment using a culture-free test in Moroccan children. *Archives of Clinical Neuropsychology, 36*(8), 1502-1510. https://doi.org/10.1093/arclin/acab005

Matuszek, C., Witbrock, M., Kahlert, R. C., Cabral, J., Schneider, D., Shah, P., & Lenat, D. (2005). Searching for common sense: Populating CycTM from the web. In *Proceedings of the 20th AAAI Conference on Artificial Intelligence* (pp. 1430–1435).

McCarthy, J. (1960). Programs with common sense. *RLE and MIT Computation Center*, 75–91.

McCarthy, J. (2007). From here to human-level AI. *Artificial Intelligence, 171*(18), 1174–1182. https://doi.org/10.1016/j.artint.2007.10.009

Milford, M. J., Wyeth, G. F., & Prasser, D. (2004). RatSLAM: A hippocampal model for simultaneous localization and mapping. In *Proceedings of the 2004 IEEE International Conference on Robotics and Automation* (pp. 403–408). https://doi.org/10.1109/robot.2004.1307183

Newell, A. (1990). *Unified theories of cognition.* Harvard University Press.

Newell, A., Shaw, J. C., & Simon, H. A. (1958). Elements of a theory of human problem solving. *Psychological Review, 65*(3), 151–166. https://doi.org/10.1037/h0048495

Oltramari, A., & Lebiere, C. (2012). Pursuing artificial general intelligence by leveraging the knowledge capabilities of ACT-R. In J. Bach, B. Goertzel, & M. Iklé (Eds.), *Artificial general intelligence. Lecture notes in computer science* (Vol. 7716, pp. 199–208). https://doi.org/10.1007/978-3-642-35506-6_21

Paik, J., & Pirolli, P. (2015). ACT-R models of information foraging in geospatial intelligence tasks. *Computational and Mathematical Organization Theory, 21*(3), 274–295. https://doi.org/10.1007/s10588-015-9185-x

Perrigo, B. (2023). OpenAI used Kenyan workers on less than $2 per hour to make ChatGPT less toxic. *Time.* Published January 18th, 2023.

Peterson, J. C., Battleday, R., Griffiths, T., & Russakovsky, O. (2019). Human uncertainty makes classification more robust. In *Proceedings of the IEEE/CVF International Conference on Computer Vision (ICCV)* (pp. 9616–9625). https://doi.org/10.1109/ICCV.2019.00971

Sternberg, R. J., Forsythe, G. B., Hedlund, J., Horvath, J. A., Wagner, R. K., Williams, W. M., ... Grigorenko, E. L. (2000). *Practical intelligence in everyday life.* Cambridge University Press.

Sun, R. (2007). The importance of cognitive architectures: An analysis based on CLARION. *Journal of Experimental and Theoretical Artificial Intelligence, 19*(2), 159–193. https://doi.org/10.1080/09528130701191560

Sutton, R. S. (2019). The bitter lesson. *Incomplete ideas* (Blog), Retrieved from http://www.incompleteideas.net/IncIdeas/BitterLesson.html

Thórisson, K., & Helgasson, H. (2012). Cognitive architectures and autonomy: A comparative review. *Journal of Artificial General Intelligence*, 3(2), 1–30. https://doi.org/10.2478/v10229-011-0015-3

Završnik, A. (2020). Criminal justice, artificial intelligence systems, and human rights. *ERA Forum*, 20(4), 567–583. https://doi.org/10.1007/s12027-020-00602-0

PART 3

Inter-subjective common sense: public discourse

AI in common sense, the public discourse and its functions, the social psychology of assimilation

7

GIAMBATTISTA VICO'S DIALOGICAL COMMON SENSE

Ivana Marková

Dialogical common sense in relation to AI

An enormous amount of evidence points to humans' attempts to develop machines that can learn and think, imitate and even conquer human intelligence, and re-produce it in other machines. One of the founders of cybernetics Norbert Wiener (1964) explored intelligence as intertwined with communication, control systems, ethics and religion, in the history of human aims to produce a Golem. Golem, an artificial and anthropomorphic being, was part of Jewish myths and folklore in different countries of the world; it was perhaps best known as the Golem of Prague, associated with the legend about Rabbi Loew. Golem, made of mud and clay, had the power and knowledge to protect Jews in the Prague ghetto against racist attacks. Variations of a mythical Golem as the product of the human mind and represented as an artificial being, ranging from an angelic saver of humans to a diabolic monster, became a favourite subject of science fictions (e.g., Karel Čapek's R.U.R).

Martin Bauer (Chapter 1, this volume) reminds us of the assumed close relation between the human mind and computers when referring to Alan Turing's vision of intelligence embodied in machines that, in future, would become indistinguishable from human intelligence. Developing this idea further, some contemporary cognitive psychologists claim (or write) that they can understand the brain, and even the mind (a cognitive psychologist often uses the term "mind/brain") as a kind of computer (a Golem). In other words, it is the Golem which comes first, and the human mind which created the Golem is relegated to second place. Such a vision, however, is not accepted universally. Among those who oppose this perspective is Gerd Gigerenzer

DOI: 10.4324/9781032626192-12

(2022). In writing about common sense and AI, Gigerenzer reminds us of fundamental strategies of human intelligence that have developed in evolution in and through struggles to cope with uncertainty; to achieve their ambitions, humans use heuristics, imagination and creativity in open and ever-changing contexts. Contrary to human intelligence, Gigerenzer argues, AI needs a stable environment to make algorithmic predictions about solutions of well-defined problems. AI is guided by formalistic rules, whilst cultural and historical experience is irrelevant to devising algorithmic paths. In other words, human intelligence and AI develop and function in different environments, and therefore, they are equipped with capacities for diverse kinds of problem-solving, some requiring the use of heuristics, while others use algorithms as their proper strategies.

Enthusiastic perspectives of cognitive psychologists about the relation between the mind and computer tend to ignore that these two systems, i.e., human minds and AI machines, are made from totally different stuff, and that the question about machines indistinguishable from human intelligence cannot be resolved without serious consideration. Wiener observed: "Living beings are living beings in all their parts; while machines are made of metals and other unorganised substances, with no fine structure relevant to their purposive or quasi-purposive function" (Wiener, 1964, p. 5). This does not mean that no commonalities could be found between these two kinds of systems. Indeed, we may witness that in some specific functions, this can be performed both by humans and by AI, e.g., physical movements, mechanistic functions of artificial limbs, carrying out surgical tasks, among others, AI easily outperforms human capacities.

Such complex and unresolved issues cannot escape readers' attention in Part 3 of this book, which is concerned with humans' intersubjective meanings of common sense in relation to AI. It is apparent that these two systems address common sense with fundamentally different concepts. Above all, in addition to structural and material differences between human and AI common senses, the dialogical perspective of common sense is underlain by historical, language-based and cultural phenomena, which are unique in each human being.

One way of embarking on such complex issues is to examine the underlying epistemology of human mental capacities by focusing on the common-sense perspective of the Italian philosopher of the 17th and 18th centuries Giambattista Vico,[1] a revolutionary and highly original scholar who, in my view, can be referred to as the precursor of dialogicality.

Dialogicality is an epistemology of the interdependence between the Self and Others (i.e., individuals, groups, institutions) in and through sense-making and sense-creating of social realities (Bakhtin, 1981, 1984) situated in history and culture. According to this epistemology, every human is capable of ethical and moral judgement; this capacity has been acquired throughout socio-historical and cultural development of the human species *as* humans. Therefore, ethics is not based on *individual rationality,* but on *dialogical rationality* (Marková, 2016, 2023). The ethics of the Self-Other interdependence contradicts the neutral and objectivist cognitive perspective and the information processing of AI.

Vico's revolutionary epistemology was ignored during his lifetime, and the ideas of the dynamic interdependence between the Self and Others reappeared, though usually without references to Vico, in the development of social sciences and humanities in the 18th and 19th centuries (Marková, 2016, 2023). Rather than exploring the full range of Vico's dialogical thinking, this chapter will focus on two ideas that characterise Vico's views of common sense: first, on language as a common-sense epistemology, and second, on action, as the truth of common sense.

Language as a common-sense epistemology

Following the ideas of rhetoric in ancient Greece, Vico viewed common sense as inseparable from moral conduct; it was a feature of civil wisdom and justice (Bayer, 2008). Vico adopted the Greek concept of justice that was conceived as a universal virtue. As justice was practised by rhetoric, it highlighted the role of language in the public discourse. Vico conceived language not only as a rhetorical device but as a common-sense epistemology: knowledge, beliefs and experience are expressed in and through language. Moreover, language emerges and develops during human communication with others and common sense manifests itself through metaphor and imagination, through the transfer of meaning from one word to another, and through myth. Fables, which describe the world in poetic language, are products of collective imagining and true histories of custom (Vico, 1744/1948, §7). All this indicates that language provides a systematic way of seeing, understanding and reacting to the world (Vico, 1744/1948, §779).

Vico viewed each culture as unique and as comprising its own realities; equally, he considered language of each culture as unique in relation to that culture. Consequently, language meanings could not be translated into another language without residue. The power of language reveals itself in using metaphors and imaginations. Metaphors aim at discovering common elements in diverse things and so transfer their meanings of these elements from one thing to another (Grassi, 1976, pp. 562–563). Vico called this enormous creative power of language the "the genius of language" (Vico, 1709/1965, p. 40). "The genius of language" enables humans to go beyond immediate sensory experience of Aristotelian common sense (CS1 as in this volume, Chapter 1). Instead, imagination and ingenium are creative capacities of common sense that are embedded in the past and orientated towards future: "Imagination is the eye of 'ingenium', judgment is the eye of understanding" (Vico, 1710/2010,

p. 98). "The genius of language" or "*ingenium*" refers to invention, to construction or arguments, capacity to synthesise and link together different things, among others.

More than anything else, "the genius of language" and its dialogical nature are realised in creating names. To name something or someone is directed not only to the object of naming, but it is a social activity because one needs others to acknowledge the name. In other words, naming is for the Self as well as for Others: it is a collective interaction, and it creates the social reality of humans. Vico explored the creation of names in concrete examples. For instance, people need to establish their ownership, and this is assured through the invention of names because a name draws up the boundaries between what is mine and what is not mine (Vico, 1744/1948, §483). Only if others accept the name the individual suggests for a particular thing, its meaning becomes a common property on which the community can act. Naming therefore has the whole history and multiple events behind. It cannot be replaced by a category or a label (Marková, 2016).

Finally, "the genius of language" reveals its power in and through the multitude of meanings that can be attached to a single word in relation to different contexts, and intentions of speakers. Each instance in which a word is used takes place in a new context, even if the difference between the previous and new context is very small. Therefore, each such instance modifies meanings of words (symbols) and of knowledge and so it generates a new representation of the referent (Karcevskij, 1929/1982, p. 51). Moreover, the creative power of language develops in and through this process and gives shape to various language modalities like irony, using similes, metaphors or other comparative expressions. All these features may disguise and reveal themselves in words, silences, ambiguities, reflective arguments, disagreements, negotiations and so on.

In his analysis of Vico's thoughts, Grassi (1976, p. 560) emphasises that Vico's idea of common sense has nothing to do with the deductive capacities put forward by rationalists or with philosophical and metaphysical concerns. Instead, it is related to the historically established interdependencies of human requirements, that is, to the needs and utilities, which Vico calls "the two origins of the natural law of nations" (Vico, 1744/1948, §141). The basis of this perspective is Vico's concept of language as a common-sense epistemology: knowledge, beliefs and experience are expressed in and through language conceived as dialogue. Dialogue is by its nature open, and without any concrete restrictions concerning the direction it should take. It is equipped to deal with uncertain problems. This is possible precisely because of the human faculties of "*ingenium*" and imagination. These capacities that have their roots in common sense (Vico, 1744/1948, §809) oppose AI algorithmic processes that are defined to solve well-defined problems.

The fundamental feature of Vico's dialogism was his emphasis on broad historical and value-based traditions and cultures. This broad and comprehensive perspective on dialogue was specifically elaborated by Mikhail Bakhtin in the 20th century in his conception of a dialogue as not only interaction between two individuals but also between groups, historical epochs and cultures. Bakhtin conceived the whole authentic human life as a continuous and open-ended dialogue:

> Life by its very nature is dialogic. To live means to participate in dialogue: to ask questions, to heed, to respond, to agree and so forth. In this dialogue a person participates wholly and throughout his whole life: with his eyes, lips, hands, soul, spirit, with his whole body and deeds.
>
> *(Bakhtin, 1984, p. 293)*

Action as the truth of common sense

In linking common sense with ingenium, imagination and action, Vico considered action as the proof of truth. Before we come to Vico's arguments that separate what is "certain" and what is "true", let us emphasise that Vico insisted that common sense arises in and through the process in which humans have created their own history (Vico, 1744/1948). Let us explain. Humans live in the physical and natural environment that exerts demands on living and on satisfying their needs. Humans must judge what their needs are, and they satisfy them by inventing tools and instruments, by means of which they make practical changes to their environments to cope with their problems. The human demands are heterogeneous: they are physical, biological and social. They repeat themselves, usually over centuries, and many of them produce in people similar experiences. For example, humans must search for food, protect themselves from danger, look after their children, and otherwise. They produce instruments and tools to build accommodation, to be warm, to save water and so on. These activities lead to what Vico called "underlying agreements". To develop "underlying agreements", humans use imagination, ingenium and action, all creating their common sense. Vico's historical approach showed that in affecting their environment by mastering power over objects, demands and their solutions, humans create their history, change their consciousness and attain knowledge not only of those objects but also of themselves. Repeated experiences become internalised as uniformities. They become fixed in the human mind and in activities; stabilised over generations, they provide further resources for common sense knowledge. Therefore, common sense is not a set of consciously formed empirical beliefs or intellectual concerns. Neither it comes from the innate cognitive capacity of the individual. Instead, it comes from the long experience of humans who share common uniformities in life over generations. As they must struggle with how to overcome their problems, sharing common uniformities is not a passive experience of regularities and repetitions: common uniformities arise from actively created "underlying agreements". Once they are fixed, common-sense ideas are unconsciously internalised. Vico characterised common sense as "judgement without reflection, shared by an entire class, an entire people, an entire nation, or the whole human race" (Vico, 1744/1948, §142).

This perspective about human action as common sense led Vico to conceptualise the distinction between truth and certainty, which is based precisely on the reality of action and of common sense. Vico thought that by studying scientific phenomena, humans cannot achieve truth because they have no power to create natural and physical phenomena (e.g., wind, forces of the sea), because they do not arise from human actions. Physical and natural phenomena were created by God and so humans can understand them only to a limited degree; all they can achieve is a specific level of certainty (certum); that is, they can reach only some probability of truth. Certainty, according to Vico, has only a grain of truth, and is not connected with common sense. Vico's distinction between truth and certainty stemmed from his religious convictions that were universally adopted during his lifetime. He was convinced that God created phenomena that are true, and humans can discover only partly and incompletely these godly products. Therefore, human knowledge about these godly products is only "certain", but not "true". However, humans have the capacity to invent and imagine things, and they create them – and to that extent and they mirror God's activity. What they create is real, it is true.

Let us recall René Descartes (1637/1955; 1641/1955) for whom the truth and certainty were due to the individual's thinking capacity, which was the source of indubitable truth. In contrast, for Vico, the source of indubitable truth rested in human action – with *verum factum*. Vico fully explained his concept of *verum factum* in his early book *On the Most Ancient Wisdom of the Italians* (Vico, 1710/2010). The proof that something is true lies entirely in the fact that humans make that something. It is not a blind production of that something, but humans make something because they imagine how that thing may look and what it would be for. So, *verum factum* goes far beyond perception: it is an imaginative and inventive action. Humans do not passively digest underlying agreements; rather, they form common sense foundations by triggering the capacity to make and invent things and to acquire knowledge of the world in and through action. Let us add that Vico was considerably influenced by his contemporary Francis Bacon who was very interested in technological advancements during the scientific revolution and in practical experience and inventions. Vico (1710/2020) stated that for Italians, *verum*, the true, and *factum*, the made, were exchangeable or convertible. This principle had proven extremely important in Vico's time in school education (Gianturco, 1990, p. xliii), where children were encouraged to search for truth actively in constructing knowledge, rather than passively adopting knowledge from what is given to them by teachers. Only what humans create, e.g., laws, mathematics, customs, language and their own history, can be referred to as the truth. For example, take mathematics or geometry. The principles of mathematics or geometry are universally true because they are inventions of humans: "We are able to demonstrate geometrical propositions because we create them!" (Vico, 1709/1965, p. 23). Equally in the *New Science* (1744/1948, §349), Vico stated that geometry was the first indubitable principle that humankind has created. Geometry subsequently modified the human mind. Vico even suggested that human actions followed patterns of geometry; when making geometrical patterns out of elements, the human mind makes them real. However, in contrast to Euclidean and Cartesian and analytic geometry (Vico, 1709/1965), Vico's geometry was concerned with very complex human affairs like the world of nations and history. Such complex phenomena are created and re-created by people, and people refer to them neither in terms of "points, lines, surfaces, nor figures" (Vico, 1744/1948, §349). This point reappeared in Alexandre Koyré (1948) in the 20th century in his argument against the measurement of dynamic natural beings. Koyré insisted that "in nature there are no circles, ellipses or direct lines; it would be ridiculous to measure exactly natural beings like horses, dogs or elephants". He suggested that geometrical and physical concepts were not applicable to the dynamic world of daily life.

As cultures inhabit different physical, biological and social environments, their "underlying agreements" are specific, as each culture follows its own rules. While underlying agreements of physical and biological nature become routinised as physical and biological pressures are experienced by humans in a similar manner (e.g., hardness and softness, birth and death), social underlying agreements are more varied and they are in constant change. Human beings create their common senses by establishing communities, social institutions, traditions and political organisations. Vico also conceived that ethical and moral norms are part of "underlying agreements" of common sense of communities and nations (Vico, 1744/1948, §145). Their transmission over generations does not need to be through verbal language; non-verbal symbolic gestures and silences have community meanings and are understood by members. Common sense is embedded in the construction of laws, rules and customs and the development of institutions as they all serve the needs and utilities of communities.

Let us return to Vico's insistence that common sense arises in and through processes in which humans have created their own history (Vico, 1744/1948). Human actions, invention and imagination are interlinked in this process of the truth (verum) building, which is the reality of living in the social world (Vico, 1744/1948, §331). Truth arises from actions and from the principles developed in civil society. By making truth the subject matter of human action, Vico placed it under human control. Truth is the reality of living in the social world and its fundamental feature is ethical *"sensus communis"*. Vico rejected an approach to ethics as an objectified moral science based on rules and propositions. In his book on the study of methods (Vico, 1709/1965, p. 33), he stated that educational methods placed too much emphasis on the natural sciences and on the intellectual development of the person, and disregarded ethics which, in fact, deals with essential social and political issues, with virtues and vices, and patterns of behaviour. He described in detail what he thought were the differences between science and common sense, the latter, in contrast to the former, being of ethical nature, and interdependent with language, *"ingenium"* and imagination. Vico (1709/1965, pp. 46–47) argued against the systematisation of rules in ethics and he pointed out that in real life, human conduct depends on sound judgement and therefore, nothing is more meaningless than the treatment of ethics as a general and objective science. Vico saw the ethical nature of common sense in history and community. We have noted above that he thought that common sense is a socially shared but not reflected upon, habitual way of thinking, communicating, and acting. It guides humans in everyday reality; it enables them to cope with obstacles, and to make instantaneous judgements and evaluations of situations.

Without discussing the epistemology of algorithms in AI, let us point out that neither of the two concepts of common sense that were fundamental in Vico's perspective, are relevant in AI, though for different reasons. First, the power of human language reveals itself by using metaphors and imagination. Imagination and ingenium are creative capacities of common sense that are embedded in the past and orientated towards the future, among which creating new names and meanings is a genuinely social phenomenon. To name something is a social activity because one needs others to acknowledge the name. In other words, naming is for the Self as well as for Others: it is a collective interaction, and it creates the social reality of humans. Dialogue is by its nature open, and without any concrete restrictions concerning the direction it should take. A single word may express a multitude of meanings as they relate to different intentions of speakers in specific contexts. Language is equipped to deal with uncertain problems that humans face. In other words, the concept of language in a dialogical sense is totally irrelevant to algorithmic thinking.

With technological and societal developments in modernity, Vico's distinction between the "truth" and "certainty" is no longer applicable to human daily experience. Products of human actions, which Vico viewed in their concrete forms such as making furniture, paintings, artistic products, or developing instruments that serve human needs, still represent the "truth" of individual's actions. Nevertheless, human actions have become very diverse and heterogeneous. The complex world engages individuals in uncontrollable activities. Common sense that inspires and regulates human actions during relatively predictable historical periods is no longer relevant when human actions become overtly constrained by uncertain and unpredictable complex domains of markets, volatile institutions, and political manipulations. In such circumstances, humans cannot control and change their environment by acting according to their intentions and are obliged to make their choices in an insecure world, and so their choices, too, are complex and uncertain.

Complexity and uncertainty

Changes in technology and science after the Second World War and rapid innovations in communication and computation had a major effect on the development of new directions in social sciences, including dialogicality. Cybernetics (Wiener, 1948), the scientific study of control, information and communication in animals and machines, re-focused the interest of sciences on investigations of big systems and their structures. Above all, Wiener's work brought to attention the concepts of information and communication. Advancements in the understanding of complex chemical, physical, biological and social systems showed that they could not really be studied by decomposing them into their elements. Instead, new fields of study were fostered by the holistic idea of Gestalt, structures and communication in their dynamics, and they adopted the non-linear concept of time (Byrne, 1998; Byrne and Callaghan, 2013). They attempted to grasp concepts of large, unpredictable and uncertain complex domains that were mutually related (e.g., Ramage and Shipp, 2009).

Modernity hardly allows for the development of fixed experiences leading to underlying agreements leading to common-sense knowledge. Consequently, social scientists became preoccupied with the question of how humans make sense of convoluted phenomena in daily life where different elements do not develop into coherent patterns, and interactions go in different and often contradictory directions. For example, how do humans understand the unpredictability of stock markets, the risks of money in banks or the risks of pandemics? Individuals have become very dependent on variable activities of others and on networks in which they participate.

Dialogicality that we defined above as an epistemology of the interdependence between the Self and Others has undergone many conceptual transformations. Among these, dialogicality of the French philosopher and sociologist Edgar Morin is particularly apt to address complex phenomena of modernity. Morin is deeply concerned with the epistemology of dialogical thinking which he has applied to explain the principles of complex systems.

His epistemology of dialogical thinking, which he calls the Dialogical Principle, has been motivated by the Hegelian/Marxian ideas about the dynamic and historical interdependencies of antagonistic processes. The Dialogical Principle, inspired by Hegelian thought, regards antagonistic processes as indissociable from one another, and as being relational complements. Whilst classic scientific thinking strictly separated order from disorder, organised from disorganised states and rationality from irrationality, Morin (2008, p.19) does not view opposites as excluding one another as was the case in ancient Greek philosophy. Instead, the logical core of dialogical complexity is to treat "separability-inseparability, whole-parts, effect-cause, product-producer, life-death, homo sapiens-homo demens" as dynamic and complementary. This means that the oppositions are not static but capable of transformation into their oppositions or complements. One cannot define what is certain or what is uncertain. Instead, one must always be aware of dynamic borders between certainty and uncertainty.

Edgar Morin extends the Dialogical Principle (e.g., 1996, 1997, 2008) into the Principle of Organisational Recursivity, and the Hologrammatic Principle, with all three principles defining complexity and complex thinking in and through self-generation and self-production. In this process, the producer-product is in a recursive loop breaking down the classic cause–effect relationship. Society arises from interactions among humans and their products, such as culture, emergencies or language. In this way, products merge with producers. Finally, the Hologrammatic Principle emphasises the special relation between the whole and its parts: the part is present in the whole, and equally important, the totality of the whole in terms of the socio-genetic heritage is part of each cell of the individual. In other words, society is present in every individual through language, social norms and culture, and equally, every individual is present in society by being able to use language and conform to social norms and cultural standards (Morin, 1996).

Although Morin's dialogicality possesses features of interdependencies between the Self and Others including ethics and aesthetics, it also shows that dialogicality and common sense have undergone transformation in the context of advancements of technology and of scientific discoveries. More generally, advancements in natural and social sciences in modernity transformed relations between humans and objects, and consequently, they transformed concepts referring to these relations. Concepts change due to a different referent, different components of a concept may take place at different rates, and the components may change in different directions (Marková, 2023). Such conceptual transformations in the rapidly developing science and technology raise fundamental questions about common senses of humans and AI.

Conclusion

This chapter has drawn attention to complex and unresolved issues about humans' intersubjective meanings of common sense in relation to AI. Above all, it has shown that these two systems address common sense with fundamentally diverse concepts. Among these, the dialogical perspective of common sense is underlain by historical, language-based, and cultural phenomena, which are unique in each human being. We examined some ideas about the common sense of Giambattista Vico, a highly original scholar, who can be referred to as the precursor of dialogicality.

Although common sense is vital to humans' coping with daily realities, it is, nevertheless, only one kind of intersubjectively shared knowledge. In unpredictable situations, humans find themselves in unfamiliar circumstances in which they experience crises, extraordinary events, moral dilemmas and changeable situations. Routines break down and the customary guides of common sense are not enough for solving unfamiliar problems, and humans need other kinds of socially shared knowledge to deal with such situations. They require learning, imagination, inventiveness, taking risks, instant actions, and otherwise, to cope with unpredictable circumstances. Although common sense is an essential feature of daily knowledge, it is necessary to explore the boundaries of common sense in relation to other kinds of socially shared knowledge.

Second, considering the basic epistemological differences between dialogicality and AI, is it appropriate to use the term "common-sense" without explaining what it means in the two systems, and what connections there are between its use in AI and dialogicality? Vico made it quite clear what he meant by "underlying agreements" leading to the establishment of common sense. In contrast, we have no clear definition of common sense in relation to AI and therefore, we have no basis for a meaningful comparison of common sense in these two systems.

The third unanswered question refers to the intersubjective meaning of common sense expressed in language and dialogue. Meanings of words and symbols are embedded in history and culture and are open to transformations affecting their nuances in concrete circumstances of social interactions. Due to these open relationships, we can rarely predict how dialogue will turn out. It can move in different directions because human invention, intuition and imaginary are without limits. Moreover, the uniqueness of dialogical rationality (see above) is corroborated by the ethics of the Self-Other interdependence, which contradicts the neutral and objectivist cognitive perspective in AI. Since common sense in AI is based on algorithmic principles which are not open to dynamic and unpredictable circumstances, AI will need to propose criteria for what counts as common sense.

Thirdly, the contents of concepts are not stable, and they change their referents, as they are interdependent of changes in environments to which they refer. As we have seen, dialogicality in Vico's conception and that in Morin's theorising related to pre-modern phenomena in the former and to advanced modern phenomena in the latter. Such changes and transformations are inevitable, and we cannot imagine, and even less predict how concepts will develop with the future advancements of AI. All these provocative questions await exploration.

Note

1 In discussing Vico's ideas about common sense, I rely on chapter 2, Towards Giambattista Vico's common sense, in Marková, I. (2016). *The Dialogical Mind: Common Sense and Ethics*. Cambridge, UK: Cambridge University Press.

Bibliography

Bakhtin, M. M. (1981). *The dialogical imagination: Four essays by M.M. Bakhtin*. M. Holquist (Ed.). University of Texas Press.

Bakhtin, M. M. (1984). *Problems of Dostoyevsky's poetics*. C. Emerson (Ed. and trans.). University of Minnesota Press.

Bayer, T. I. (2008). Vico's principle of *sensus communis* and forensic eloquence, *Chicago-Kent Law Review, 83*, 1131–1155.

Byrne, D. (1998). *Complexity theory and the social sciences: An introduction*. Routledge.

Byrne, D., & Callaghan, G. (2013). *Complexity theory and the social sciences: The state of art*. Routledge.

Descartes, R. (1637/1955). Discourse on the method of rightly conducting the reason and seeking for truth in science. In E. S. Haldane and G. R. T. Ross (trans. and Eds.), *The philosophical works of Descartes* (Vol. I., pp. 79–130). Cambridge University Press.

Descartes, R. (1641/1955). Meditations on first philosophy. In E. S. Haldane and G. R. T. Ross (trans. and Eds.), *The philosophical works of Descartes* (Vol. I, pp. 131–199). Cambridge University Press.

Gianturco, E. (1990). Introduction. In G. Vico (1709/1990). *On the study of methods of our time* (pp. xxi–xlv). Cornell University Press.

Gigerenzer, G. (2022). *How to stay smart in a smart world*. Allen Lane.

Grassi, E. (1976). The priority of common sense and imagination: Vico's philosophical relevance today. *Social Research, 43*, 553–575.

Karcevskij, S. (1929/1982). Du dualisme asymetrique du sign linguistique. *Travaux du Cercle Linguistique de Prague, 1*, 33–38. Reprinted as The asymmetric dualism of the linguistic sign. In F. Steiner (Ed.), *The Prague School: Selected writings, 1919–1946* (pp. 47–54). University of Texas Press.

Koyré, A. (1948). Du monde de l' «à-peu-près» à l'univers de la précision [From the world of 'very nearly' to the universe of precision]. *Critique, 28*, 806–823.

Marková, I. (2016). *The dialogical mind: Common sense and ethics*. Cambridge University Press.

Marková, I. (2023). *The making of a dialogical theory: Social representations and communication*. Cambridge University Press.

Marková, I. S. (2023). Empathy: A case study in the historical epistemology of psychiatry, *History of Psychiatry, 34*. http://doi.org/10.1177/0957154X231163764

Morin, E. (1996, February). A new way of thinking. *The UNESCO Courier.*

Morin, E. (1997). *Comprendre la complexité dans les organisations de soins.* ASPEPS.

Morin, E. (2008). Restricted complexity, general complexity. arXiv:cs/0610049v1[csCC] 10 Oct 2006.

Ramage, M., & Shipp, K. (2009). *System thinkers.* Open University and Springer Verlag.

Vico, G. (1709/1965). *On the study of methods of our time* (E. Gianturco, Trans., Introduction and notes). The Bobbs-Merrill Company.

Vico, G. (1710/2010). *On the most ancient wisdom of the Italians* (J. Taylor, trans.; R. Miner, introduction). Yale University Press.

Vico, G. (1744/1948). *The new science of Giambattista Vico* (T. G. Bergin & M. H. Fisch, trans.). Cornell University Press.

Wiener, N. (1948). *Cybernetics, or control and communication in the animal and the machine.* Wiley.

Wiener, N. (1964). *God and Golem: A comment on certain points where cybernetics impinges on religion.* M.I.T. Press.

8

THE A-SOCIABILITY OF AI

Knowledge, social interactions and
the dynamics of common sense

Bernard Schiele and Alexandre Schiele

There are a number of obstacles to the development of AI with common sense.

First, the very notion of common sense is polysemic, with many, often contradictory, definitions, and without a minimum consensus among researchers (see Bauer, Chapter 1 this volume). Second, when common sense is spoken of in pragmatic terms, as the "immediate understanding of the way familiar things work in the broadest sense" (Andler, 2023, p. 227), the issue remains intact because much is implicit in daily life, with people resolving arising difficulties more often than not without even "taking notice" (ibid.). Third, the notion of "context" often describes everything that is known, consciously or not, by any social actor at the moment he or she acts in a specific situation, towards a goal for instance, and which remains independent from that action itself at the moment it takes place. Thus, the context provides information which may not be explicit but no less indispensable. In other words, the "context", although implicit, is crucial to the intelligibility of the action through the information it provides to both the social actor and the eventual observer to interpret it and appreciate its scope. In this perspective, common sense "refers to both what can be understood as knowledge [...] and what is of the order of judgment, i.e. to complete most plausibly the necessarily incomplete description of a given situation" (ibid., p. 228). How then to formulate and formalise what is implicit under the form of explicit propositions? And how to assess that the proposed solution is the right one since other explanations exist? This is why, the problem of the "representation of knowledge", present in any potentially arising situation, continues to stump the development of AI.

DOI: 10.4324/9781032626192-13

The fourth, rarely, if ever, mentioned, difficulty is that although common sense refers to a collectivity – the "common" being what "belongs to a great number or a majority of individuals" (Trésor de la langue française, 2023), within AI it is still tackled from an individual standpoint, the "common" being reduced to the mere aggregation of individual behaviours. As a brief reminder, research in AI first sought to develop a "general theory of rationality which endeavoured to be the general theory of intelligent systems" (Andler, 2023, p. 242). However, "we have now shifted from theory to data, i.e. specific cases" (ibid.). Such a reversal was made possible, as Andler underlines, by the massive increases in computing power. Thus, rather than attempting to apply a small number of principles to a great number of situations, the mass processing of individual data is now preferred. This is not the place to determine whether it is the effect of computing power, the residual influence of behaviouralism or the reflection of a dominant narrative which centres contemporary life around the individual (Harvey, 2005). Was it not Margaret Thatcher, the spearhead of Neoliberalism, who asserted in 1987 contrary to decades (centuries?) of scholarship: "who is society? There's no such thing! There are individual men and women and there are families".

Still, the collective dimension – what is "shared" – is omitted in AI. Of course, developments in Deep Learning and Large Language Models over the last decade could be said to have remedied the issue through the processing of big data and the big datafication of relationships, as long favoured by sociology, anthropology and social psychology. But as Mayer-Schönberger and Cukier (2013) observed:

> Social networking platforms don't simply offer us a way to find and stay in touch with friends and colleagues, they take intangible elements of our everyday life and transform them into data that can be used to do new things. (...) Datafication is not just about rendering attitudes and sentiments into an analysable form, but human behavior as well. This is otherwise hard to track, especially in the context of the broader community and subgroups within it.
>
> *(pp. 91–93)*

It would appear as though the recent developments in AI modelling interactions between individuals to extract useful data and reducing common sense to the sum of individualities are blind to a fundamental social dimension: the "group" as the structuring intermediary between individuals and between individuals and society. If common sense still eludes AI, it is because it is blind to the role of the "group", yet the challenge of modelling and datafying it, if possible at all, will not be solved overnight.

First, it must be recalled that when Piaget investigated the production of knowledge, he held that the "datum" to know only becomes a "known object" through the interdependence which links the subject, after the interactions have taken place, to the known object. Thus, three elements are crucial: the knowing subject, the known object and the relation which links them. In the same spirit, but going further, Moscovici (2008) introduces another just as crucial element, an *other*: the interrelation of the self with the datum to know is simultaneously mediated by the self's linguistic and symbolic interactions with this other. In short, for Moscovici, we do not know the "real" alone, but with an other. Thus, the object, the explicit or implicit known, is constructed in a given context, in and through the dynamic of the communicational interactions and exchanges which simultaneously link the self with the other and both to the constructed object. In other words, in the footsteps of Moscovici (1961, 2008) and Marková (2023), who rediscovered the role of the other, we hold that common sense can only be understood on the basis of the interdependence of relations between the self, the other and the mutually constructed object.

Of course, this methodology leads to an individual cognitive structuration, but it only realises itself in the subject's social environment, and specifically the group environment (see below). We could add, in passing, that the information which circulates is only contextualised for those who participate in it. For the others, this information remains structurally decontextualised, free statements in circulation. Thus, information, regardless of its complexity, is relative to the conditions of its contextualisation, with as many distinct objects as there are specific knowledge contexts. In other words, to speak of objects with forever fixed characteristics is misleading, obfuscating the complexity of the issues of knowledge production, diffusion and appropriation.

Imaginary, real and language

To our eyes, three levels of analysis should be distinguished: knowledge production – common sense being one form of knowledge, knowledge diffusion and the weight of social factors in the production and diffusion processes.

(A) To tackle the issue of knowledge production as the representation of this knowledge is to tackle the process of objectivation, i.e., decentration of the subject vis-à-vis his or her own viewpoint, and, beyond, the process of validation of constructed objects. It should be acknowledged that the legitimacy of objects, in the spirit of what was said above, remains in flux and does not derive from some fixed intrinsic value. To the contrary, it must be seized and resituated within the transformations of the social process: (1) the knowledge production process cannot be understood separately from the social relations within which it takes place (Latour & Woolgar, 1979; Latour, 1987; Jovchelovitch, 2007); (2) within the social sphere are scattered distinct and distinctive practices and discourses. Is it necessary to stress that they constitute as many specific cognitive configurations that an actor may mobilise according to circumstances (Jovchelovitch, 2007); and (3) the social sphere is a totality, it is structured by all the discourses in circulation and the mobilised practices at a given moment in a given society (Angenot, 2006).

This being said, these discourses and the practices they encompass do not enjoy the same status. They exist within a hierarchy, both implicit and explicit, which determines the relative legitimacy of their objects, and by extension, of the modes of knowledge that underpin them and of their links – allowing some, forbidding others (without necessarily excluding or even limiting them) (Bourdieu, 1972, p. 162). It is already a known fact (Schiele & Bauer, 2023).

(B) Diffusion presents itself as the regulatory interactions and interrelations between hierarchised discourses and practices. If there are legitimate filiations (e.g., laboratory → school; or school → practice), there exist others, parallel, more occult, but just as efficient, propagating both legitimate and illegitimate knowledges everyone encounters. To understand the dialectic of legitimate and illegitimate objects, one must understand the dynamics of the exchange, borrowing and transformation of objects. If, thanks to Moscovici (1961, 2008) and Boltanski (1968), we can now understand the genesis of a number of common-sense discourses, we can only observe the diversity of factors governing the assimilation of knowledge, the complex relations between different cognitive configurations, and, thus, observe a polyphasia which each and every social actor must necessarily face (Jovchelovitch, 2007). Let us add, in passing, that although scientific thought always endeavours to eliminate social factors (to preserve itself from the encroachments of other forms of knowledge?) (Habermas, 1990), they remain nonetheless crucial in the knowledge production and diffusion processes.

To attempt to tackle the issue of the diversity of relations of objectivation and of their relations in all their complexity, it would be necessary to state it as a dual question: (1) Is it possible to think about the genesis of cognitive modes without automatically posing a hierarchy or its absence? (2) Is it possible to think the specificity of these modes, of their transformations and of their interactions, even their interdependence without the a priori exclusion of their independence or subordination? These two questions are of prime importance when AI is at play, especially because it tends to evacuate them.

The points raised above presuppose: first, (§A), the intrinsic properties of a majorated relation of objectivation fix the limits of the potential development of individuals. Even from a constructivist standpoint, which holds that the subject reconstructs these properties by actively assimilating them, the antecedence of the structuration of the cognitive field as a hosting structure predominates. The collective properties largely impose themselves upon the subjects because they pre-exist, but also because they constitute the individual as a specific subject anchored in concrete temporal and situational frames. Second, (§B), the dominant relation of objectivation within a given society tends to favour a cognitive mode at the expense of coexisting others.

Knowledges, individuals and groups

In both cases, the properties of the relation of objectivation would internally delimit the development of the subjects or the actualisation of a cognitive mode to the detriment of another. Would it be possible to tackle the relation of objectivation from another angle, taking into consideration the group, rather than limiting ourselves to the interindividual self-other relation? To this end, it would be necessary to substitute it with a ternary relation. Is it conceivable that the structures of the group mediate both the forms of the relation of objectivation and those of the cognitive activities manifested by the individual? If it were the case, the forms would imply themselves in and through the group to which they are immanent. But this point requires the prior analysis of the articulation of the properties of the relation of objectivation and of those of the relation of the subject to the group.

It is from the dialectic of the individual cognitive processes and social processes of the group that the structuration and transformation of the relations of objectivation result. In other words, the question is to determine how the weight of the social processes influences the structuration of cognitive processes, having shown that they manifest themselves in and through symbolic and discursive processes. It is thus the issue of the autonomy of those processes and of their internal rules that is raised, and, as a corollary, that of the capacity of AI to apprehend them. To the contrary, if we limit ourselves to the level of discourse, should the autonomy and dissociation of the relations of causality which generates discourses and the links of implication between their elements be retained? In this case, a given discourse could manifest itself within the processes of distinct groups and *vice versa*.

To describe the phenomena that we are trying to grasp, we must substitute an Aristotelian logic for a non-Aristotelian one, shift from immobile objects to objects which cannot be stabilised, determine in which conditions they can be considered at "rest" (Bachelard, 1973, p. 105 ss.), favour processes over states and consider cognitive fields from the standpoint of processes in constant evolution (regardless of their legitimacy within a given social context). These fields have the characteristic of preserving their form only through an uninterrupted flux of exchange with their environment. Thus, we must constantly think about regulations and anchorages which constantly modulate themselves (Foucault, 1971). This transition from states to processes implies a methodology which attempts to simultaneously conceptually dissociate and concretely articulate diachronic and synchronic processes (Piaget, 1967a), on the one hand, and structural and situational processes (Granger, 1967), on the other. It seems to us that it is necessary to articulate processes over time and the equilibrium of these processes at specific junctures to grasp how the coordination of structural rules of transformation and those just as structural of equilibrium actualise themselves in a concrete situation involving a margin of indetermination.

In the same spirit, the ever-reactuated opposition between objective and subjective conditions should be abandoned in favour of a standpoint which asserts the dialectic of the imaginary and the factual. The position we defend is the following: the imaginary and the factual constantly codetermine each other. The distinction between objective fact and subjective fact is questionable. If we postulate a reality independent from the knowing subject, or at the very least if we consider this reality as a plausible hypothesis (Bourdieu, 2001), knowledge results from such a construction that the "observed real" is indissociable from the structure of observation; what we call the "real" is the product of a coordination between the properties of the object of knowledge ("known real") and the properties of the subject and an other, also understood as a social subject, as it has been argued by constructivism (see above) (Ulmo, 1967, 1969; Piaget, 1967a, 1967b, 1967c). In fact, the "real" can only be grasped through and by a structuring and structured process of coordination, the product of which is reinjected as a new element, as a new fact, added to the preceding ones and which transforms the relation of knowledge. The conditions of possibility of such a construction presuppose a "real" imbued with enduring properties, at the very least for a given threshold of interaction (i.e., for a given level of apprehended reality).

This merely supposes that the discourse is a means through which a coordination is manifested. For example, to speak of concrete "material relations" between human beings implies a discourse upon materiality which produces it as an observable effect. The imaginary presides over any understanding of the fact, i.e., there is such a structuring effect that the very notion of the "real" and the resulting effect of knowledge itself are simply the preservation of a subjective structuration. To our eyes, the imaginary is present at all levels of the process of the construction of observable reality. Just as there is no degree zero of human interactions, there is no degree zero of signification. Human beings are thrust in the universe of meaning. Every element of the real participates of a structure from which it draws its meaning, and it cannot be constituted independently of this structure. The question as to when and how we transitioned from ignorance to knowledge is irrelevant: human beings have always been in a relation of knowledge because they have always been in interaction with their environment (and with others, see below).

As a first approximation, we will call structured imaginary all the symbolic productions from which human beings stake a claim to the knowledge and mastery of the "real". Under this denomination, we can group representations, myths, theories, magics, etc. Common sense and scientific thought thus belong to the order of imaginaries and characterise thresholds of coordination, i.e., moments of knowledge. Human beings do not think of reality in a partial manner, but in a complex one since this reality proceeds from the coordination of the relations they have with the factual and other humans and from which the "real" is itself assimilated by the individual. The "materiality" of the "real" is but the attribution of properties which, through their socialisation over time, became longer lasting (Berger & Luckmann, 1967; Luckmann, 1987).

The opposition, even dialectical, between objective and subjective relations, e.g., representations, appears too partial to be preserved in its entirety. Representations are not a by-product: they exercise a hold as crucial as the "material fact" (Moscovici, 2008). Even if we assimilate objective reality to a structured entity, which is distinct from an explicative discourse which can be produced upon this reality, action is only possible through the production of a discourse which makes possible its appropriation. What we call objective relations, in the final instance, can only be grasped and understood through the production of a cognitive scheme which allows for the conception of an objective totality. How to understand the relations of human beings with the "real" without understanding the discursive relations with the "real"? But, how to understand the production of this discourse without articulating human beings with the social whole and *vice versa*? Furthermore, how to understand the specificity of cognitive processes which allow for the construction of an explicative system designed to account for these very relations? Finally, how to understand this specificity without articulating the nature and organisation of cognitive structures specific to human beings (ontogenesis) to social determination (sociogenesis)? A subject cannot think of himself in psychological or sociological terms without referring to a sociality which establishes a signifier order and thus frees the development of structuring interactions thus made possible.

Discourses represent a modality of the structured imaginary. They are at the same time symbolic function and expression. Human beings only take hold in the world and acquire the objective practice of the world through the appropriation of discourses which regulate its flow. Any *action* upon the world presupposes an imaginary to think and transform it, i.e., the importance of interactions between the structured imaginaries: they are not word-plays, they have a structure, an organisation, a "reality" just as pregnant as the "objective reality" they make possible to construct and understand. Discourses thus appear as the specific locus of the imaginary and the nodal point of the integration of synchronic and diachronic levels, on the one hand, and structural and situational levels, on the other.

This is why we must now examine the relations between group and language. We will defend the following idea: a relation of knowledge is such that the properties of both the subject and the object are constituted, preserved and transformed by the very structuration of this relation of knowledge which unites the one with the other; this relation develops within a social relation mediated by the group, and this social relation is carried by the discourse and, at the very least, by a structured symbolic relation.

Drawing upon Cassirer (1933), Humbolt (1969), Whorf (1969) and Bertalanffy (1973), we hold that language and by extension discourse as an intermediary instance (Robin, 1973; Pecheux, 1975; Greimas, 1976) are not simply descriptive but also constitutive of the relation of knowledge. "Language is not the mere transposition of thought under a verbal form, it essentially participates in the primitive act which enables this transposition", as long ago Ernst Cassirer wrote (1933, pp. 18–44). The conceptual structuring varies from language to language, and the conceptual proliferation or dissociation corresponds to distinctions between properties of the "real" (Lévi-Strauss, 1962, p. 5).

Individuals, others and groups

The articulation of the relation of objectivation is tributary to its social conditions of production, i.e., the cognitive operations of a subject must be understood in the context which makes them possible. The relation of knowledge between a subject and an object rests upon the mediation acted by a third term which makes it possible, as we have already stressed. Therefore, the production of a discourse of knowledge takes place within the context of social relations which generate its conditions. The articulation of the discourse to its genesis requires the reintroduction of the centrality of norms, values, motivations, etc., contingent parameters systematically set aside by the legitimate scientific discourse and, up to now, AI (Andler, 2023). All the preceding considerations rest upon the notion of interaction, which can be defined as "behaviors modifying each other (from struggle to synergy)" (Piaget, 1967b, p. 19), or, even, as the "reciprocal effect(s) between two persons, resulting from their sustained contact" (Purushottam, 1979, p. 155). Interactions are constitutive of a flux of information between totalities of which they ensure the regulation.

From the preceding remarks, it is legitimate to infer that a relation of objectivation rests upon a structuring relation between individuals, groups and society in and through symbolic interactions, such as discourses. Let us clarify.

Firstly, it is the multiplicity of interactions between human subjects which constitutes the fundamental fabric of society, which confers to it both existence and life (Berger & Luckmann, 1967; Rocher, 1968). It is

essentially a system of activities, the basic interactions of which consist in actions – in the true sense of the word – modifying one another according to specific laws of organization or equilibrium [, and] it is from the analysis of these interactions within behavior itself that then proceed the explanation for collective representations, or interactions modifying the conscience of individuals.

(Piaget, 1967b, p. 30)

Society is thus a "system of relations" which binds individuals together. However, we must distinguish society and the social sphere, with society being a specific moment of the social sphere. It is the manifestation of a situational state of a structural phenomenon.

Secondly, society, a historical conjuncture, and the social sphere, a generic form, can be characterised as the moment of a synergistic or conflictual relationship between the elements that constitute them. However, these elements are not single individuals, but groups of individuals. Since Linton we know that "every society, from the primitive band to the modern state, is in effect an organized aggregate of small groups themselves organized" (Linton, 1959, p. 56). The social whole, the product of the structuring interactions between these totalities, is the regulated product of the relations between its constitutive groups. The concepts of social stratification, sub-culture, social classes, etc., reflect the composite nature of society and not distinct and specific subdivisions. The opposition of human beings and society thus obscures the fundamental fact that every human being exists first and foremost in groups and that each group is the locus where human beings realise themselves as existential and epistemic social subjects. It could be said that society and the subject "live" themselves through and by the group which anchors the processes of integration (socialisation, acculturation) and social and existential relations. In other words, the subject, group and society form a triad, and any analysis of the process of objectivation requires for each specific case the description of the properties of the triad under consideration.

Thirdly, the group is a structured subset of the social whole, a "system of activities", and a "system of constructive interdependencies", i.e.,

the elements which constitute it have at the beginning no other characteristic than the relation which binds each element to the whole it is a part of, progressively acquiring new structural properties from the very fact that they are covered by a web of internal relations.

(Greimas, 1976, p. 119)

The group, as a structural object, possesses the characteristics of a system: it can be described by the laws of composition and the rules of transformation; as a situational object, it has a concrete history which specifies and differentiates it; and as a strategic object, it is the locus where behaviours, schemes of action are constructed, and where decisions are made. It is an operator. It allows for a process of communication since behaviour and communication imply one another. Watzlawick et al. (1972) insisted that every behaviour and every action have the value of a message. At any given moment, messages are produced, exchanged and reinterpreted. Finally, the group preserves a state of relative equilibrium which results from the conservation of its characteristics as a system, conservation without which the group would simply not exist.

Fourthly, society, group and individual characterise three orders of totality, and each interacts with the other. It is within the group that psychogenesis and sociogenesis are articulated. Should we stress anew that the individual does not pre-exist to society, but is a "function of this totality". Long ago, Auguste Comte argued that human beings should be explained by humankind. The individual constructs representations through the coordination of acts and operations, while the group, through the coordination of individual representations, generates collective representations (Moscovici, 2008). As such, it ensures coherence between subjects through the regulation of interdependency: it is upon this basis that it adapts itself to other groups to preserve its integrity and that of its members (ibid.).

It follows that individuals and group are supportive of a joint form of thought since psychological and sociological subjects codetermine each other while one cannot be understood without the other. It would therefore be impossible, unless new data prove otherwise, to dissociate the operations of the psychological subject from those necessary to the emergence of the sociological subject. Individuals, groups and objects are closely articulated, and, ultimately, cannot be understood in isolation. So far, as pointed out before, AI has aggregated individuals without addressing the question of the group, or, rather, of groups. Furthermore, the group allows for the construction of the context of knowledge, and this knowledge cannot exist outside of this context, as already pointed out. The process of production of an object of knowledge implies the designation of a knowing subject and of coordinated subjects. This object preserves the coordination accomplished between subjects. In other words, social facts (structuring interactions) and cognitive facts (designation of an object by the coordination of individual representations) are closely interwoven. A group thus constitutes an object of knowledge which fixes and preserves the relations established between its constitutive members. Individuals coordinate themselves through the constitution of common objects of knowledge, which in turn orient and preserve their interrelations.

This being said, any individual belongs to many groups and moves between them. Thus, he applies and adjusts his array of virtual norms, behaviours and discourses in accordance with the rules of each group. The individual corresponds to a layering of group relations, reactualised in each new situation. The existential group and subject refer to the production of a concrete

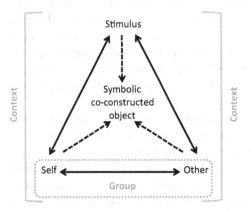

FIGURE 8.1 Co-construction of the symbolic object in any given context by social actors in a group dynamic.

individual history marked by historical social relations. The individual within a group represents a concrete element of a whole, just as concrete. This space is in fact the socialised space of knowledge. Yet, from another standpoint, the group, like the individual, can be defined by the totality of its properties, regardless of the individual attributes of its members.

We stressed the importance of social structurations and the fact that it first and foremost consisted of groups in constant interaction. Each group, to an extent, is a subculture, and from this standpoint, society can be defined as the reunion of subcultures in interrelation. We have stressed how both the subject and the group are involved by specifying that the structuration of the real rested upon the structuration of the norms of the group. We must now specify that the known object, the grasped "real", is entirely contained within the symbolic expression which allows for this conceptual structuring. In other words, we must consider the subject, the group and the object as being inseparable, collectively forming what we will call the *symbolic co-constructed object (SCO)* (Figure 8.1).

Within a group, discourses and practices are sutured: this is why knowledge is not exempt from norms, it is a norm. For instance, in scientific knowledge, there is a convergence, and it is its major specificity, between the modes of production of knowledge and the norms constitutive of the group to the extent that the expression of the scientific norm is also that of the group, i.e., the rules of production, exchange and circulation of knowledge characterise the rules of the constitution of the group (Bourdieu, 2001). The "truth" of the "real", not its "reality", for a given group corresponds, to be recognised as such, to the rules of production of this truth, and this truth is never but the expression of the common, accepted and shared rule of the members of the group. It defines the sphere of validity which results from the history of the group, summarising it. From another standpoint, this "truth" is but the production of predictable answers in the context of a system of rules. It satisfies the rules of exchanges at a given moment of the equilibrium of the group. In this spirit, the objectivation of the norm in an explicit system is a specific case of the relations between norms and knowledges (Foucault, 1971).

Conclusion

We can now better grasp the three functions of the discursive-social dynamic: (a) cognitive, it determines the mode of knowledge by favouring a structuration of the relation of objectivation in relation with a specific social formation; (b) communicational, it governs the exchanges between the members of this social formation; and (c) normative, it allows for the preservation of the structures of exchanges and of the modes of knowledge.

In these conditions, two types of questions arise: (1) what is the effect of the social conditions of the production of a discursive system upon its structuration, and what is the effect of the properties of a discursive system upon the structuration of social relations? (2) What is the effect of social relations upon the constitution of the cognitive properties of discursive systems, and what is the effect of discursive systems upon the cognitive abilities of social subjects? Could we envisage such a relation between a group and the discursive manifestations which take place within it that every given level is the manifestation of a group relation of structuration and of a specific relation of objectivation?

A specific type of discourse would determine, in turn, a specific group relation, a specific state of social structuration, a specific relation of objectivation and a specific mode of knowledge. To our eyes, the mode of knowledge, of individual and of collective knowledge, is not intrinsic to individuals, contrary to what Piaget's (1967d, 1976) conception of cognitive development and of knowledge development would suggest. In fact, individual cognitive development can only be realised within a group process mediated by a discursive structure which facilitates or inhibits specific cognitive operations accomplished by the members of the group. The cognitive functions of the discourse follow from its syntactic structure, which, in accordance with the rules, governs the process of operations and, beyond, the processes of actions and interactions. The internal limitations of the discursive processes inherent to any formatting operation have a structuring effect on the development and the product of cognitive activities. Is it not Piaget who said that the "real" is but the product of a coordination of actions and operations of a subject observing and deducing with the formalism on hand, framing these actions and operations. Precisely: a social subject, socially constituted, in interrelation with groups just as socially constituted.

In short, we have defended the thesis that any given group organisation frees or inhibits the cognitive virtualities of its members. The group is a boundary condition of individual expression: there is such a relation between the virtual capabilities of the subject that they can only be realised within the limits imposed by the group. There is thus a relation between individual cognitive expression and group structure. The cognitive capabilities of a subject cannot be understood in and of themselves: they can only be realised in the dialectical relation which binds the subject to the object of knowledge, yet this relation is also dependent upon the other subjects with whom he or she is in relation. And this dynamic has so far not seemed to be taken into consideration by AI, if it can at all.

Bibliography

Andler, D. (2023). *Intelligence artificielle, intelligence humaine. La double énigme.* Gallimard.

Angenot, M. (2006). Théorie du discours social. *COnTEXTES, 1.* http://journals .openedition.org/contextes/51. https://doi.org/10.4000/contextes.51

Bachelard, G. (1973). *La philosophie du non.* Presses Universitaires de France.

Berger, P. L., & Luckmann, T. (1967). *The social construction of reality.* DoubleDay Company Inc.

Boltanski, L. (1968). *Prime éducation et morale de classe, Cahiers du Centre de Sociologie européenne.* Mouton.

Bourdieu, P. (1972). *Esquisse d'une théorie de la pratique.* Droz.

Bourdieu, P. (2001). *Science de la science et réflexivité.* Editions RAISONS D'AGIR.

Cassirer, E. (1933). Le langage et la construction du monde des objets. *Journal de psychologie normale et pathologique,* XXXe année, Paris, 18–44.

Foucault, M. (1971). *L'Ordre du discours.* Gallimard.

Granger, G.-G. (1967). *Pensée formelle et sciences de l'homme.* Aubier-Montaigne.

Greimas, A. J. (1976). *Sémiotique et sciences sociales.* Seuil.

Habermas, J. (1990). *La technique et la science comme 'idéologie'.* Gallimard.

Harvey, D. (2005). *A brief history of neoliberalism.* Oxford University Press.

Jovchelovitch, S. (2003). *Knowledge in context. Representations, community and culture.* Routledge.

Jovchelovitch, S. (2007). *Social representations, public life and social constructions* [online]. LSE Research online. http://eprints.lse.ac.uk/2649

Latour, B., & Woolgar, S. (1979). *Laboratory life. The social construction of scientific facts.* Sage Publications.

Latour, B. (1987). *Science in action.* Harvard University Press.

Lévi-Strauss, C. (1962). *La Pensée sauvage.* Plon.

Linton, R. (1959). *Le Fondement culturel de la personnalité.* Dunod.

Luckmann, T. (1987). Some thoughts on commons sense and science. In F. van Holthoon & D. R. Olson (Eds.), *Common sense. The foundations for social science* (pp. 179–197). University Press of America.

Margaret Thatcher Foundation. https://www.margaretthatcher.org/document /106689

Marková, I. (2023). *The making of a dialogical theory. Social representations and communication.* Cambridge University Press.

Mayer-Schönberger, V., & Cukier, K. (2013). *Big data.* Houghton Mifflin Harcourt.

Moscovici, S. (1961). *La Psychanalyse, son image et son public.* Presses Universitaires de France.

Moscovici, S. (2008). *Psychoanalysis. Its image and its public.* Polity Press.

Pêcheux, M. (1975). Analyse du discours, langue et ideologies. *Langages, 37,* 7–126. mars, Didier, Larousse.

Piaget, J. (1967a). Nature et méthodes de l'épistémologie. In J. Piaget (Ed.), *Logique et connaissance scientifique* (pp. 3–132). Gallimard.

Piaget, J. (1967b). *Études sociologiques.* Droz.

Piaget, J. (1967c). *Biologie et connaissance.* Gallimard.

Piaget, J. (1967d). Les relations entre le sujet et l'objet dans la connaissance physique. In J. Piaget (Ed.), *Logique et connaissance scientifique* (pp. 754–778). Gallimard.

Piaget, J. (1976). *La formation du symbole chez l'enfant.* Delachaux et Niestlé Éditeurs.

Purushottam, J. (1979). Psychologie du groupe, analyse et perspective des relations du groupe et de l'individu. In G. Begin & J. Purushottam (Eds.), *Psychologie sociale* (pp. 137–186). Les Presses de l'Université Laval.

Robin, R. (1973). *Histoire et linguistique.* Armand Colin.

Rocher, G. (1968). *Sociologie générale.* HMH.

Schiele, B., & Bauer, M. W. (2023). Looking forward: The *Graoullys* – Blind spot in science communication. In M. W. Bauer & B. Schiele (Eds.), *Science communication: Taking a step back to move forward* (pp. 472–480). CNRS Éditions.

Trésor de la langue française. (2023). http://atilf.atilf.fr/tlf.htm

Ullmo, J. (1967). Les concepts physiques. In J. Piaget (Ed.), *Logique et connaissance scientifique* (pp. 623–705). Gallimard.

Ullmo, J. (1969). *La pensée scientifique modern.* Gallimard.

Von Bertalanffy, L. (1973). *Théorie générale des systems.* Dunod.

Von Humbolt, W. (1969). *De l'origine des formes grammaticales et de leur influence sur le développement des idées.* Éditions Ducros.

Watzlawick, P., Helmick Beavin, J., & Jackson, J. D. (1972). *Une logique de la communication.* Seuil.

Whorf, B. L. (1969). *Linguistique et anthropologie, les origines de la sémiologie.* Denoël-Gonthier.

9

EXPLORING THE COMMON WISDOM ON ARTIFICIAL INTELLIGENCE AND ITS POLITICAL CONSEQUENCES

The case of Germany

Frank Marcinkowski and Florian Golo Flaßhoff

The question of whether artificial intelligence (AI) can exhibit common sense (CS) has guided the development of this technology from its very beginnings. It also concerns most of the contributions to this volume. This chapter poses the question a little differently by not looking at the technology itself but at the society in which it is deployed. We therefore ask: Is there a common sense *about* AI emerging in modern society, and if so, what does it say in detail? For this purpose, the term CS is used in its most basic understanding, namely as a body of widely shared knowledge. A stock of knowledge is considered to be common if it is accepted as valid by more or less large parts of the public over a longer period of time. It includes not only cognitions (AI can make predictions) but also evaluative judgements (AI is useful) and even emotions (AI is frightening) which are taken for granted without further justification. Common wisdom is considered true at the time it is held, but may turn out to be false in retrospect. Furthermore, common wisdom can differ between social groups, so it does not necessarily involve the entire population. In the common wisdom of trade unions, for example, wages are naturally understood as buying power. For employers' representatives, wages are just as naturally to be recorded as costs. Consequently, within a given society, there may be competing bodies of knowledge about a certain matter that are unquestionably taken for granted within groups but disputed between them. In any case, every common wisdom is useful or viable for a particular purpose and is therefore retained.

In this chapter, we are particularly interested in political purposes that seek to benefit from the commonly held beliefs about AI. Such efforts take advantage of the fact that common wisdom is the ideal appeal body if one

DOI: 10.4324/9781032626192-14

wants to mobilise political support. It can be used to demand for certain behaviours or thinking and to solicit acceptance for political decisions (see Bauer, Chapter 1 this volume). This feature of common wisdom is based on three social functions identified by the German sociologist Siegwart Lindenberg (1987). First, common wisdom forms a universally available (or group-specific) basis for social interaction between people since shared knowledge forms a basis for common action, experience, and communication. This is why Lindenberg speaks of the baseline function. In the reference function, the author refers to the observation that CS can regularly be used as a yardstick for the correctness of factual assertions, subjective judgements or individual behaviour. If an assertion contradicts common wisdom, one will for that reason alone regard it as untrustworthy and not consider it necessary to make any further effort to test it. Finally, common wisdom has an appeal function. It occurs when an assumption is asserted as true or correct because it is consistent with what the speaker defines as the common wisdom on the matter in question. Lindenberg describes the latter function by using the example of a courtroom, but one can easily imagine appeals of that kind in the economic or educational realm, but also in everyday situations in the lifeworld of normal people. There is, however, one area of modern societies where appeals to the common wisdom of people are ubiquitous, which is the politics of democratic states. If evidence-based decisions are regarded as the standard of good politics and, at the same time, the common wisdom of the population on any issue can be made available at any time through professional opinion research, proposals and demands that refer to the demoscopically manifested majority opinion will become the standard case of political appeals. Many examples could be given to show that political proposals and positions will most likely be successful if they are based on what a majority of people think they know and feel is right, which is the common wisdom of the public.

From this, it follows that the emergence and consolidation of a common wisdom on AI are of enormous political importance, because its content and valence determine which political appeals are reasonably possible on this basis and which are not. In other words, the common wisdom on AI is not politically neutral. Quite the opposite, a certain expression of conventional wisdom favours certain political interests that can appeal to alleged self-evident truths, and it disadvantages others that have to stand their ground against the supposedly obvious. The political consequences of such a constellation can be illustrated by two contrasting variants of a CS on AI. One can imagine a common sense that regards artificial intelligence as a technological contribution to solving nearly all problems of modern societies, economically, ecologically and socially. Evgeny Morozov (2013) has identified such a mindset within the Silicon Valley community and coined it "digital solutionism" – the belief in simple, technical solutions for everything. Where this belief prevails – we call it AI *as part of the solution* – political appeals for more private and public investment in AI while reducing legal barriers to its use will fall on fertile ground. In contrast, one can imagine a common sense – we call it AI *part of the problem* – that perceives this technology as the origin of new problems: economic because of the elimination of thousands of jobs, ecological because of its enormous energy consumption, social because of the loss of privacy, political because of the new possibilities of social control, to name just these. Such thinking would be the ideal basis to support political demands for careful technology assessment before use, strict legal regulation and even bans if necessary.

In a nutshell: depending on how it is shaped, common wisdom favours two completely different ways of dealing with artificial intelligence, which could be described as politicisation and depoliticisation. Therefore, the question raised in this chapter is of utmost interest in terms of public policy. The next section we will briefly discuss what dominant political intentions are associated with AI in contemporary Western societies. It is argued that the political and economic elites of Western democracies have a vital interest in depoliticising the penetration of artificial intelligence into their societies wherever possible. Since politicisation involves accepting a social issue as a possible subject of collectively binding decision-making and that its need for political control is acknowledged, this also means that the elites hope for common wisdom that views AI as part of the solution.

AI and the current crisis of democratic capitalism

Given the current state of the economy and society of the European states in the outgoing neoliberalism, one can assume that the depoliticisation of technologies with artificial intelligence is an urgent interest of the economic and political elites in Germany and Europe. Since the great financial and economic crisis of 2008/09, Europe has observed the creeping end of the era of neoliberal capitalism (see Streeck, 2021). It failed because of its own contradictions, which manifested themselves as crises (not least as financial and debt crises), and because of the resistance of the population in the developed OECD countries. This epoch was based on the abandonment of state intervention in national economies, the disappearance of national economies in favour of the globalisation of goods, labour and financial markets, the stealthy replacement of nation-states by transnational entities, including the EU, both incapable and unwilling of intervention, and an increasing financialisation of global capitalism. Since then, weak growth has returned across the board in all OECD countries, national debt (not least as a result of the need to rescue the deregulated banking system) and private household debt have become overwhelming, social inequality has grown to almost obscene levels, and national governments have proven incapable of formulating consistent and credible policies to effectively counter these crises. The same is true of the collateral damage of global capitalism that is currently particularly virulent, such as global warming, global migration movements and pandemics, to name just these three. As a result, national governments are losing legitimacy and trust, and the statist popular parties of the post-war era (primarily the social democratic parties) are disintegrating or beginning to dissolve. They are being replaced by new kinds of movement parties without a solid foundation and firm anchoring in the social fabric of society, as well as populist movements from the right and left that are fundamentally incapable of governing. At the same time, this disintegration of national statehood – quite different from what the neoliberal credo suggests – is a serious threat to capitalist society, which needs a functioning state or state system to keep the contradictions described above latent through ever new policy arrangements – the now proverbial "buying time" (Streeck, 2015).

In this situation of European democracies, the digital revolution (including AI) has a dual function in terms of legitimation, which can be described as a contribution to system and social integration. First, digitisation is supposed to revive the belief in the technocratic steering capacity of nation-states weakened by globalisation and thus mobilise fresh willingness to follow national governments that have largely lost popular support and trust. To this end, it is functional to reinforce digital-technocratic fantasies among the population and to promote technical solutionism, according to which there is a technical solution for every social problem – and "digitisation", data and artificial intelligence are at the top of the list of solution technologies. The resounding "success" of the technocratic narrative and solutionist promises is countered by the fact that the majority of people lack a credible idea of how data technologies can contribute to solving social problems (pensions, migration, mobility, energy supply, environment, etc.) due to a lack of interest and concrete knowledge about digitality, big data and artificial intelligence. The data presented in the following section show that there is still some work to be done in this area in terms of political communication. Second, digital technologies including AI should revive hopes for economic growth and "prosperity for all" in a future digital capitalism and thereby regain acceptance of precarious employment, high living costs, stagnant real wages and growing social inequality. Since the mass of employees can currently hardly see how social advancement can be realised as a result of ever greater effort in their working lives, they need at least an idea of where the prosperity of the future will come from (cf. also the analysis of AI narratives in the study by Bareis and Katzenbach, 2021). In this context, digitisation, digital data ("the oil of the post-industrial society") and artificial intelligence are claimed by politics, business and the media to be the hope of the economic prosperity of tomorrow and the day after tomorrow. A third legitimising function has recently entered the consciousness of

European publics, namely the importance of artificial intelligence for external security. Not least the war between Russia and Ukraine has brought the military significance of artificial intelligence into focus. Where states are planning to expand their military capabilities, such as Germany after many decades of weakening its forces, they will be dependent on the availability of the most modern technologies, including artificial intelligence. But AI is not only indispensable on the battlefields of the future, intelligent machines are also fighting each other in the "New Cold War", which is currently being battled out in cyberspace.

Due to the described significance of smart technologies for the security and legitimacy of the western democratic states, from the viewpoint of governments it is essential to avoid digitisation and artificial intelligence becoming the subject of polarised public disputes. What is desired instead is a common sense that unquestioningly recognises the necessity and usefulness of this technology, or, to use the phrase coined above, a common belief in AI as part of the solution. The shaping of the public discourse on digitisation and artificial intelligence on the part of the political–economic elites is consequently designed for depoliticisation and quietism, and in doing so may rely – as far as can be seen – on the friendly support of the mainstream media. In short, AI is a "political technology" in the sense of Michel Claessens (2023), on which not only economic interests are directed but which is also associated with political intentions and hopes. This has consequences for the nature of public communication about this technology and, as a consequence, for the development of public opinion. Against this backdrop, the next section addresses the question of whether a common sense of AI is beginning to emerge that is functional or dysfunctional for these political purposes. Given the lack of international comparative data on this topic, we use the largest political economy in Europe, Germany, whose population has long been notorious for its supposedly technophobic attitude (Metag & Marcinkowski, 2014), as a case study.

Indications of a common wisdom on AI in Germany

All of the following analyses are conducted using the extensive datasets of the "Opinion Monitor: Artificial Intelligence" project (https://www.cais -research.de/forschung/memoki/), which the main author has been leading since January 2020. The project permanently monitors public opinion on artificial intelligence via monthly population surveys, analyses of media coverage as well as communication about AI on X (previously Twitter). To describe the development of popular wisdom about AI, around 1,000 German citizens over the age of 18 who are online at least occasionally are surveyed every month. All interviews are conducted online using a standardised questionnaire by a professional service provider. The duration of the monthly interviews is 7 to 9 minutes. Samples are based on stratified random selection, representative for age, gender and place of residence (federal state). Since the first survey wave in May 2020, responses have been collected from around 41,000 respondents (as of June 2023). For some of the following analyses, data collected on a monthly basis have been aggregated on an annual level. To capture the diversity of issues related to AI, the Monitor also conducts special surveys on particular topics. This chapter draws on several data sets from this series to provide the most comprehensive and up-to-date answers possible to the initial question.

Interest in AI

The formation of shared knowledge about any given subject presupposes, first of all, that people are interested in that subject. Of course, this also applies to AI. Without widespread interest in this technology, no common wisdom can be established within society or individual social groups. What is the situation in Germany with regard to this prerequisite? In the years 2020 and 2021, the Monitor measured only moderate interest in artificial intelligence among the German population. According to this, less than one-fifth of the population (18%) claimed that they are highly interested in the technology. About half of the population had little or no interest. At this time, one should have concluded that an essential prerequisite for the emergence of common wisdom about AI is simply missing. This picture has changed significantly since 2022. In the current surveys, around 40% of respondents regularly claim to be very interested in artificial intelligence. In contrast, the proportion of those who are not or only slightly interested has fallen to around one-third of the population. The remaining quarter claim to have a moderate interest in AI. It should be noted that the survey measurement of interest is necessarily based on self-reports. The significantly increased levels may therefore be partly due to the feeling that artificial intelligence has become much more important as a topic of public discourse in the post-Corona era. This creates the impression that this technology is a thoroughly important matter to be interested in as an awake citizen, even if one is otherwise just as untech-savvy as before. The widespread feeling that it is socially desirable to engage with the topic of artificial intelligence has grown significantly in Germany, as elsewhere in the Western world, especially after the release of ChatGPT by the American tech company OpenAI in November 2022. The project is evaluating the coverage of the thirty news media (print and online) with the highest reach in Germany on a monthly basis. The data reveal a clear ChatGPT effect on German journalism: in 2022, the thirty media outlets mentioned published an average of 113 articles on AI per month. In 2023, they averaged a full 550 articles in the first six months of the year, nearly five times as many as the previous year. This media hype has probably reinforced the impression that one has to be interested in AI as a good citizen. At the same time, the actual use of this information supply has risen sharply. In 2022, one-third of all respondents (32.7%) say they have received a media article on the topic of AI at least once a week. In 2023, a good 48% of respondents say they read at least one media article on the topic every week. Not surprisingly, there is a clear statistical correlation between interest in the technology and the frequency of use of media information on the topic. Close inspection of the data reveals those with a high level of interest and previously moderate media consumption receive AI reporting more frequently since the ChatGPT hype began. Those with little interest in the technology, who have so far completely ignored the information available in the media, are now at least occasionally exposed to a relevant media article. As a result, those with a high level of interest will benefit more than those with a low level of interest from the expanded range of information, which is why the differences between the groups will become more entrenched rather than dissolve. The data also suggest that artificial intelligence is unlikely to ever become a top area of interest for a majority of people. From what we can see, the proportion of people with an above-average interest will be from one-third to a maximum of 40% of the German population in the long run. This puts the meaning of *common* in the phrase common wisdom into perspective. With that in mind, we now turn to the question of what people commonly perceive as AI.

Common images of AI

A second necessary condition for the development of a common knowledge about AI is that people know at least roughly what this technology is about. Where do we stand with this? What are the German population's perceptions of AI? Do people even recognise AI when they encounter it? The Monitor project provides strong evidence for the assumption that a majority of people understand artificial intelligence to be something material, physical and tangible. The image of the robot is a prototype for this view. Between May 2020 and April 2021, all respondents to the monthly survey were asked to indicate in an open-ended question what they first think of when they think of artificial intelligence. As around 5,000 analysable responses show, nearly all respondents who named at least one intuition referred to a technical artefact or a specific application of AI (89%). Furthermore, the data illustrate that AI is mainly associated with three societal fields: the mobility sector and especially autonomous vehicles (35%); the personal everyday life and applications at home (18%; typical mentions were smart home; smart speakers; entertainment media); and healthcare including both medical use and care of elderly persons, especially using care robots (17%). All three applications can be linked to concrete objects in people's minds, which support the

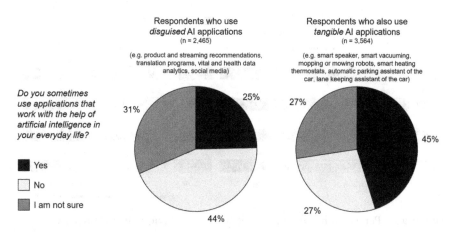

FIGURE 9.1 Conscious and non-conscious use of artificial intelligence.

previous conclusion. Other areas such as police and security (2.0%), education (1.0%) or public administration (0.6%) that use AI in recommendation or decision-making software are not figuratively represented in people's minds and are probably mentioned less frequently for that very reason.

Since February 2023, the Monitor has approached the issue by asking two closed-ended questions. First, we ask respondents whether they sometimes use artificial intelligence in their daily lives (options: yes, no, I don't know). In the next step, we ask about the use of various devices, services and applications that we know work with artificial intelligence. Figure 9.1 is based on a cross-tabulation of both questions, with additional distinctions made between technical artefacts and computer-based applications, between hardware and software if you will.

As you would expect, it is much easier for people to recognise that they are using AI if this can be experienced directly, for example through the steering wheel of their car, which turns itself as if by magic when the parking assistant is switched on. As many as 45% of respondents can tell they are using AI in such and similar cases. Among those who exclusively use services such as recommendation algorithms, translation programs or data analytics, just a quarter of users are aware that this is what is now called AI. In both subgroups, however, it is also clear how widespread the uncertainty still is about what to think of as AI. More than a quarter of respondents openly admit to not knowing whether they use AI or not. Physical experience and direct observability are apparently indispensable prerequisites for the emergence of common wisdom on AI. The fact that AI often operates covertly and is usually not even recognisable as such by end users complicates the formation of shared knowledge. If this is true, then one must assume that

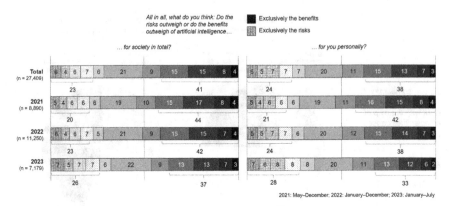

FIGURE 9.2   Perceived harm and benefit from AI: individually and socially.

the popularisation of large language models and in particular the release of ChatGPT has ushered in a new stage in the development of acommon wisdom on AI. This service, which is undoubtedly identified in the media as the prototype of current artificial intelligence, probably made a large number of people aware for the first time that AI can also be something that is encountered as a mere screen interface with an input window. One may assume that this insight will become common in the future: AI is sometimes just computer code processed by some chip that could be stuck in any inconspicuous gadget.

Evaluative judgments about AI

This widespread image of AI forms the foundation for various basal assessments of this technology among the general population. Figure 9.2 shows the distribution of answers to a well-established question in technology research about benefit and risk assessments. Since May 2021 the monitoring project regularly asks this question in two variants, namely on an individual and on a collective level of perceived loss and gain. In order to track developments over time, the figures are not only given for the entire observation period (first line) but also in comparison for the last three years. It turns out that the group of respondents who consider AI to be mostly beneficial used to be twice as large as the group of those who expect more harm from AI on both individual and societal levels. At least that's what the figures for 2021 say. Since then, there have been significant shifts in the direction of increased risk awareness.

The most substantive change occurred between 2022 and 2023 and it is reasonable to assume that there is another ChatGPT effect behind this development. With regard to social consequences, the proportion of those who expect more benefit than harm is currently still ten percentage points larger than the proportion of AI sceptics, but has become significantly smaller over the last three years. This tendency is even clearer when it comes to the question of the individual consequences of AI. Here, too, the proportion of optimists is currently still larger than the percentage of those who tend to expect disadvantages for themselves. But the group of optimists has shrunk by almost ten percentage points in the past three years. At present, it is difficult to predict in which direction this assessment will develop further. However, our data strengthen the assumption that with the personal and conscious use of applications such as ChatGPT, the perceived benefit of AI increases significantly. In this respect, the development visible in Figure 9.2 is possibly a consequence of the alarmed public discourse about ChatGPT in Germany. As the use of these and similar technologies increases and people no longer rely on second-hand experience, this development could reverse just as quickly.

Since a larger part of the population's assessment of the benefits and risks of AI is not based on their own experience or conscious use of smart technologies, it is interesting to know what capabilities people attribute to AI and what they do not assume it has. To clarify this, the monitoring project regularly asks what people think AI does particularly well and what it does fairly poorly (or is not capable of at all). A majority of respondents rate AI's capabilities as very strong when it comes to moving physical objects such as machines or vehicles (e.g., by industrial robots). A good portion of respondents also have high confidence in the technology when it comes to classification tasks, of images, text or sounds. Finally, autonomous learning from data, as well as the generation of text, images and sound, is also considered a domain of today's AI. More people are sceptical about AI's ability to have meaningful conversations with human interlocutors and about its ability to make recommendations for human action. In both cases, the proportion of those who have a lot of confidence in AI in these fields is only slightly larger than the proportion of those who do not think AI is particularly competent in these tasks. However, the level of confidence in the AI's ability is lower than the level of assumed incapacity in only one of the nine skills surveyed. This is the ability of AI to make autonomous decisions (see Figure 9.3, first column).

Once again, it is appropriate to distinguish between the assessments made in the post-ChatGPT period and the period prior to the release of OpenAI's large language model. Comparing these two periods, the attributed generativity and the assumed ability to engage in meaningful conversations have increased. Surprisingly, over the same period, the proportion of those who believe AI has the ability to learn from data is getting smaller, albeit marginally. This suggests that more people have learned what AI can do by now, but not what this ability is technically based on.

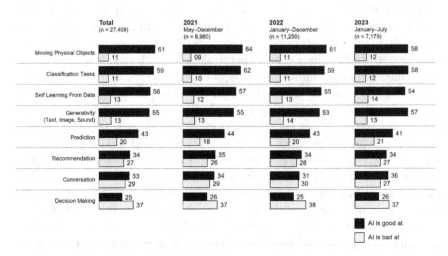

FIGURE 9.3   Perceived capabilities of AI.

The Monitor asks not only about technical functionalities but also about the perceived ability of AI to help solve specific crises all western countries are currently facing. The data show a mixed picture. Although people attribute a range of capabilities to AI, as shown in the previous section, their belief in the technology's problem-solving ability is by majority low (Figure 9.4). Only in the case of the climate crisis and its associated natural disasters do a relative majority of respondents expect AI to make significant contributions to addressing these problems. Otherwise, the importance of AI in overcoming the major challenges of modern societies is considered low by a majority of respondents. In the observed period, the belief in problem-solving ability is decreasing in all categories. Whether the growing scepticism is due to the fact that the crisis phenomena are worsening despite the fact that mankind disposes of intelligent technologies, or due to the fact that there is no comprehensible idea of how artificial intelligence can be used in concrete terms to deal with the problems mentioned, must remain an open question.

To understand the graph correctly, it must be said that the measurement of digital solutionism is based on a unipolar scale. This means that even some of the respondents represented by the light bar attribute a certain, albeit not decisive, importance to smart technologies for solving problems. Moreover, it would be possible that respondents have little confidence in AI for the problems mentioned, but much more confidence in it in other cases. Finally, individual perceptions of problems also play a role. Someone who does not see social inequality or migration as a problem is unlikely to have a high opinion of using technology to eliminate these phenomena. In any case, we can conclude that the digital solutionism mentioned above is not

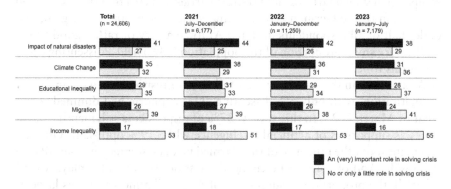

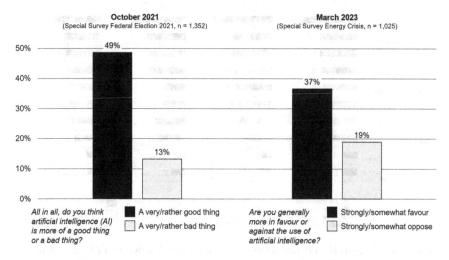

FIGURE 9.4   Perceived problem-solving capacity of AI.

currently a particularly dominant part of the common wisdom about AI among the German population.

General attitudes

The monitor provides two different measurements to determine the direction of mass opinion on AI in Germany. The first one is a very simple and straightforward question that was first asked in a special survey for the German federal election in autumn 2021: "Do you think AI is – all things considered – a good thing or a bad thing?" This question was asked again (in a slightly different wording) in the March 2023 monthly survey. As can be seen (Figure 9.5), in 2021, under the impression of a federal election

FIGURE 9.5   General approval and rejection of artificial intelligence.

campaign in which virtually all political parties had declared the accelerated digitisation of the German economy and society to be an urgent goal, just under half of all respondents declared AI to be a very or rather good thing. Only a very small proportion of the population (13%) held a dissenting opinion at this time.

As an aside, in the same survey, a full 75% of respondents were in favour of digitisation, with only 5% dissenting. This euphoria had dimmed somewhat by March 2023. In this survey, 37% of respondents still identify themselves as supporters of artificial intelligence while 19% oppose it. One can speculate about the influence of the alarmed media coverage on ChatGPT on this result. And of course, the changed question wording also plays a role. After all, the proportion of supporters of AI is still almost twice as large as the proportion of opponents. These figures are probably also more realistic than the exaggeratedly clear approval in 2021, with a relatively large share of citizens locating themselves somewhere between these two opinion poles.

In order to obtain a more nuanced picture, the Opinion Monitor regularly surveys whether respondents oppose or support the use of artificial intelligence in different areas of social activity. Figure 9.6 shows the approval rate (top two boxes of a five-point Likert scale) for each field.

It reveals overwhelming support for AI in the financing system with well over half of respondents strongly in favour of fintech AI. Somewhat smaller but still notable is the share of supporters for the use of artificial intelligence in healthcare, industry (i.e., the use of industrial robots), transportation, private homes and education. Thus, in areas where technology plays a major

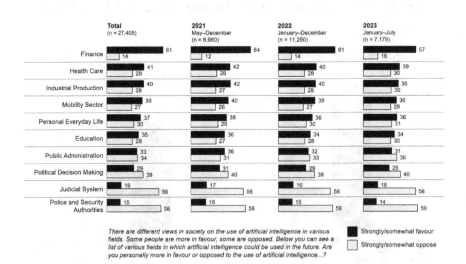

FIGURE 9.6 Approval and rejection of artificial intelligence in different fields of application.

role anyway (industrial production, mobility), the application of AI does not seem to be a problem, but rather desired. At the same time, there is only little support for AI in political decision-making, law enforcement and policing. Since 2022, the use of AI in public administration has also been rejected by a narrow majority of Germans. In areas where power is at issue or where decisions are made with a lot at stake, AI seems to trigger more refusal. However, in most areas of application, we find more approval than rejection, so that overall there is a rather AI-friendly climate of opinion on this question as well. As with much of the previous evaluation, it can be seen in this one that the generally positive basic attitude of the German population toward AI has recently become a little more sceptical. That seems to be the general trend. If there is anything to be learned about common sense from the numbers, it is probably that the state apparatus should be kept free of artificial intelligence.

Common wisdom and AI governance: preliminary conclusions

The current state of collective knowledge and public opinion formation within German society hardly justifies speaking of a common sense about artificial intelligence in a strict meaning of the term. In fact, many assessments are still in flux and some ideas are just emerging. This is not surprising and should be no different in other countries. After all, the technology is only just coming to the attention of many people. Interest in it has been increasing noticeably recently, and with it, presumably, the feeling of having to form an opinion about it. The publication of ChatGPT has contributed significantly to this, as the longitudinal analyses show, and one may assume that this process will continue. Some contours of a possible common sense are nevertheless already apparent. First of all, in the minds of many people AI is connected with concrete devices, something that can be touched and observed, i.e., a technical artefact rather than a technology. AI that hides in bureaucratic processes or economic transactions will hardly ever become an object of common sense. The power of these intelligent apparatuses that constitute AI in the minds of most people is widely recognised. This is evidenced by both widely shared perceptions of utility and the capabilities attributed in detail. At the same time, only a minority see the technology as predominantly risky. The high hopes for AI are all the more surprising given that the majority of people have so far lacked a clear vision of how AI can contribute to solving major human problems. *AI as part of the solution* to the climate crisis, growing inequality, deficiencies in education, and others is definitely not common sense at present. Nevertheless, relative majorities favour the use of AI in many areas of society though not in government and politics. And overall, more people are positive than negative about the technology.

Today's dominant views of AI, this brings us back to the chapter's initial concern, apparently favours political calls for more state support and less legal regulation of artificial intelligence. Such appeals, without being able to prove their effectiveness, do not seem to have missed their target. This is shown once again by the data from the Monitor project.

The project uses a battery of three questions to explore what governmental approach to AI is preferred by the majority of citizens. Each question contrasts two opposing stances on the dimensions of regulation, funding and responsiveness. The battery has run twice so far, in the autumn of 2021 and the summer of 2023. Again the data show that there is still some movement in the public's views. When asked about legal regulation in 2021, just under half of the respondents are in favour of the state staying out of it and leaving the further development of the technology to science and industry. Just under a third of respondents were considering government regulation. In 2023, the share of those in favour of deregulation has dropped to 40%, while support for regulatory technology policies has increased by two percentage points. More than half of respondents envision the government's role as a technology promoter and call for more public funding for AI development in 2021. Less tax money for AI is desired by only a quarter of the population. With public debt growing, support for more public funding has fallen to 43% in 2023; less public funding for AI is preferred by 30%. Finally, there is the question of how to deal with critics of AI. In 2021, only a quarter of the population thought that critical voices should be taken seriously. More than half of the respondents at that time expressed the view that the non-believers should be convinced. Preferences have also shifted on this dimension. In the recent survey, while more than 40% of respondents still believe that critics need to be convinced of what they believe to be the correct assessment (the common sense), more than 30% are in favour of taking critical voices seriously.

Even if the majority support for a deregulated laissez-faire approach to AI policy is currently crumbling, on the other hand there are no signs of a heated polarised debate about this technology in Germany. In this respect, the hopes of depoliticising the technological change induced by AI are certainly intact. Just under a third of the population tend to view some aspects of the transition critically. This contrasts with a proportion of around 40% of the population who predominantly see advantages and are politically in favour of state support for technological change. In any case, no resistance to it is to be expected from them, just as little as from a good quarter of the population, which has no clear political preference when it comes to dealing with AI. Especially the growing white part of the bar (Figure 9.7) is a cause for concern. It points to an eminent segment of the population that views the penetration of artificial intelligence into society as a self-directing process of ongoing technological innovation that sweeps across

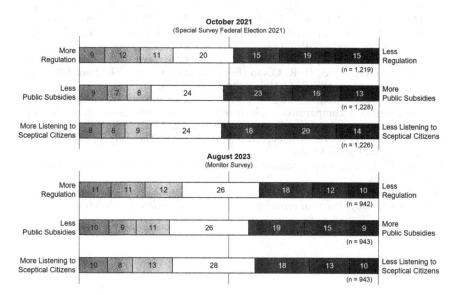

FIGURE 9.7   Support for opposing concepts of AI governance.

modern societies like a natural phenomenon and can no more be controlled or stopped than the tidal wave of a tsunami. This mentality is accompanied by the hope that the development of AI does not need to be controlled at all, because – unlike a natural disaster – it brings predominantly positive consequences, representing, as it were, a merciful fate. Those who think this way will see no need or even possibility for political intervention and thus contribute to the depoliticisation of technological change. Given the non-participation of a considerable part of the population, it can be assumed that the social implementation and shaping of new AI technologies will remain the domain of interested industry, accompanied by symbolic politics at the national and European levels. The profound societal change driven by the development of AI could thus be accomplished not only to the exclusion of the public but also under the condition of widespread policy abstention. These are not good prospects for the hopes of "human-centred AI" enthusiastically promised by national governments and the European Union.

Bibliography

Bareis, J., & Katzenbach, C. (2022). Talking AI into being: The narratives and imaginaries of national AI strategies and their performative politics. *Science, Technology, & Human Values, 47*(5), 855–881. https://doi.org/10.1177/01622439211030007

Claessens, M. (2023). Political technology mystifies science communication for general public, *Research Outreach, 137*. https://doi:10.32907/RO-137-4989867834

Fukuyama, F. (1989). The end of history? *The National Interest, 16*, 3–18. http://www.jstor.org/stable/24027184

Lindenberg, S. M. (1987). Common sense and social structure: A sociological view. In F. van Hothoon & D. R. Olson (Eds.). *Common sense: The foundations for social science* (pp. 199–215). University Press of America.

Metag, J., & Marcinkowski, F. (2014). Technophobia towards emerging technologies? A comparative analysis of the media coverage of nanotechnology in Austria, Switzerland and Germany. *Journalism, 15*(4), 463–481.

Morozov, E. (2013). *To save everything, click here: The folly of technological solutionism*. Public Affairs.

Streeck, W. (2014). *Buying time. The delayed crisis of democratic capitalism*. Versobooks.

Streeck, W. (2021). *Zwischen Globalismus und Demokratie (Between globalism and democracy: Political economics in late neoliberalism)*. Suhrkamp.

10

ASSOCIATIONS OF AI AND COMMON SENSE IN THE NEWS

Anouk de Jong and Anne M. Dijkstra

The development of artificial intelligence (AI) increasingly impacts society. Applications of AI already influence various aspects of peoples' daily lives, including work, play, travel, communication, domestic tasks and security (Kitchin, 2017). Nevertheless, current developments in science and technology, including AI, are complex and relatively detached from society. Therefore, most citizens largely rely on news media to receive information about new developments in this area (Schäfer, 2017). How news media cover topics related to AI, and what role common sense plays in the coverage of this highly specialised topic can offer a new perspective on the public discourse about AI. Although studies exist that analysed media coverage about AI (e.g. Chuan et al., 2019; de Jong et al., 2023; Vergeer, 2020), to our knowledge no research has focused on AI and common sense in the Dutch public domain.

In this chapter, we describe the role of common sense in the public discourse about artificial intelligence in the Netherlands. We aim to increase understanding of this discourse by building on an analysis of the philosophical debate about AI, combined with a two-step media analysis of Dutch newspaper articles about AI (see also de Jong et al., 2023). In our analysis, we focused on AI and common sense. The studies, however, were conducted before the discourse expanded with the launch of ChatGPT in December 2022.

In Dutch, the most used translation of common sense is "gezond verstand", which seems similar to the German "gesunder Menschenverstand" and "Vernunft" or the French "bon sens". The Dutch term "gezond verstand" can be used in different ways, but relates most closely to common

DOI: 10.4324/9781032626192-15

sense as the stock of universal principles and knowledge, and the ability to make good use of it (Bauer, Chapter 1, this volume). In addition, it is commonly used as a political appeal to be reasonable and can refer to a sense of community, especially for moral and political guidance (Bauer, Chapter 1 this volume). Therefore, in this contribution, our understanding of common sense in the Dutch context is that common sense refers to shared knowledge that every Dutch citizen is supposed to know and apply in their daily life.

For our studies we used the definition of artificial intelligence (AI) given by the European Commissions' High-Level Expert Group on Artificial Intelligence (AIHLEG):

> Artificial intelligence refers to systems that display intelligent behaviour by analysing their environment and taking actions – with some degree of autonomy – to achieve specific goals. AI-based systems can be purely software-based, acting in the virtual world (e.g. voice assistants, image analysis software, search engines, speech and face recognition systems) or AI can be embedded in hardware devices (e.g. advanced robots, autonomous cars, drones or Internet of Things applications).
>
> *(AIHLEG, 2019a).*

In our view, this definition is sufficiently detailed to provide a distinguishable description of AI, whilst still being applicable to various types of AI systems and applications.

The remainder of this chapter provides a frame for our studies in the section "Artificial intelligence in the public discourse", whereupon a description of the methods is given in the section "Methods", followed by an overview of the main concepts in the philosophical debate about AI in relation to common sense in the section "Philosophical debate about AI". Next, the sections "News articles about AI" and "News articles about AI and common sense" describe the results of the media analysis about AI. We discuss our findings and draw conclusions in the section "Discussion". We found a duality in how common sense enters the public debate about AI. We include a reflection on recent developments with large language models, such as ChatGPT.

Artificial intelligence in the public discourse

AI systems increasingly influence numerous aspects of society. Therefore, Kitchin (2017) called for more critical and empirical research on software, algorithms and the work they do. He emphasised the need to think of algorithms as contingent and embedded in socio-technical systems, which can make it difficult to uncover the impact of algorithms. Nevertheless, algorithms affect many tasks and practices, through pattern recognition, predictions, simulations and optimisations, which shape social and economic processes (Kitchin, 2017). The influence of AI applications on society has continued to increase over the past few years through new technical and societal developments. For example, many new AI tools were introduced to monitor and manage the COVID-19 pandemic and its impact on the world (Galetsi et al., 2022).

Another recent development in AI that has received much attention is the launch of ChatGPT, a language model optimised for dialogue (OpenAI, 2022). ChatGPT has sparked calls for research on potential uses and effects of large language models (Van Dis et al., 2023). Furthermore, researchers have questioned how they can use ChatGPT in their work and how this may affect the quality of scientific research (Stokel-Walker & Van Noorden, 2023). Since OpenAI has launched a free research preview of ChatGPT, many people have shared their experiences with prompts and results (OpenAI, 2022). This has led to considerable media coverage and a lively public discourse about ChatGPT (e.g., McCue, 2023).

Since AI increasingly affects citizens' daily lives, it is important that they can access information about AI applications and their potential impact. As stated, many citizens rely to a large extent on news media to provide them with information about developments in science and technology (Schäfer, 2017). Studying news articles about AI can enhance understanding of public perceptions and attitudes towards AI and of the science–society relationship in general (Dijkstra & Schuijff, 2016).

Previous research about AI in Dutch media focused on an analysis of topics and trends (Vergeer, 2020). Vergeer (2020) identified 16 interpretable/salient topics using topic modelling, with the three most common ones being "robot and football", "tech giants and fake news" and "smart assistants". Other topics, which are relevant to our study, included "humanity, Turing test and Blade Runner", "philosophy and writers" and "consciousness and philosophy". Vergeer (2020) also found that the sentiment of newspaper articles published between 2000 and 2018 was balanced, and that reporting about AI increased steadily from 2014 onwards.

Chuan et al. (2019) found a similar increase in the amount of newspaper articles about AI, starting in 2015. They studied the frames, topics and occurrence of risks and benefits in articles about AI in five major newspapers in the US. They reported that benefit frames occurred slightly more often than risk frames in coverage of AI. The main types of benefits included economic benefits, improvements in human well-being and reductions of human biases and inequalities. The main types of risks included shortcomings of the technology, loss of jobs, privacy concerns, misuse, ethics and threats to human existence (Chuan et al., 2019).

Recurring topics in other studies regarding media coverage of AI in the US included robots, speech recognition, big data, machine learning, autonomy, prejudice, privacy and the militarisation of AI (Ouchchy et al., 2020; Zhai et al., 2020). In addition, Brennen et al. (2018) showed that news articles about AI in the UK mainly discussed products, initiatives and announcements, while AI is often portrayed as a solution to public problems. Furthermore, Johnson and Verdicchio (2017) argued that two main problems with news coverage of AI are that AI is wrongly attributed a type of autonomy similar to that of humans and that the role of humans in the development and deployment of AI is underplayed.

Common sense has not been studied in any of the aforementioned publications. Nevertheless, this concept is relevant to the development and expert discourse concerning AI, which led us to consider if and how it recurs in the public discourse.

Methods

To get an overview of the public discourse about AI and common sense, we re-analysed data derived from an earlier study on expert and public discourses about AI in the Netherlands (see de Jong et al., 2023) and added newly collected data from a media analysis.

The first part of our study consisted of an analysis of philosophical literature about AI, which, based on previous lists (e.g., AIHLEG, 2019b; Hayes et al., 2020) identified six main philosophical concepts related to AI, namely: autonomy, bias, fairness, explainability, responsibility and risk (see de Jong et al., 2023). In this chapter, we discuss these concepts as a base for our analysis of the public discourse about AI and common sense. We analysed how the six selected concepts were discussed in news articles in Dutch news media by means of a thematic analysis. In addition, we performed a qualitative media analysis in which we aimed to specifically identify discussions about artificial intelligence and common sense in Dutch news media.

In the first part of the media analysis, we compared the philosophical and public discourse on AI (see de Jong et al., 2023). Between 1 September 2019 and 31 August 2020, the seven main Dutch national newspapers published 740 unique newspaper articles mentioning AI (kunstmatige intelligentie). We selected a sample of 53 newspaper articles from this time period for a thematic analysis of which philosophical concepts and other themes recurred. The selection was made by searching for newspaper articles mentioning "kunstmatige intelligentie" in the NexisUni database, which automatically sorted the articles based on relevance to the search term. The first 80 articles (10%) were downloaded for a full read. Articles consisting of less than 500 words and articles that did not discuss AI as a main topic were removed. This resulted in the sample of 53 articles.

By using a combination of deductive and inductive coding, a code book was developed and the articles were coded. The first version of the codebook was based on the six concepts from the philosophical analysis. The codebook was adapted through an iterative process of coding the first few articles and adding codes for relevant recurring themes. The final codebook was independently applied by two researchers to ten articles from the sample to calculate the intercoder reliability, resulting in a cumulative Krippendorff's alpha of 0.811, which is above the recommended minimum of 0.8 (Stewart, 2023).

The same process was applied to an additional media analysis we conducted to study how specifically common sense appears in the public discourse about AI in the Netherlands. We searched for articles in all Dutch newspapers published between 1 January 2015 and 31 December 2022 that mentioned both "kunstmatige intelligentie" (artificial intelligence) and "gezond verstand" (common sense) in NexisUni. This resulted in a sample of 39 unique articles, of which 22 articles included relevant discussions about AI and common sense. We read and coded these articles and identified recurring themes. Furthermore, to compare the public discourse about AI and common sense to the general discourse about AI, a timeline was created of all articles about AI that were published in Dutch newspapers between January 2015 and December 2022. In the next sections, results are presented.

Philosophical debate about AI

In our review of the philosophical literature about AI, we selected six concepts to focus on, based on existing lists of relevant philosophical concepts concerning AI. The European Commissions' High-Level Expert Group on Artificial Intelligence (AI HLEG, 2019b) identified respect for human autonomy, prevention of harm, fairness and explicability as main ethical principles to consider in the development and deployment of AI. Hayes, van de Poel and Steen (2020) created a list of values to be considered in the use of machine learning algorithms in the domain of justice and security, consisting of accuracy, autonomy, privacy, fairness and equality, ownership and property, and accountability and transparency. Vakkuri and Abrahamsson (2018) conducted a systematic mapping study of recurring keywords in academic papers about ethics of AI and found that autonomy and responsibility occurred most often, followed by consciousness, free will, existential risk and moral agency.

Based on the overlap and differences between the aforementioned lists of principles, values and keywords, we decided to focus on the six concepts of autonomy, bias, explainability fairness, responsibility and risk in our analysis of philosophical literature about AI. In this section, we discuss each of these concepts briefly.

The philosophical debate about artificial intelligence and *autonomy* centres around two main trends. Since AI is often described as having some degree of autonomy, the first trend focuses on what autonomy means and questions how autonomous AI can become. When the term "artificial intelligence" was first introduced, it was expected that one computer system would be able to outperform people in many different tasks (Helm et al., 2020, p. 69). However, instead of working towards such a general AI system, most research is currently focusing on developing AI systems that can perform one specific task more quickly, efficiently or accurately than human experts (Helm et al., 2020, p. 70). Nevertheless, discussions about the possibility of fully autonomous, general AI are still ongoing (Helm et al., 2020).

The second trend concerns how various AI applications might impact the autonomy of people who interact with or are affected by these applications. Hayes et al. (2020) explained how judicial decision-making algorithms can limit the autonomy of decision-makers because they often lack the required skills to critically reflect on outputs of complex and opaque algorithms. At the same time, these algorithms can also limit the autonomy of the subjects of decisions, by making them look suspicious and foreclosing future opportunities and freedoms (Hayes et al., 2020). Regarding AI in general, the European High-Level Expert Group on Artificial Intelligence (AIHLEG 2019b) included the principle of respect for human autonomy to prevent AI systems from unjustifiably manipulating, deceiving or subordinating people.

Philosophical literature about AI and the concept of *responsibility* mainly concentrates on the question of who should be responsible for the consequences of the use of AI systems (Hayes et al., 2020; Johnson & Verdicchio, 2018). Johnson and Verdicchio (2018) distinguished three different types of responsibility, and have argued that it should always be possible to trace back responsibility to the human(s) who made the decision to design the AI in a certain way, because even a hypothetical superintelligent AI system cannot be held morally and legally responsible. In addition, Hayes et al. (2020) emphasised the need for transparency in AI systems in order to clarify who can be held responsible for outcomes of AI systems.

The concept of *fairness* is especially relevant in philosophical discussions about specific types of AI, such as decision-making algorithms. Several definitions of fairness have been developed specifically to prevent arbitrary unfair treatment of people affected by outcomes of decision-making algorithms and AI (Saxena et al., 2020). In addition, the related concept of *bias* is often mentioned as a possible cause of unfairness in AI. However, biases do not always lead to unfair treatments, and some types of bias are necessary for AI systems to categorise, sort and group data. Therefore, Kitchin (2017) argued that algorithms should always be understood as a relational and contingent element in the context in which they are used. Algorithms may reform the categorising, sorting and grouping of data, but it is more likely that they accelerate these existing processes, which may or may not be unfair (Kitchin, 2017).

Philosophical discussions about the concept of *explainability* are usually closely related to biases in AI and fairness as well. When deciding whether a decision is fair, people usually want an explanation of how the decision was made. However, this is often complicated when machine learning algorithms are used, since they usually lack transparency of this decision-making process. Hayes et al. (2020) argued that transparency of AI is important for fairness, accountability, autonomy and privacy. They use a definition of transparency as the possibility to get knowledge about something or some event "characterized by availability, accessibility, understandability and explainability of relevant information" (Hayes et al., 2020, p. 15). Knowledge of an algorithm can help to judge if the decisions made by the algorithms are fair and to counteract the ways in which algorithms may limit the autonomy of people who interact with them (Hayes et al., 2020).

The final concept we extracted from philosophical literature about AI was *risk*, which includes several mentions of risks of AI that were not related to the other concepts. First, the risk that AI could harm privacy has received much attention in ethics guidelines for AI (Hayes et al., 2020; Raab, 2020). Second, there is an environmental risk, related to the computing power the development of AI requires. Several estimations have been made of the resources needed and emissions resulting from the development of AI (e.g., Ensmenger, 2018; Strubell et al., 2020). Other risks of AI that were mentioned in philosophical literature, but did not receive as much in-depth attention, include risks related to the safety, accuracy and technical robustness of AI, as well as risks related to AI's potential impact on ownership and property legislation (AIHLEG, 2019b; Hayes et al., 2020).

News articles about AI

First, to detect main trends in the public debate about AI, a timeline (Figure 10.1) was created of all newspaper articles mentioning AI that were published in Dutch newspapers between 1 January 2015 and 31 December 2022. Using the search term "kunstmatige intelligentie" in the database NexisUni resulted in 11,952 articles, after excluding results classified as advertisements, this led to a sample of 11,821 articles. The sample included different versions of articles that were published in multiple newspapers. In the Netherlands, several press offices publish multiple regional newspapers which produce their own regional news, and regularly use the same content for national and international matters. Since these newspapers are read by different people, all versions of those articles were included in the timeline.

The timeline in Figure 10.1 shows that overall there is a slight increase in the amount of newspaper articles about AI over time. The timeline visualises

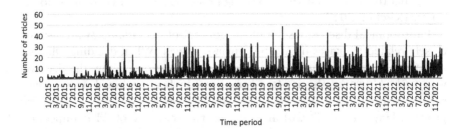

FIGURE 10.1 Timeline showing the amount of Dutch newspaper articles published per day between 2015 and 2022.

several periods with less coverage of AI, some of which correspond with peaks of COVID-19 infections in the Netherlands, around May 2020, October 2020, December 2020, April 2021, July 2021 and November 2021 (Rijksoverheid, 2023). In addition, several large peaks in the number of publications are visible, with nine days on which more than forty newspaper articles mentioning AI were published.

The largest peak of 48 articles occurred on 11 October 2019, including four articles that were published in multiple regional newspapers. The main topics of the articles concerned new investments in AI and a feud between two companies to provide the fastest internet. There were two days on which there were 45 publications about AI. On 4 February 2020 the major news topic was that the national telecom watchdog would start monitoring AI. On 24 June 2021 almost all articles concerned the opening of an exhibition of Rembrandt's "The Night Watch", of which missing pieces had been reconstructed using AI.

Second, for the qualitative thematic analysis of newspaper articles about AI, we selected a sample of 53 articles published in the seven main national Dutch newspapers within the period from 1 September 2019 till 31 December 2020. During the analysis, we concentrated on the occurrence of the selected philosophical concepts and other recurring themes. The non-philosophical themes that recurred most often in news articles about AI were geopolitics (57), regulation (51), healthcare and the coronavirus (22) and climate change (17). All of the philosophical concepts were discussed at least a few times in the newspaper articles, as shown in Table 10.1. For each of the concepts, an example quotation (translated from Dutch) is provided.

The newspaper coverage of the concepts of autonomy, responsibility and risk in relation to AI is discussed more in-depth in this chapter, since these concepts recurred most often in the newspaper articles about AI and common sense.

TABLE 10.1 Philosophical concepts in newspaper articles about AI

Category	Frequency	Example quotation
Autonomy	7	"If it concerns matters of life and dead, it cannot be the case that the computer operates completely autonomously, according to the [European] Commission" (Schiffers, 2020).
Bias	22	"People make a lot more mistakes than machines. Although biases are also ingrained in algorithms" (Winkel, 2019).
Explainability	14	"A problem is that even the creators of those algorithms don't know exactly how they arrive at their translation or image qualification" (Schoonen, 2020).
Fairness	18	"Too often the gain is for companies and the costs are for society" (Het Financieele Dagblad, 2020b).
Responsibility	27	"It is often unclear where the responsibility for "the product" begins and ends" (Broekhuizen, 2019).
Risk (privacy)	34	"Meanwhile privacy disappears, as an expensive downside of the fact that everything appears to be free" (Funnekotter et al., 2020).

Autonomy

A few newspaper articles mentioned fears of AI becoming fully autonomous and overpowering people. The quote in Table 10.1 exemplifies how people tried to reduce fears by emphasising the presence of meaningful human control over current AI applications. However, fears of autonomous AI were usually discussed as far-fetched examples promoted in science fiction stories that audiences were encouraged not to worry about. For example, one article stated (Westerterp, 2019): "There are many visions of fear surrounding AI: What if the computer autonomously develops itself into something we don't want, like robots that see people as subordinate and destroy them?". Similarly, multiple articles compared artificial intelligence to human intelligence and concluded that AI cannot be autonomous and conscious like people. One article (Verhagen, 2019) argued: "Intelligence includes a lot more than carrying out calculation tasks. A computer that has consciousness? Unthinkable".

Responsibility

Some news articles specifically addressed the question of who should be responsible for AI systems or argued that certain companies did not take enough responsibility. For example, in one article a professor was quoted, stating: "We have to force companies to contribute to society, it is a question of taking responsibility" (Het Financieele Dagblad, 2020b). In articles about new applications of AI, it was often stressed that the people using the AI application were responsible for checking the AI and making final decisions. For example, in an article about the use of AI in a military context, a general stated: "We apply a policy of meaningful human control, of human judgement" (Van Benthem, 2020). As mentioned before, the idea of meaningful human control came up in discussions about the autonomy of AI as well.

Risk

Many newspaper articles described risks of AI, the most commonly mentioned specific risk concerned the impact AI might have on privacy, as shown in Table 10.1. Risks related to the accuracy and safety of AI systems were discussed as well, although most articles that focused on specific applications of AI emphasised their positive aspects. Despite climate change being a common topic in news articles about AI, the risk of AI negatively impacting climate change was not mentioned. Instead, most articles focused on how AI applications can help to reduce climate change and prevent its negative effects. For example, an article that discussed the use of AI in the design of building projects stated: "If you try to build sustainably you have to give up on other requirements, or it becomes less affordable. A computer can find that optimal balance, a person cannot" (Het Financieele Dagblad, 2020a).

News articles about AI and common sense

We performed an additional search for newspaper articles in which both AI (kunstmatige intelligentie) and common sense (gezond verstand) were explicitly mentioned. Of the 39 newspaper articles published between 2015 and 2022, only 22 articles discussed AI and common sense in relation to each other. In the thematic analysis of those 22 articles, we focused on definitions of AI and common sense, the recurrence of the six philosophical concepts and extracted new themes related specifically to discussions of AI and common sense.

Most newspaper articles did not include a general definition of AI, but focused on a specific application of AI. For example, Mols (2020) explained generative language models like GPT-3, stating: "All these language generators are able to derive the meaning of words and word groups from their context, without actually understanding or knowing the world". Other articles, especially those that were shorter or focused on broader reflections on AI in general, just mentioned the term "artificial intelligence" without any definition or explanation.

Similarly, most articles mentioned common sense without providing a definition. Only three articles explained their claim that AI did not have common sense, stating that it lacks the ability to combine knowledge in a way that has not been done before and anticipate (Van Bergen, 2017; Haarlems Dagblad, 2017; Mols, 2016). One article (Riemersma, 2022) reflected on the lack of definitions and explanations of common sense in relation to AI, stating: "AI lacks common sense (…), but what that means exactly remains unclear". The author went on to provide his own definition: "It's all human knowledge that is so self-evident it's rarely spoken about" (Riemersma, 2022).

In the articles about AI and common sense, all of the six philosophical concepts previously identified recurred. Table 10.2 provides an overview of how often each of the concepts occurred, with an example quotation translated from Dutch from one of the newspaper articles. Interestingly, the concept of autonomy occurred most often in this sample, whereas it was the least discussed concept in news articles about AI in general. Below, the concepts of autonomy, responsibility and risk will be discussed in relation to the two main themes regarding AI and common sense.

In addition to the philosophical discussions, two main themes related to AI and common sense were identified. The first theme considers AI's lack of

TABLE 10.2 Philosophical concepts in newspaper articles about AI and common sense

Category	Frequency	Example quotation
Autonomy	10	"The development of AI will eventually need to change if humanity wants to avoid being overpowered by a technology they created" (Van Bergen, 2017).
Bias	2	"[AI] works based on existing data, which always contain some kind of prejudice" (Verhoef, 2022).
Explainability	2	"Data-driven models are often very complex and hard to explain. This leads to a black box that policy makers just have to trust" (Verhoef, 2022).
Fairness	4	"Companies are already patenting basic ideas of AI. That creates even bigger inequalities than we already have" (Mols, 2017).
Responsibility	7	"With killer robots the human involvement and responsibility in conflicts disappears" (de Koning, 2015).
Risk	6	"The question is if common sense can keep up with the pace of change. Whilst discussions about risks of blind trust in data are starting up, smart cities are arising quickly" (Van Noort, 2017).

common sense to be its main limitation, especially in comparisons between artificial intelligence and human intelligence. The second theme considers AI's lack of common sense as an opportunity to revalue human's unique abilities and to reduce fears of fully autonomous AI systems taking over jobs and society as a whole.

Regarding the first theme, the lack of common sense as a limitation of AI was discussed most frequently (15 times). For example, an article pointing out the impressive aspects as well as the limitations of the GPT-3 language model stated: "The machine lacks common sense. It has an incredibly large amount of data, but no models of the world" (Mols, 2020). In another article, titled "Computer loses from toddler intuition" the same journalist wrote: "the gap between the systems we currently have and what our brain does, is enormous" (Mols, 2018). This exemplifies how in many cases the limitations of AI were highlighted through comparisons with human intelligence.

Discussions about AI's lack of common sense as a limitation are related to the concepts of autonomy and responsibility as well. An article with arguments for and against the use of "killer robots" included two examples of this, with an argument against autonomous weapons: "Robots have no common sense and are less good at distinguishing soldiers from citizens. It's an illusion to think that autonomous weapons perform better than people" and one in favour: "People remain responsible for programming, activating and deploying the weapons" (de Koning, 2015). In these examples, AI's lack of common sense is seen as a main limitation of autonomous weapons, and a proposed solution is to hold people responsible if a mistake is made.

In the second theme, artificial and human intelligence are compared in a different way. Here, the lack of common sense in AI systems was seen as a positive factor that highlights the unique abilities of people and can increase their perceived value in the workplace. Within this theme, seven articles described worries that AI will continue to take over tasks from people, which means that certain types of jobs will have to adapt or disappear. These worries were exemplified in an interview with an author who called for a revaluation of manual labour and common sense, in order to reduce inequalities between citizens with different levels of education (Sommer, 2020). He argued that intelligence might automatically become less valued because artificial intelligence is expected to take over much knowledge work in the near future, making jobs that require common sense more important again (Sommer, 2020).

In many of the articles that see AI's lack of common sense as an advantage, common sense is seen as a uniquely human characteristic. These articles often discussed the perceived risk that fully autonomous AI systems will completely change society and overpower people. A clear example was an article by Van Noort (2017) which discussed several science fiction scenarios as well as current developments in AI. The article concluded, "Scenarios about an end to personal freedoms, human autonomy and the rise of new types of totalitarian regimes through faith in data sound extreme, and maybe they are. (...) If we're going to apply this technology on a large scale, a large dose of (human) common sense is needed" (Van Noort, 2017). This quote exemplifies how human common sense can be seen as an antidote to the perceived risks and fears of fully autonomous AI systems that take over societies.

Discussion

In this chapter, we looked at the public discourse about AI and common sense from different angles. To get an overview of the public discourse about AI in general, we created a timeline of all articles mentioning "kunstmatige intelligentie" (AI) that were published in newspapers in the Netherlands between 2015 and 2022. This timeline confirmed that coverage of AI in Dutch newspapers increased from 2015 onwards (Vergeer, 2020). Our time-line shows that the increase continued until at least December 2022, despite some dips in the attention for AI due to the COVID-19 pandemic. The re-analysis of 53 newspaper articles published between September 2019 and December 2020 provided more insight into the content of the public discourse about AI in the Netherlands (see de Jong et al., 2023).

Focusing on six main concepts from philosophical literature about AI (based on AIHLEG, 2019b; Hayes et al., 2020; Vakkuri & Abrahmsson, 2018) allowed us to get a better understanding of reflections on the impact of AI in the public discourse and how common sense enters into those discussions. All selected concepts of autonomy, bias, explainability, fairness, responsibility and risk recurred in news about AI in general as well as in the articles that discussed AI and common sense. The concepts of autonomy, responsibility and risk were most salient in the latter discussions, despite not being the most common ones in the public discourse about AI in general.

Previous studies have described several aspects of the public discourse about AI (e.g., Ouchchy et al., 2020; Vergeer, 2020). Offering a new perspective by focusing on how common sense has entered into the public discourse about AI, we found a duality. On the one hand, the lack of common of AI systems is seen as a main limitation of AI, and a challenge to overcome for AI developers. On the other hand, AIs lack of common sense is seen as an advantage. In this sense, the lack of common sense of AI applications is mentioned to reduce fears of AI becoming fully autonomous or taking over too much work. In addition, several newspaper articles called for a revaluation of common sense and manual labour as AI applications are seemingly beginning to take over more knowledge work.

When AI's lack of common sense is seen as one of its main limitations, references were made to autonomy and responsibility. Especially in comparisons of artificial and human intelligence, AI is found to be less autonomous due to its lack of common sense. Consequently, the public discourse emphasised that humans should remain responsible for the development and deployment of AI. This position corresponds with discussions about AI and responsibility in philosophical literature, which focus on who should be held responsible to what extent in situations in which AI is used (Hayes et al., 2020; Johnson & Verdicchio, 2018).

News articles that mentioned AI's lack of common sense as a positive aspect focused on risks of AI taking over jobs or even completely overpowering people. Despite the major focus on risks in the philosophical debate, such fears generally received little attention in the philosophical articles included in the literature review. In the newspaper articles on this topic, common sense was seen as a uniquely human trait that could help to prevent AI from becoming too autonomous. Interestingly, the question of how autonomous AI can become was discussed in philosophical literature as well, even though the impact of current AI systems on human autonomy received more attention (Hayes et al., 2020; Helm et al., 2020).

Limitations and further research

Our study of the public discourse about AI and common sense in the Netherlands is limited by the small amount of newspaper articles that mentioned AI and common sense explicitly. We compared the themes in these news articles to our earlier analysis of the expert and public discourse about AI in general, which focused on the philosophical concepts of autonomy, bias, explainability, fairness, responsibility and risk (de Jong et al, 2023). We recommend further research by means of a data-driven analysis with a larger sample, potentially including newspaper articles as well as other media, to show the broader public discourse over a longer time.

As stated, our sample of newspaper articles ended in December 2022, before the release of ChatGPT received major news coverage (e.g., McCue, 2023). Vergeer (2019) noted that the theme of algorithmic journalism was absent in their analysis of Dutch newspaper coverage of AI. This has changed since the release of ChatGPT, with several journalists covering how ChatGPT could affect their work (e.g., Eijsvoogel, 2023; Kist, 2023). Despite several articles mentioning GPT-3, the language model behind the first version of ChatGPT, these discussions were not included in our sample. Therefore, we join Schäfer (2023) in recommending further research on public communication about AI and generative language models specifically, including studies on if and how common sense enters into those debates.

Conclusion

Through our analyses of newspaper articles, we found that coverage of AI in the Netherlands has increased between 2015 and 2022, despite small decreases due to the COVID-19 pandemic. Newspaper articles that discuss AI and common sense in relation to each other are rare. Nevertheless, they offer an interesting perspective on the public debate about AI and its impact on society. Common sense enters the public debate in seemingly contrasting ways. On the one hand, its lack of common sense is seen as a main limitation of current AI systems, especially in comparisons of AI and human intelligence. On the other hand, AI's lack of common sense is seen as an advantage, reducing worries of autonomous AI systems taking over jobs and leading to calls to revalue human common sense.

When AI's lack of common sense was discussed as a limitation, news articles emphasised that humans should remain in control of the development and deployment of AI, echoing the philosophical discourse on autonomy, responsibility and AI. Nevertheless, in these news articles, AI's lack of common sense is mainly considered as a challenge to overcome in its development. In contrast, news articles that see AI's lack of common sense as an advantage focus on AI becoming autonomous as a risk, with fears of AI systems overpowering people. In these discussions, common sense is considered to be a uniquely human characteristic, which needs to be valued more when AI increasingly takes over knowledge work. This duality in how common sense is included in the public debate highlights that AI with common sense is both feared and wished for.

Bibliography

AIHLEG. (2019a). *A definition of AI: Main capabilities and disciplines.* https://ec .europa.eu/digital-single-market/en/news/definition-artificial-intelligence-main -capabilities-and-scientific-disciplines

AIHLEG. (2019b). *Ethics guidelines for trustworthy AI.* https://ec.europa.eu/digital -single-market/en/high-level-expert-group-artificial-intelligence

Brennen, J. S., Howard, P. N., & Nielsen, R. K. (2018). *An industry-led debate: How UK media cover artificial intelligence.* https://ora.ox.ac.uk/objects/ uuid:02126b4c-f4f9-4582-83a0-f8a9d9a65079/download_file?safe_filename =Brennen%2B-%2BUK%2BMedia%2BCoverage%2Bof%2BAI%2BFINAL.pdf &file_format=application%2Fpdf&type_of_work=Report

Broekhuizen, K. (2019). Ik wil meer vijanden kunnen doden per liter kerosine. *Het Financieele Dagblad*, 10.

Chuan, C.-H., Tsai, W.-H. S., & Cho, S. Y. (2019). Framing artificial intelligence in American newspapers. *In Proceedings of the 2019 AAAI/ACM Conference on AI, Ethics, and Society.* pp. 339–344. Association for Computing Machinery, Inc. New York, NY, USA. ISBN 9781450363242

de Jong, A., Dijkstra, A. M., & MacLeod, M. A. J. (2023). (Mis)alignment of expert and public discourse of AI in the Netherlands. In M. W. Bauer & B. Schiele (Eds.), *Science communication: Taking a step back to move forward.* 202-211. CNRS Éditions. Paris, France. ISBN 978-2-271-14839-1

De Koning, B. (2015, August 15). Het debat; stelling: Killer robots moeten verboden worden. *Vrij Nederland*.

Dijkstra, A. M., & Schuijff, M. (2016). Public opinions about human enhancement can enhance the expert-only debate: A review study. *Public Understanding of Science, 25*(5), 588–602. https://doi.org/10.1177/0963662514566748

Eijsvoogel, J. (2023, March 25). ChatGPT kan verdienmodel journalistiek ondermijnen. *NRC Handelsblad*.

Ensmenger, N. (2018). The environmental history of computing. *Technology and Culture, 59*(4), S7–S33. https://doi.org/10.1353/tech.2018.0148

Funnekotter, B., Aan de Brugh, M., Voormolen, S., Verhuizen, G., Spiering, H., Molijn, C., & Korteweg, N. (2020, 4 January). Van oermens tot kunstmatige intelligentie; 2020 van klimaat tot crispr: Een vooruitblik. *NRC Hadelsblad*.

Galetsi, P., Katsaliaki, K., & Kumar, S. (2022). The medical and societal impact of big data analytics and artificial intelligence applications in combating pandemics: A review focused on Covid-19. *Social Science & Medicine, 301*, 114973. https://doi.org/10.1016/j.socscimed.2022.114973

Haarlems Dagblad. (2017, February 24). Auto's voorzien van gezond verstand. *Haarlems Dagblad*, 6.

Hayes, P., Van de Poel, I., & Steen, M. (2020). Algorithms and values in justice and security. *AI and Society, 35*, 533–555. https://doi.org/https://doi.org/10.1007/s00146-019-00932-9

Helm, J. M., Swiergosz, A. M., Haeberle, H. S., Karnuta, J. M., Schaffer, J. L., Krebs, V. E., Spitzer, A. I., & Ramkumar, P. N. (2020). Machine learning and artificial intelligence: Definitions, applications, and future directions. *Current Reviews in Musculoskeletal Medicine, 13*(1), 69–76. https://doi.org/10.1007/s12178-020-09600-8

Het Financieele Dagblad. (2020a, June 25). Dankzij data zit je in de nieuwe Kuip altijd goed. *Het Financieele Dagblad*, 6.

Het Financieele Dagblad. (2020b, March 7). Het Poldermodel is ideaal voor techkwesties. *Het Financieele Dagblad*.

Johnson, D. G., & Verdicchio, M. (2017). Reframing AI discourse. *Minds and Machines, 27*(4), 575–590. https://doi.org/10.1007/s11023-017-9417-6

Johnson, D. G., & Verdicchio, M. (2018). AI, agency and responsibility: The VW fraud case and beyond. *AI and Society, 34*(3), 639–647. https://doi.org/10.1007/s00146-017-0781-9

Kist, R. (2023, April 24). AI kan journalist 'superpowers' geven - Maar moet dat ook? *NRC Handelsblad*.

Kitchin, R. (2017). Thinking critically about and researching algorithms. *Information Communication and Society, 20*(1), 14–29. https://doi.org/10.1080/1369118X.2016.1154087

McCue, T. (2023, February 26). *Most popular ChatGPT prompts and how to improve them*. Forbes. https://www.forbes.com/sites/tjmccue/2023/02/26/most-popular-chatgpt-prompts-and-how-to-improve-them/?sh=5667478c3064

Mols, B. (2016, April 30). En toen ging de computer zelf leren. *NRC Next*, 30–31.

Mols, B. (2017, October 21). Robots lijken vaak best knap, tot je dieper gaat graven. *NRC Next*.

Mols, B. (2018, November 10). Computer legt het af tegen peuterintuïtie. *NRC Next*.

Mols, B. (2020, October 24). Onbetrouwbaar, gammel en bewonderenswaardig; Laat de robot maar tikken; Nieuwe kunstmatige intelligentie verraste deze zomer de wereld. *NRC Handelsblad*.

OpenAI. (2022). *ChatGPT: Optimizing language models for dialogue*. https://openai.com/blog/chatgpt/

Ouchchy, L., Coin, A., & Dubljević, V. (2020). AI in the headlines: The portrayal of the ethical issues of artificial intelligence in the media. *AI & Society*, *35*(4), 927–936. https://doi.org/10.1007/s00146-020-00965-5

Raab, C. D. (2020). Information privacy, impact assessment, and the place of ethics. *Computer Law and Security Review*, *37*. https://doi.org/10.1016/j.clsr.2020.105404

Riemersma, T. (2022, June 08). Kunstmatige intelligentie stuit op filosofische grenzen. *Trouw*, 11.

Rijksoverheid. (2023). *Coronadashboard landelijk*. https://coronadashboard.rijksoverheid.nl/landelijk

Saxena, N. A., Huang, K., DeFilippis, E., Radanovic, G., Parkes, D. C., & Liu, Y. (2020). How do fairness definitions fare? Testing public attitudes towards three algorithmic definitions of fairness in loan allocations. *Artificial Intelligence*, *283*. https://doi.org/10.1016/j.artint.2020.103238

Schäfer, M. S. (2017). How changing media structures are affecting science news coverage. In K. H. Jamieson, D. M. Kahan, & D. A. Scheufele (Eds.), *Oxford handbook on the science of science communication*. Oxford University Press. pp. 51–60.

Schäfer, M. S. (2023). The notorious GPT: Science communication in the age of artificial intelligence. *Journal of Science Communication*, *22*(02), Y02. https://doi.org/10.22323/2.22020402

Schiffers, M. (2020). Brussel wil wedloop om kunstmatige intelligentie op ethische wijze winnen. *Het Financieele Dagblad*, 8.

Schoonen, W. (2020). Laat kunstmatige intelligentie haar eigen gang gaan. *Trouw*, 14, 15.

Sommer, M. (2020, October 10). De advocaat zal brood gaan bakken. *de Volkskrant*, 24–27.

Stewart, L. (2023). *Inter-rater reliability and inter-coder agreement in ATLAS.ti*. ATLAS.Ti. https://atlasti.com/research-hub/measuring-inter-coder-agreement-why-cohen-s-kappa-is-not-a-good-choice

Stokel-Walker, C., & Van Noorden, R. (2023). What ChatGPT and generative AI mean for science. *Nature*, *614*, 214–216. *https://doi-org.ezproxy2.utwente.nl/10.1038/d41586-023-00340-6*

Strubell, E., Ganesh, A., & McCallum, A. (2020). Energy and policy considerations for deep learning in NLP. In *ACL 2019 –57th Annual Meeting of the Association for Computational Linguistics*, pp.3645–3650, Association for Computational Logistics. Florence, Italy. https://doi.org/10.18653/v1/P19-1355

Vakkuri, V., & Abrahamsson, P. (2018). The key concepts of ethics of artificial intelligence. *Technology and Innovation*. https://doi.org/10.1109/ICE.2018.8436265

Van Benthem, J. (2020, January 23). Geen autonome dodelijke wapens zegt VS-generaal. *Nederlands Dagblad*.

Van Bergen, W. (2017, October 13). Leer machine menselijke waarden. *De Telegraaf*.

Van Dis, E. A. M., Bollen, J., Zuidema, W., Van Rooij, R., & Bockting, C. L. (2023). ChatGPT: Five priorities for research. *Nature*, *614*, 224–226.

Van Noort, W. (2017, 12 April). Spartelen in een rivier van data; Datadictatuur. *De Groene Amsterdammer*.

Vergeer, M. (2020). Artificial intelligence in the Dutch press: An analysis of topics and trends. *Communication Studies*, *71*(3), 373–392. https://doi.org/10.1080/10510974.2020.1733038

Verhagen, L. (2019, December 21). Kunstmatige intelligentie is de mens steeds vaker te slim af. *De Volkskrant*.

Verhoef, P. (2022, October 12). Modellen zijn prima, maar gebruik ook je gezonde verstand. *Nederlands Dagblad*, 14.

Westerterp, M. (2019, November 13). Games en kunstmatige intelligentie helpen elkaar ontwikkelen. *Nederlands Dagblad*.

Winkel, R. (2019). Kunstmatige intelligentie bij werving staat nog aan begin. *Het Financieele Dagblad*.

Zhai, Y., Yan, J., Zhang, H., & Lu, W. (2020). Tracing the evolution of AI: Conceptualization of artificial intelligence in mass media discourse. *Information Discovery and Delivery*, 48(3), 137–149. https://doi.org/10.1108/IDD-01 -2020–0007

11

MEANWHILE IN JAPAN

The possibility of techhno-animism for engaging deliberation for emerging technology

Mikihito Tanaka

The direction of the development of social elements is primarily determined by the imaginary shared within a society (Castoriadis, 1998). One typical example is emerging technologies, of which artificial intelligence (AI) is perhaps the most representative. Emerging technologies are recursively shaped by imaginaries that are shared socially among citizens, which influence the scientists who develop the technology and the policymakers and corporate executives who control the power to promote scientific research (e.g., Jasanoff & Kim, 2015).

The imaginary has become available as a media representation. Today, the Internet is no longer "downstream" of the mass media, and discussions that take place on the Internet sometimes flow into the mass media and set the social agenda. The public is exposed daily to representations of emerging science and technology in this hybrid media system, and it posts its impressions online to overwrite the representations (Chadwick, 2017). These hybrid media systems have introduced possibilities for deliberation about emerging science and technology, and their analysis allows us to understand the present state of the imaginary regarding them.

Furthermore, the source for the diverse imaginaries represented in the media is the *common sense* that is shared by the real world. The common sense of the present and future functions as a frame of reference for technological development; those who research emerging technology, such as AI, are influenced by common sense, and they choose their own research directions. Citizens who enjoy the technological results of such research may actively examine and use the technology according to their common sense. The direction of technological development is determined by actions that

DOI: 10.4324/9781032626192-16

are born of socially constructed and shared common sense mediated by the imaginary.

However, a significant element of common sense is rooted in the community. Alternatively, it could be said that the differences in common sense between communities define what we call *culture*. Nevertheless, the following question arises: To what extent do differences in common sense and culture as a source affect the direction of technological development? This question is difficult because science and technology are now universal among cultures.

The direction of the development of emerging technology is influenced by the imaginary shared by society through the media. The imaginary is generated from the source of common sense. However, even though emerging science and technology globally and synchronously develop, how they develop and how they are accepted is intertwined with culture, and each culture may have a different common sense. In this light, it is relevant to scrutinise the state of budding technologies in the context of culture and common sense.

With this in mind, this section explores the current state of Japanese social norms regarding AI through discourse in the media space. In Anglophone social media, the meme "meanwhile in Japan" is often used to refer to Japan as having unique or odd media representations of AI and robotics (Robertson, 2018; Tanaka, 2023). Indeed, Japan forms a semi-closed cultural sphere that self-mockingly refers to itself as "Galapagos". This characteristic should serve as an important reference point for analysing the relative role of common sense in the development of AI. This chapter analyses Japanese common sense regarding the relationship between AI and humans embedded in the media.

The common sense in this chapter is related to CS-2: common sense as a stock of universally recognisable knowledge, CS-3: quasi-rational judgement call, and especially CS-5: what social psychology is all about, which were classified in Chapter 1. Bauer states about CS-2 that "In China, this CS was part of the school curriculum as *"Changshi"* [常識], what every young Chinese does and should know" (See Chapter 1). The word "common sense" or *Jo-shiki* [常識] in Japan, which uses Chinese characters, is lexically equivalent to this. However, in addition to this overt connotation, common sense in Japanese culture is based on intuitive rationality (CS-3) and, more importantly, is a ritual norm (CS-5) that binds a community together and indicates an agreement that underlies collective moral judgment. The phrase *kare ha joshiki ga nai*, which is often used in Japanese society, can be directly translated into English as "he has no common sense"; it also means that the person lacks ethics and morals as a community member.

The specific case of common sense of Japanese society, which is crucial in considering the relationship between AI and humans, can be called by another name: *techno-animism*. At the very least, techno-animism seems to permeate the discourses related to robots, AIs and other things that imitate human activities. This chapter aims to shed light on how this common sense of techno-animism biases the understanding of AI held by Japanese society and to present, through an analysis of this bias, some ideas that can be used as a reference for non-Japanese readers.

Techno-animism as the common sense

The Japanese people's worldview has been nurtured by a mix of Shintoism, which is based on the ancient primitive religion, and other imported religions, such as Buddhism, Confucianism and Taoism. As a keyword that characterises this religious worldview or reverence for nature, the term *animism* has been repeatedly used by critics and scholars in Japanese religious studies, cultural anthropology and folklore to describe support for the Japanese worldview (Umehara, 1995; Baba, 2021).

The concept of animism has been extended to the concept of "techno-animism" as an expression of the Japanese people's unique affinity for robotics, AI science and technology, and it is often used to describe Japanese society (Okuno, 1983). Although the scope of this concept is broad, it is commonly rooted in the social tendency to find spirituality in technology and could be defined as the attitude that recognises the *soul* in artefacts, including robots, and tries to build an affinity with them (Okuno, 2002), or attitudes that accept the idea that "the entire world here is built from a bricolage of assorted and interchangeable (machine/organic/human) parts where familiar forms have been broken down and reassembled into new hybridities" (Allison, 2006, p. 13).

This concept has been used by foreign observers of Japanese culture to describe its peculiarity – with the careful avoidance of Orientalism – which helps make sense of Japan as a country where the boundaries among humans, machines and media imaginaries, such as Anime or Manga, are blurred (Jensen & Block, 2013; Robertson, 2017; Hagerty & Rubinov, 2019). In her book *Millennial Monsters: Japanese Toys and the Global Imagination* (2006), Anne Allison uses the concept of techno-animism in a vivid depiction of Japanese culture's playful indulgence in the capitalistic and materialistic fantasies that are now known worldwide.

However, it can be argued that this concept of techno-animism has also been used to justify the negligence of the ethical, legal and social issues that surround AI and robots. Kureha (2021), citing many recent international public opinion polls, argues that Japanese society's willingness to believe itself to be a techno-animistic culture is unfounded (Kureha, 2021, p. 3). He highlights that there is no reason to believe that Japanese society's intimacy with and aversion to AI and robots is very different from those of other countries. For example, Americans show more positive attitudes toward robots than the Japanese (Bartneck et al., 2007). More importantly, in a survey of Europe and Japan, no difference was found between the latent positive attitudes of Europeans and Japanese, although Europeans explicitly showed negative attitudes, whereas Japanese showed positive attitudes (Haring et al., 2014). Kureha then highlights that techno-animism has functioned instead as a distraction from the ELSI problems posed by AI and robots.

However, Takahashi (2023) recently refuted Kureha's position, arguing that he fails to understand the difference between the Japanese and Western senses of techno-animism. She draws on Piaget (1929) and Reeves and Nass (1996), but she also argues that in the "West"[1] there is an ideological tradition in which techno-animism is similar to idolatry (a term that is itself controversial) at the superficial level and is therefore intuitively unacceptable or untenable. In other words, even if one is feeling intimacy with AI as same as with humans, there may be cultural inhibitions against affirming them in West. However, such restraints do not work in Japanese society. In the West, there is an explicit sense of prohibition against techno-animism, but in Japan, there is no such prohibition. In Europe and Japan, there is a latent affinity toward robots. According to Takahashi's argument, techno-animism is a name for the absence of a taboo. Takahashi then takes issue with Kureha's disregard for Allison's argument, which he sees as leading to a disregard for pop culture as a practice of techno-animism.

However, we will refrain from discussing the explanatory power or validity of techno-animism in the social acceptance of AI in Japanese society. To be more precise, this chapter, like Kureha, is critical of the attitude of Japanese discourse that avoids discussing issues that arise in accepting emerging technology in Japanese society, using techno-animism as a reason. However, as Takahashi defends Allison's argument, this chapter accepts that we cannot ignore the influence of techno-animist thoughts on the new common sense that emerges from the public dialogue through pop culture.

In other words, the problem of this chapter is that such techno-animism is widely accepted in Japanese society as persuasive, and it forms the basis of the AI debate in Japan as a kind of common sense. From this standpoint, we observe the state of lay discourse among the public in Japan, where techno-animism is welcomed and supports ethical attitudes toward AI, and we analyse how lay discourse functions as a bias in the name of common sense. Through examination, this chapter shows that some of the ethical, legal and social issues to be considered in humanity's intersection with AI can be derived by the acceptance of the concept of techno-animism.

The confrontation between humankind and AI on board

In discussing AI in Japanese society, we first focus on "Shogi", which is a Japanese-style chess game. In our former research, we confirmed that it is in the field of games that invoke the active and casual conversations online, and thus likely techno-animistic tendencies of Japanese citizens, are concentrated in AI discussions (Yoshinaga et al., 2017).

Games such as Go, chess and Shogi have served as testing grounds for the development of AI, and they have been the stage of historical confrontations between humans and AI. Major turning points of this human–machine confrontation to the present day include Grandmaster Kasparov's loss to IBM's *Deep Blue* supercomputer in 1997 in chess and Lee Sedol's loss to *AlphaGo* in Go in 2016. In Shogi, humans and AI have repeatedly played against each other, and the dominance of AI was judged to be unassailable in the Second Round of the Den-Ou Tournament in 2017.

The mass media's framing of the gaming field has been more straightforward and more open than that of AI use, such as surveillance society and economic impact (Yoshinaga et al., 2017). In other words, the media framed that AI is a threat that could eventually surpass human intelligence, and the defeat of humans on a game board as a prelude to this threat is linked to the dystopia that will eventually come.

Despite this mass media emphasis on the threat of AI, it is interesting to note the anthropocentric attitude in comments on news articles and in the social media discourse of players and spectators of the games between humans and AI. For example, the top chess players in the West and the Japanese Shogi players reacted similarly to a struggle against an AI after admitting their loss and the subsequent change of mindset in the West and East. Their first impression while playing against the AI was that the AI's tactics were "overly optimised for winning and lacking aesthetic value". However, by the time the players had repeatedly played against AI while developing tactics and losing, the universal opinion was that AI would positively influence the association between humans and the game (Okawa, 2016; Simonite, 2020). Although it may be possible to interpret this as the players being sore losers, given the universal human response described in the previous section, it could also be due to the emergence of latent tendencies of tolerance, or affinities that are unique to the top players, that led them to tolerate their opponents through repeated matches.

However, after the players admitted defeat, the tendencies of the reflective discussion differed between East and West. For example, the West proposed to change the rules of chess with the help of AI and to transform the game itself to make it more interesting (Simonite, 2020). This could be described as an orientation toward social change through AI. In contrast, the Shogi discussion demonstrated a naive anthropocentrism: the rules remain the same, defeat is acceptable, and there is an optimistic expectation that humans will change their perceptions and bring new developments to the enjoyment of the game (Habu & NHK, 2017; Otsu, 2019).

The expectations of Japanese society concerning AI in Shogi games are extremely techno-animistic in that they consider the rules, which are supposedly created by humans, to be natural and to conform to the human's understanding of rules. More importantly, this sense is widely shared. To confirm this trend, we consider another recent incident between machines and humans that did not involve AI.

"Moral should be tuned"

To further illustrate the attitude of Japanese society toward the relationship between humanity and machine-generated judgements, which is a slight departure from AI, let us look at a recent case of video-assisted referee (VAR) at the World Cup soccer tournament. The incident occurred on 2 December 2022, during the Qatar FIFA World Cup match between Japan and Spain. The ball was turned in by midfielder Kaoru Mitoma at the goal line six minutes into the second half. Tens of millions of people in Japan were probably waiting with bated breath for the referee's decision. A few minutes later, the ball was officially judged by VAR as "in", which led to Japan's comeback goal. The drama created by VAR, dubbed "Mitoma Miracle of a Millimeter", thrilled the entire country of Japan and dismayed the Spanish supporters. Of course, this is not AI. However, what was initially judged "out" by human subjectivity was overturned by meticulous machine measurements, which must be a case that places measurements above human sensibilities.

However, a few days later a controversy akin to the Shogi defeat occurred that illustrated the techno-animistic attitude of Japanese society regarding common sense. The trigger was the VAR incident, which prompted former England captain Stanley Victor Collymore to say in an interview with the Mirror:

> I can't believe we have now got ourselves into a situation whereby all but a millimetre of the ball has crossed the white line yet it is still deemed to be in. Look, I don't really give two hoots that Germany are out, that's great from an English perspective, but it still seems morally wrong and lacking in common sense that that ball was ruled in.
>
> *(Hopkinson, 2022).*

When this statement was introduced in the Japanese media, it sparked considerable debate. Particular attention was paid to the last part, "morally wrong and lacking in common sense". Collymore's concern about this common sense, whether one agrees or not, would be understandable to many Westerners. However, for many Japanese people, this comment directly opposed their common sense. One Japanese person posted the following sentence on Japan's most popular web platform, Yahoo! Japan:

In that case, I think it would be correct to change the criteria for judging the ball, for example, to include a numerical value for offside, such as how much the ball has to be out of play. It seems that would be fair for everyone to change the criteria for judging the ball on line as well, such as whether the ball's point of contact is online or not. But that is a stretch, so I guess we could just define how to fix what's morally wrong or what's common sense.

A comment by a citizen on Yahoo! Japan News

This wild discourse, which is difficult to translate, may also be difficult to understand because of its roundaboutness. However, the assertion that "even if it was one millimetre, the defined numbers made as criteria for judgment is superior, and morality and common sense should be modified accordingly" which can still hardly be understood, will be surprising to many readers. However, this radical rule-centred way of thinking was widely accepted by the Japanese public.

The same arguments we presented about the relationship between games and people are repeated here. Simply put, while Western society argues that if the rules are morally wrong, they should be changed, Japanese citizens point out that if the rules are wrong, morality and common sense should be modified.

Of course, behind these reactions is a backlash that is rooted in self-orientalism, the attitude that insists on excessive relativity of East against West, which is historically built up in Japanese society, which says that "Western societies change the rules at their convenience when they are at a disadvantage". Even so, blind faith in the "objectivity" of numbers – even though all standard numbers are the product of expediency, politics, and compromise, as well as science (cf. Porter, 2020) – is characteristic of Japanese society. This absolute trust in science and technology is a characteristic of Japanese society. Nevertheless, as in the case of Shogi, what should be understood here is a techno-animistic attitude of finding a divine deity in the rules after the rules are made and changing human thinking accordingly.

Tuning common sense

The optimistic opinion of Japanese society that AI is not a threat to humanity, but rather an opportunity to expand human capabilities, may be realistic. According to a study published in 2021, the Go game has improved by 30% since the introduction of *AlphaGo* (Choi et al., 2022). It is interesting to note that this enhancement effect is more pronounced for the younger generation.

However, a similar study on Shogi shows a widening gap between professionals since the introduction of AI (Saito & Ito, 2022). According to this study, there are five levels of professional Shogi players; however, since 2017, only the highest level, the A-level, has become better by utilising AI. In other words, only the highest-level professionals could read and learn from the tactics created by AI and further improve their skills. This Shogi case foreshadows a "digital divide" problem with the human use of AI that is often highlighted in Western ethical debates. To date, these conflicting findings of enhancement and digital divide point to a future in which AI will indeed augment human capabilities: "all humans will be equally augmented, but some humans will be more augmented than others".

If the effect of technology on humans is an elitist enhancement or divide effect, how can the difference in "common sense" between West and East, trying to adapt machines to humans or humans to machines, act on and be affected by this possible eventuality, the contours of which are now becoming clear? The scope of the social impact of generative AI, beginning with large-scale language models such as ChatGPT, is currently being debated around the world.

In response to the turmoil brought by the rapid development of generative AI, Western societies appear to be rotten about how to tame it. Of course, there is a difference in that the European Parliament focuses on how AI models are developed, whereas the US is orientated toward an approach that focuses on the risks associated with the actual use of these models (e.g., Martin et al., 2023). Nevertheless, as one might expect from the discussion so far, Japanese society is cynical about such attempts to tame AI. This is supported by optimism that could be described as a kind of resignation to the idea of tuning the current common sense to machines. In other words, Japanese society upholds the idea that domination by AI is inevitable and that if this is the case, we should change our common sense.

Is techno-animism, then, as Kureha (2021) points out, merely a self-referential tool to distract Japanese society from ethical debates? Let us finally explore both the properly and improperly of this idea.

Techno-animism in AI representations

We have seen how techno-animistic tendencies in Japanese society mitigate the reflections about AI from the ethical compendium of Western philosophy. In fact, from the perspective in which the classical Western–Eastern framework tends to function (and this essay itself dares to take such an attitude), such side effects of techno-animism are truly apparent. The site of this mitigating reaction to ethical issues is the representation of pop culture, the medium of techno-animism and the symbol of contemporary Japan. As has often been pointed out, the Japanese cultural sphere is awash in *manga* (Japanese comics and illustrations) and *anime* (Japanese animations). People not only consume them but also write their own *manga*, post them on social media and critique others' manga daily. Japan has perhaps one of the world's most pervasive manga and illustration writing cultures.

Manga itself, as a visual medium of techno-animism and a medium for connecting people, illustrates the problems and possibilities of techno-animistic responses. This is represented by one key incident in the Japanese debate on AI: the cover of the publication of Artificial Intelligence and its aftermath in 2014.

The controversy was over the cover of the 2014 Vol. 29, No. 1 issue of the *Japanese Society for Artificial Intelligence (JSAI)*. With this issue, the journal underwent a bold reform and began using manga-style illustrations on its cover. However, the cover of this memorable first issue caused a great deal of controversy. Sociologists and feminists pointed out that the cover, which depicted a female robot connected to a cable and cleaning a house, was inappropriate because it reproduced stereotypical gender roles and depicted slavery of women.[2]

The *JSAI* was quick to react, and the journal's next issue was a special one. They used big data to analyse the controversy (Toriumi et al., 2014) and invited researchers from other fields to contribute papers to fill in the gaps in the imaginary of AI experts. For example, guest scholars on gender and representation theory pointed out that the cover's representation was nostalgic and drew on classical gendered and old AI and robot perspectives, but also expected AI researchers to learn from the ongoing argument to create a new set of values (Ikeda & Yamazaki, 2014). AI experts adopted the experimental cover illustration to their journal in a self-referential way about the techno-animistic tendencies of Japanese society that support their field of study. Moreover, researchers have used the flaming incident of their journal as an opportunity to study gender sociology and representation theory, have sought to harmonise their findings with findings in other fields and have made efforts to connect the lesson to the future.

However, the social memory of the incident among many net-citizens is different. This incident is still referred to today as "one of the first incidents in which feminists and sociologists tortured us with the 'politically correct' thinking imported from the West".[3] The arguments about cover illustration are remembered by many net citizens as the dispute against external pressure, such as feminism or sociology, from an incompatible Western ethic that disrupts the harmony of their culture. This reaction of the net citizens may be an example of using techno-animism to avoid ethical issues, as Kureha (2021) stated.

Potential consequences of the debate over AI-*éshi*

As Allison (2006) highlighted, techno-animism is hedonistic and materialistic. We have witnessed from the *Japanese Journal of Artificial Intelligence* cover issue that it is, therefore, in line with current materialism and works against attitudes that seek to overcome and modify it ethically.

However, we would rather see examples of best practices where techno-animism is widely shared as common sense: a public debate that takes techno-animism as a starting point can uncover important issues. Following is the debate over generative AI that occurred just recently.

As mentioned earlier, Japanese pop culture is unique in terms of the extreme permeation of manga into everyday life. People routinely write and share manga using social media. As with most user-generated content, there is no question of skill, but artists who create good content are respected and have been called *éshi*.[4]

In 2022, generative AI such as StyleGAN2 (NVidia) and DALL-E (OpenAI) became popular. These algorithms quickly learned the patterns created by existing illustrators and created "new" content. When this wave reached Japan, based on techno-animistic conventions, this generative AI was called an AI-*éshi* and was given pseudo-personal rights.

As far as the author has observed Anglophone and Japanese discussions since then, Japanese debate over the AI-*éshi* seems to have kept the world on the cutting edge in 2022 with regard to various issues involving artistic creativity and generative AI. Issues were raised that related to moral rights, rights to the content from which art is learned, and other similar issues that would later become popular topics in the English-speaking world. However, the problems that were pointed out in the discussion of the techno-animistic attitude of treating AI as an AI-*éshi* unearthed a different aspect of the AI problem as a wild philosophy because of the sensitivity it presupposes. This can be seen, for example, in the user-generated content from AtWiki, titled "Why are AI-*éshi* problematic?",[5] which summarises the discussion of ethical, legal and social issues.

> Some people imagine that AI has a personality, saying, "AI-*kun* (AI-*chan*)[6] drew a picture for me" or "AI understands *Kawaii*".

- By recognising image-generating AI with the characterisation "AI drew this picture," the feeling of "interesting" precedes an understanding of the problematic nature of the mechanism of image-generating AI.
- Different interpretations of "AI" by different people, including anthropomorphism toward AI, sometimes create confusion in discussions about the problematic nature of AI generation.
- In some cases, the responsibility for AI image generation tools is also confused by the interpellation of anthropomorphic "AI" when

it is supposed to be humans who are using and directing the AI image generation tools.

(atwiki, 2023; translated by the author)

Although these are just a few of the large number of issues, the vast number of issues that were omitted is also interesting and anticipates the debate on generative AI that is ongoing. It is beyond the scope of this studyr to revisit the details of the points raised. Nevertheless, we can see in this description a condensation of issues that people have begun to think about from a techno-animistic perspective that assumes a bricolage of AI and humans and still proceeds to reflect on. All these alarming phrases, which emerged from the Japanese discussion space, are based on the premise of techno-animism. Nevertheless, they transcend techno-animism and are excellent reflections on the art produced by generative AI.

There is one possibility here. In the West, a sense of crisis over the erosion of humanity and society by AI has led to various ethical debates. In Japan, alternatively, the ethical arguments that are repeatedly imported from the West seem to be relativised and ignored under the common sense of techno-animism. However, the human tendency to be attracted to and feel affinity with robots and AI is common in the East and West. In this context, even though Japanese society glorifies techno-animism, it produces a moral bewilderment that is found only in excessive familiarity and from a more down-to-earth agenda.

Conclusion

The sense that AI should tune morality is not a guide to how it should be tuned. The problem here, as Takahashi highlights, is that techno-animism cannot serve as an ethical guide.

> The Japanese should be aware that the ideals of animism have never actually been the driving force for the betterment of the world and that they have, in fact, acted in an anthropocentric manner. A consensus must then be formed on the necessary value hierarchy (which may be paraphrased as relative-relativism).
>
> *(Takahashi, 2023, p. 15; translated by the author)*

I agree with Takahashi's proposal. Thus, I would like to propose an ethical discussion of science communication that is practical rather than ideological. This would introduce the possibility of examining issues from a different perspective through the acceptance of techno-animism, which is unacceptable in the West.

The current debate on AI ethics in Japan is importing the debate that is flourishing in the West, such as the trolley problem of self-driving cars and the issue of personal recognition by surveillance cameras. Science communication activities, agenda setting on science and technology studies, and discussions provoked by journalists to uncover citizens' ethical debates through citizen dialogue are also associated with these issues (Ema, 2019; Kishimoto et al., 2023; Taira, 2019). However, as we have seen, not only is the response of Japanese citizens to such an agenda insouciance, but as in the case of the AI Society cover issue, the issue itself is made to disappear through a cynicism rooted in techno-animism. Alternatively, Japanese citizens are enthusiastically discussing more esoteric issues they have discovered and are generating important questions from a common sense that differs from that of Western discussions – even if it is paradoxical. It is the "possibility of rethinking morality itself" that is presented through the topic of Shogi and soccer VAR judgement, or the group of issues found only in techno-animism, which is a vague boundary created by people and AI, formed in a user-generated-content style through discussions brought about by AI-*éshi*.

This suggests that the true potential of bottom-up agenda setting based on public engagement, which has been one of the ideals of recent scientific communication, may be contained in what people discover when they awaken from the disillusionment caused by techno-animism. The ethical debate in the West is robust. Therefore, the questions that emerge from the speculations of great scholars are solid, and even if one intends deliberation, citizens may be forced into the position of being the respondents to those questions. If this is the case, it is not a good idea to keep the dialogue between strange people insular in the Far East, thus blurring the boundary between themselves and AI, and to keep the dialogue within the perspective of Orientalism. Universal questions for humanity could be found in the issues that emerge from such techno-animistic dialogues based on an imaginary rooted in odd common sense.

The well-known meme "meanwhile in Japan" should not be used to consume Japan's strange debates but simply to find in the debates of Japanese citizens rooted in techno-animism a germ of heterodox thinking of which they themselves may be unaware.

Notes

1 Although some may criticise that the term "West" is too crude, considering the main purpose of this paper, I hope that you will forgive us for continuing to use such a large subject line in this chapter.
2 The cover of the controversial illustration can be found on the JSAI website: https://www.ai-gakkai.or.jp/whats-new/new_name_cover/ (Retrieved 23 September 2023).

3 Togetter, 11.24.2019 (last updated 4.20.2022) "Looking back 'Journal of AI society cover incident': Feminists' attack on Moe-representations [Femi no Moe-e Tataki no Hottan "Jinkou Chinou Gakkai Hyoushi Jiken wo Furikaeru]," https://togetter.com/li/1434382, Retrieved 2023.8.21, [Japanese].

4 In the literal sense, the word *é-shi* consists of two Chinese characters: "絵(*é*: picture, art)" and "師(*shi*: master, meister)". It could be translated as "master of art".

5 atwiki (last updated 8.23.2023) "Why does visual generative AI matter? [Gazou Seisei AI ha nani ga Mondai nanoka?]," https://w.atwiki.jp/genai_problem/pages/10.html, Retrieved 8.25.2023, [Japanese].

6 "-kun" and "-chan" are suffixes. Both are mostly used to call children affectionately; however, the former is used for boys and the latter for girls. Both words are frequently used for unanimated artefacts, including machines or programs, to give personality in a techno-animistic manner.

Bibliography

Allison, A. (2023). *Millennial monsters: Japanese toys and the global imagination.* University of California Press.

atwiki (2023). What is the problem with image-generating AI? [Gazou Seisei AI no naniga mondai nanoka?]. by sankakuyama, last updated Aug. 23, 2023. https://w.atwiki.jp/genai_problem/pages/10.html [Japanese].

Baba, Y. (2021). An overview of animism studies in Japan [Nihon ni okeru Animism Kenkyushi Gaikan]. *Tohoku Journal of Religious Studies, 17,* 41–75.

Bartneck, C., Suzuki, T., Kanda, T., & Nomura, T. (2007). The influence of people's culture and prior experiences with Aibo on their attitude towards robots. *AI & Society, 21*(1–2), 217–230.

Castoriadis, C. (1998). *The imaginary institution of society.* The MIT Press.

Chadwick, A. (2017). *The hybrid media system.* Oxford University Press.

Choi, S., Kim, N., Kim, J., & Kang, H, (2022, forthcoming). "How does AI improve human decision-making? Evidence from the AI-powered go program" USC Marshall School of Business Research Paper Sponsored by iORB, No. https://ssrn.com/abstract=3893835 or http://dx.doi.org/10.2139/ssrn.3893835

Ema, A. (2019). *A guidebook for AI society - How to deal with artificial intelligence [AI Shakai no Arukikata: Jinkou Chinou to Dou Tsukiau ka].* Kagaku Dojin. [Japanese]

Habu, Y., & NHK. (2017). *The essence of the artificial intelligence [Jinkou Chinou no Kakushin].* NHK Shuppan. [Japanese]

Hagerty, A., & Rubinov, I. (2019). Global AI ethics: A review of the social impacts and ethical implications of artificial intelligence. *arXiv preprint,* 1907.07892.

Haring, K. S., Mougenot, C., Ono, F., & Watanabe, K. (2014). Cultural differences in perception and attitude towards robots. *International Journal of Affective Engineering, 13*(3), 149–157.

Hopkinson, T. (2022, December 3). Stan Collymore gives 'persuasive argument' to ditch VAR for World Cup 2022 knockout games. *Mirror.* https://www.mirror.co.uk/sport/football/news/stan-collymore-highlights-persuasive-argument-28640444

Ikeda, S., & Yamasaki, A. (2014). Analyses on opinions and arguments of the cover design of "Journal of the Japanese Society for Artificial Intelligence": From the viewpoint of visual representation studies [Jinkou Chinou Shi no Hyoushi Design Iken Giron ni Sesshite: Shikaku Hyousyou Kenkyu no Shiten kara]. *Jinkou Chinou, 29*(2), 167–171. [Japanese]

Jasanoff, S., & Kim, S.-H. (2015). *Dreamscapes of modernity: Sociotechnical imaginaries and the fabrication of power*. Chicago University Press.

Jensen, C. B., & Blok, A. (2013). Techno-animism in Japan: Shinto cosmograms, actor- network theory, and the enabling powers of non-human agencies. *Theory, Culture & Society, 30*(2), 84–115.

Keidanren. (2022). Playing Game as communication [Taikyoku to iu Communication]. https://www.keidanren.or.jp/journal/monthly/2022/04_taidan.html [Japanese]

Kishimoto, A., Katirai, A., Ide, K. (2023). Overview of ethical, legal, and social issues (ELSI) in generative AI: August 2023 Edition: Focusing on global policy trends [Seisei AI no ELSI kadai], Osaka University Research Center on Ethical, Legal and Social Issues. https://hdl.handle.net/11094/92475 [Japanese]

Kureha, M. (2021). Japanese and robot: A critical study of techno-animism [Nihonjin to Robot: Techono-Animism heno Hihan]. *Contemporary and Applied Philosophy, 13*, 62–82.

Martin, P., Deutsch, J., & Edgerton, A. (2023, October 6). US warns EU's landmark AI policy will only benefit Big Tech. *Bloomberg*. https://www.bloomberg.com/news/articles/2023-10-06/us-warns-eu-s-landmark-ai-policy-will-only-benefit-big-tech

Okawa, S. (2016). *Indomitable players [Fukutsu no Kishi]*. Kodansya.

Okuno, T. (1983). Introduction to Techno-animism: Anthropology of present society [Techno-Animisum Josetsu: Gendai Shakai no Jinruigaku]. In *Shiso-no-Kagaku Dai 7 ji, 30*, 40–49. [Japanese]

Okuno, T. (2002). *Humans, animals, machines: Techno animism [Ningen, Doubutsu, Kikai -Techno Animism]*. Kadokawa. [Japanese]

Otsu, T. (2019, May 12). [Singularity Japan] Strongest AI: Do humans checkmated? [Singularity Nippon. Ningen ha mou tsunda noka?]. Asashi-Shimbun. [Japanese]. https://digital.asahi.com/articles/DA3S14010751.html

Piaget, J. (1926). La représentation du monde chez l'enfant, Felix Allan [English version: The child's conception of the world, trans. J. Tomlinson & A. Tomlinson]. Rowan & Littlefield Publishers, Inc., 1929, 2007.

Porter, T. (2020). *Trust in numbers: The pursuit of objectivity in science and public life*. Princeton University Press.

Reeves, B., & Nass, C. (1996). *The media equation: How people treat computers, television, and new media like real people and places*. CSLI Publications.

Robertson, J. (2017). *Robo sapiens Japanicus: Robots, gender, Family and the Japanese nation*. University of California Press.

Saito, M., & Ito, T. (2022). The influence of Shogi AI on professional player's records: A study from quantitative snalysis. In *The 27th Game Programming Workshop 2022* (pp. 159–166). [Japanese]. https://ipsj.ixsq.nii.ac.jp/ej/?action=repository_uri&item_id=222008

Simonite, T. (2020, September 9). AI ruined chess. Now, it's making the game beautiful again: A former world champion teams up with the makers of AlphaZero to test variants on the age-old game that can jolt players into creative patterns. *Wired*. https://www.wired.com/story/ai-ruined-chess-now-making-game-beautiful/

Taira, K. (2019). *An evil AI study: You are so far dominated [Aku no AI ron: Anata ha kokomade Shihai sareteiru]*. Asahi Shinsyo. [Japanese]

Takahashi, Y. (2023). Toward the construction of an ethic between humans and others: Limitations and possibilities of the concepts of "animism" and "techno-animism" [Hito to Hito igai tono Rinri Kouchiku ni mukete: "Animism" "Techno-animism" Gainen no Genkai to Kanousei]. *Contemporary and Applied Philosophy, 14*, 1–19. [Japanese]

Tanaka, M. (2023). On Japanese imagining of AI: A case study of digital necromancy. In M. Bauer & B. Schiele (Eds.), *Science communication: Taking a step back to move forward*. CNRS Éditions. 194–201.

Toriumi, F., Sakaki, T., & Okazaki, N. (2014). "Jinkou Chinou" no Hyoushi ni Kansuru Tweet no Bunseki [Analyzing tweets for mining opinions about the renewal of the cover design of "artificial intelligence"]. *Jinkou Chinou, 29*(2), 172–181. [Japanese]

Umehara, T. (1995). *The philosophy of the forest will save mankind [Mori no Shisou ga Jinrui wo Sukuu]*. Shogakukan.

Yoshinaga, D., Obata, T., & Tanaka, M. (2017). Gendai no Media kukan ni okeru jinkou chinou no katararekata [The representation of 'artificial intelligence' in contemporary hybrid media systems]. *Jinkou Chinou, 32*(6), 943–948. [Japanese]

PART 4

Unsettling or highlighting common sense?

AI against common sense and the social psychology of accommodation: common sense challenged by AI and challenging the emergent technology

12

COMMON-SENSE ATTRIBUTIONS OF AI AGENCY

Evidence from an experiment with ChatGPT

Fabian Anicker and Florian Golo Flaßhoff

If a bank denies a loan due to a bad score by a credit scoring algorithm: Who decided, the bank accountant or the algorithm she used? If large parts of a speech you gave were written by a large language model: Is it your co-author? Almost since its inception, AI has raised questions about the line separating humans and artificially intelligent computers. These become more pressing as computers successfully mimic human competencies in more and more areas. If we want to understand the transformation of social relations through AI, we need concepts that help us to take account of the growing recognition AI systems enjoy as partners in all kinds of interaction and their effect on the course of action. Are some AI systems already actors capable of choosing to behave intelligently? However, concepts like "choice", "action" and "intelligence" are anthropocentric terms and there are no straightforward rules for applying them to nonhuman entities. In this article, we propose a solution to the problem of agency that follows a strategy championed, among others, by Alan Turing. Turing advocated a pragmatic and empirical strategy toward the attribution of intelligence to computers. In the empirical section of this study, we present results from an empirical experiment on the use of ChatGPT showing that the mode of interaction with systems influences the common-sense strategies of situational agency attributions.

Turing's twist: From a substantial to a relational view of agency

Already at a time when computers were still simple calculation devices filling huge buildings, the question of whether these machines could ever be considered intelligent was debated. Alan Turing had an interesting take on this. He proposed the "imitation game", a famous test now known as the Turing test.

DOI: 10.4324/9781032626192-18

The idea is as simple as brilliant. The Turing test specifies that computers should be considered intelligent if a human interrogator cannot distinguish their answers from those of a human being (Turing, 1950). Turing thereby circumvents messy and possibly insolvable questions about the nature of intelligence and consciousness in favour of a functional approach. If you cannot systematically distinguish the outputs of two systems, Turing argues that there is no reason to not attribute the same competence to them.

Turing thereby transforms the problem of how to think about the applicability of anthropocentric concepts to nonhuman entities. There are two marked characteristics of this transformation. First, it leads to a functional view of competencies. Intelligence simply *is* the ability to perform functions that are recognised as intelligent. Second, he emphasises the important role of social attributions. Turing proposes to call a computer intelligent if people treat its outputs as signs of intelligence. But while this is still a very helpful starting point in many discussions in philosophy and computer science (Epstein et al., 2009; Hofstadter, 1982; Pinar Saygin et al., 2000), we depart from Turing in two ways. First, we prefer not to talk about machine intelligence but about machine *agency*. Machine agency may be much more relevant than "intelligence" to elucidate the *societal* impact of AI. For machines to influence social life, it may not be necessary that their intelligence operates similarly to the intelligence of humans, but whether they count as *doing* something and are relied upon as trustworthy *agents*, that is, as originators of choices with practical significance. What matters is how artificially intelligent computers influence structurally relevant social processes, what social status they acquire in these processes, and what social consequences are likely to ensue. This leads to a view of agency as an attributed social status. Second, unlike Turing, we are not interested in designing an agency test that makes its attribution as hard as possible. In real social life, people are not trying to prove that the systems they encounter "are not really agents", they just observe what these systems do, react to them, and use the schemes which seem to be the best fit. Therefore, instead of trying to say what a computer program should be able to do to count as an agent in a situation of critical examination, we propose to look at the *actual, practical attribution* of agency in human-machine encounters. The following section will develop this perspective on agency and its empirical implications.

Common-sense schemes in the attribution of agency: Agency as social institution and social attribution

This social relational view of agency allows us, following Turing, to treat the question of whether some computers can have agency as an empirical rather than an ontological question. The question of whether machines can have agency is ultimately not a question about the properties of individuals but about social rules of attribution and recognition. In the context of this volume, it is interesting to look at these social rules of agency attribution through the lens of *common sense*. The rules of how to apply agency categories are not consciously known by the actors. Also, they are widely shared. Whether someone counts as acting, not doing anything at the moment, currently unable to act, or in principle incapable of acting rarely needs to be debated. This common knowledge forms a tacit basis of interaction and can only become conscious in moments of crisis when the status of some entity as an agent is in doubt. Also, infringements of the default rules of agency ascriptions are normatively sanctioned (try starting an argument with your coffee mug in front of other people and you will see what we mean). Referring to Martin Bauer's distinction between different meanings of common sense (in Chapter 1, this volume), we can see that this complex of practical knowledge unites properties of universally recognisable knowledge ("CS-2") and practical judgement strategy ("CS-3").

But what does it actually mean to treat something as an agent and what difference does it make? Here we take Daniel Dennett's theory of intentional systems (1971) as a starting point. Dennett describes the ascription of intentionality and agency as a practical explanatory "stance" taken by actors. The application of terms like intentionality, agency, choice or rationality is understood by looking at their "role in practical reasoning, and hence in the prediction of the behaviour of practical reasoners" (Dennett, 2009, p. 339). From this point of view, it is perfectly reasonable to think that a cat is striding around nervously because it *wants* to be fed or that your computer is moving the knight because it *believes* in its chances to checkmate you on the kingside. Dennett argues that this kind of talk about the purposes, beliefs and intentions of animals and things has nothing metaphorical or questionable about it; it is simply in many cases the only way we can make sense of some systems that are too complex to predict by looking at the past states of their components and the causal factors influencing them. The ascription of agency is a way of practically dealing with entities as it makes their behaviour more predictable and allows us to know what to expect and how to react to them. Agents, then, are entities that are practically dealt with by ascribing choices, beliefs and desires to them rather than by ascribing fixed behavioural dispositions or by regarding them as points in chains of causal relations.

This view of agency as culturally embedded, practical attribution allows us to move beyond a restrictive conception of agency as a human monopoly. Being consistent about seeing agency as a function of attribution, we must acknowledge that agents are all around us. In many situations, we cannot even begin to practically make heads or tails of our pets, the postal service, or our e-mail spam filter without attributing some kind of knowledge and purpose to them (regardless of whether we also hold a more or less meta-physical belief about them 'ultimately' being deterministic systems).

We refine this scheme by distinguishing two kinds of agentic status that entities can have. They can either be considered entities of a type that automatically should be considered agents. This means that it is socially appropriate to treat these kinds of entities as agents. We call this "default agency". Second, they can be pragmatically treated as agents in a given situation. We call this "situational agency". Both are social statuses that entities can acquire or lose in time, but the latter is much more dynamic than the first one.

Situational agency

An entity with situational agency is one that is treated by other actors as an originator of actions with beliefs and purposes in a given situation. From the pragmatic standpoint taken here, it is obvious that we practically attribute purposive motives to many other entities than human beings. Indeed, putting on agency glasses when dealing with phenomena that require a differentiated reaction seems to be something like a cognitive default strategy. A classical experiment by Fritz Heider and Marianne Simmel (1944) showed that even the movements of geometrical figures (two triangles and a circle on a two-dimensional plane) are interpreted by observers as deliberate actions of animate beings. Practically, agency attributions serve as a way to come up with quick hypotheses of how to react to entities: My cat "wants" me to feed her, my computer does not "understand" my command, the neighbour's dog "hates" me and so on. The situational agency ascription provides causes for observed behaviour and helps to predict future events. As this attribution mostly happens on the level of unconscious pragmatic know-how, little pressure arises to apply situational agency consistently to the same entity across different situations. We may switch effortlessly in pragmatic stances by treating a chess engine first as an intentional agent if we try to beat it as an opponent, second as a complex system if we try to reprogram it, and next as a physical object if the computer is broken (cf. Dennett, 1971, p. 91).

Default agency

For many system types, there is a widely shared socially instituted default for the kind of agency they are supposed to possess. This default status of objects as agents or non-agents is – as shown before – not an ontological quality but a social institution relative to a culture. Who counts as an agent is not predetermined by biological criteria. Even a base anthropocentric category like humanity is by no means universally applied to all biological entities of the species *Homo sapiens* (cf. Fuller, 2023). And human traits like personality or rationality are frequently applied to non-human animals, especially complex animals like primates or pets (Stamps & Groothuis, 2010). However, compared to situational agency, default agency is much more stable. At a given time, usually, a broad common sense exists on the inclusion or exclusion of entities into the realm of recognised agents. In modern Western culture, all sane and adult human beings are usually treated as "full" agents who are accountable for their actions. If a dog bites a man, it can be controversial who to blame: it or its owner. If a man bites a dog, usually the case is clear. There are concepts of restricted agency as in the case of toddlers or people with mental illness. There are also complex conditional notions of agency. For example, for people with Tourette's syndrome, the overwhelming part of their verbal utterances is treated as meaningful communicative action while some part is treated as non-agentic noise. These complex notions form a part of the latent pragmatic background knowledge – a type of common sense that regulates interaction and governs the ascription of agency and responsibility to people. However, the cultural common sense of default agency is not fixed (see Meyer & Jepperson, 2000 for the historical roots of the Western concept of agency). In large-scale cultural processes of a longue durée, entities drift inside or outside the spectrum of recognised social actors. The process of rationalisation in Western civilisation and the accompanying "disenchantment of the world" (see also Joas, 2017; Weber, 1922) can for example be regarded as a huge deflation in the attribution of agency. Forces of nature, animals and gods lost their social status as intentional agents. A similar restriction of default agency attributions can be observed during the ontogenesis of human infants who typically start with an over-inclusive notion of agency (being angry at objects that hit them or talking to their plush toys). During ontogenesis, they acquire a differentiated common sense about when and how to distinguish agents from non-agents (Chandrashekar et al., 2022; Malle & Knobe, 1997; Perez-Osorio & Wykowska, 2020, pp. 372–375).

The link between situational and default agency

Situational and default agency attributions mutually influence each other. In their review of studies on stance-taking in human–robot interaction, Perez-Osirio and Wykowska summarise that adopting the intentional stance "can influence the interpretation of basic social signals, and as a consequence, activates fundamental mechanisms of social cognition" (Perez-Osorio & Wykowska, 2020, p. 383). Default agents may benefit from a "principle of charity" (Davidson, 1973) by the interpreters, who try to maintain accountability presuppositions even under difficult circumstances. On the other hand, entities conventionally considered non-agents may need to show extraordinary performances to acquire default agency. However, it is also established that the situational attribution of competencies (including agency) can lead to attitude-building about the default status of entities as agents or non-agents. This causal path was first analysed by competence attribution theory first proposed by Heider and later on developed in correspondent inference theory (Crittenden, 1983; Heider, 1952; Howard, 1985; Jones & Davis, 1965; Jones & McGillis, 1976). Heider argues that competencies are inferred from behaviour as "[t] he most direct recognition that p can do something is given by his actual behaviour" (Heider, 1952, p. 87). This is also supported by experimental evidence on stance adoption that shows that agency attributions are modified to account for observed behaviour (Marchesi et al., 2022). If an observable pattern of behaviour systematically cannot be interpreted in terms of purposive action, default ascriptions of full agency may be modified or retracted completely.

Agency of AI systems

The interesting thing about computers, and AI agents in particular, is that they hold a somewhat liminal status between agents and non-agents. Findings from prior research suggest that categories of *situational agency* are frequently attributed to computers or computer programs. Experiments have shown that in many cases even simple personal computers from the 1990s were unconsciously treated as actors with a recognised social status. For example, when subjects were asked to rate the performance of a computer in a mutual task, they rated the machine significantly more favourably if the questionnaire was filled out on the same computer than if they used another machine; a finding which indicates the application of norms of social desirability (Gambino et al., 2020; Nass et al., 1994). However, it is hard to imagine that many people translate this situational attribution into a conscious appraisal of, in this case, desktop computers as *default agents*.

This may not hold for more complex, generative AI systems anymore. While there is certainly less agency ascribed to AI systems and robots, previous research has shown that people deliberately attribute some degree of agency to them, e.g., by assigning moral blame for wrongful behaviour (Wiese et al., 2017; Wilson et al., 2022). Research on strongly anthropomorphic companionship chatbots has shown that people attribute personality, memory, feelings, and even sexual desire to the bot (Skjuve et al., 2021, 2022). Some studies that used Dennett's theory of stance-taking as a framework looked at the attribution of intentionality to robots by asking people to describe their behaviour and checking whether (and how quickly) they choose mechanistic or mental vocabulary to explain robot behaviour (Marchesi et al., 2019; Marchesi et al., 2021). The studies show that the adoption of an intentional stance and the degree of anthropomorphism can be influenced by subtle differences in the behaviour of AI agents and also depends on personality traits (Epley et al., 2007). Overall, it seems that a substantial share of people is practically inclined to attribute situational agency to AI systems while a socially instituted default for interacting with the most recent AI systems has not yet been instituted (on public attitudes on AI see Marcinkowski in Chapter 9, this volume). Many people interact with systems whose capabilities they do not know and are forced to make practical decisions about recognising or denying agency without relying on an established social framework of the default agentic status of these systems.

Experimental study: The agency of ChatGPT

Breakthroughs, especially in the field of large neural networks and the amazing speed at which these are implemented in society, open up the possibility of new kinds of machine agency. Among the most interesting recently developed systems are *large language models* (LLMs). Unlike simple preprogrammed chatbots, LLMs are generative models with substantial inferential power and huge stocks of knowledge that can flexibly adapt to the context of a conversation. The systems are also prone to hallucinate from time to time, confidently making up facts as they go along. Our object of study is ChatGPT, a large language model developed by OpenAI which received considerable public attention since its release in November 2022. Its rapid rise to worldwide fame (ChatGPT was the fastest-growing web application in the history of the internet) suggests enormous public interest in the app. ChatGPT can be addressed with sentences in natural language through a simple chat interface. Its outputs are limited to language (in a broad sense including code) as the medium of expression. However, within this medium, ChatGPT incorporates abilities across lots of domains, knowledge about special fields as well as general knowledge, the ability to understand and write code, tell jokes, write poems, give advice and so on – in most domains worse than most experts in the specific field, but in the breadth of its linguistic capabilities superior to any human being.

Unlike companionship chatbots, ChatGPT is not designed to be strongly anthropomorphic. Due to ethical safety measures implemented by the developers, ChatGPT routinely reminds its users of it being a large language model, instead of trying to lure them into the illusion of talking to a "digital person". ChatGPT never initiates a conversation, rarely poses direct questions and uses a rather formal tone of conversation. Due to these design features, the conversation with ChatGPT is unlike any with a human being. ChatGPT was therefore a challenging case for its early users as there iswas no established cultural default agency. As Mahowald et al. persuasively claim "heuristics that emerged from our language experience with other humans—are broken" (Mahowald et al., 2023, p. 3). To assess how people nevertheless navigate their interaction with ChatGPT, we designed an empirical experiment.

Design of the empirical experiment

Based on our theoretical framework, we designed an experiment on the attribution of agency to ChatGPT. In particular, we wanted to assess the situational attribution of agency and the attitude formation about the default status of ChatGPT as agent or non-agent. The experiment was conducted as a laboratory study at Heinrich-Heine-Universität Düsseldorf in June 2023.

Each participant provided written informed consent before taking part in the experiment. All participants (mostly from the student population) were naïve to the purpose of the experiment. Data from 23 participants were excluded from the analyses due to non-completion. The final sample was N = 166 participants, of which 68 are male, 97 female and 1 nonbinary).

Two experimental groups were invited for three sessions of interaction with ChatGPT. Sessions were timed to be between five and nine days apart. A control group only answered the pre- and postexperimental questionnaire in two sessions which were three weeks apart.

In the two experimental groups, we manipulated whether ChatGPT would be the conscious object of attention or whether it would be used as a means to an end to reach some other goal. Subjects in the first condition were asked to critically assess the competencies of ChatGPT in a variety of domains from logical thinking through moral reasoning to factual knowledge (this treatment specified nine domains for a 3 by 3 distribution of tasks over the sessions). In the second condition, subjects were asked to use ChatGPT to work out a plan for their own business startup in nine steps from researching their interests to estimating their capital requirements (also three distinct tasks per session). Participants in both conditions documented their results during the sessions on a working sheet. Additionally, the chat protocols were saved and linked to the pseudonymised data for later analysis. The explicit attribution of agency to ChatGPT was assessed in a post-treatment questionnaire that was also administered to members of the control group who reported that they use ChatGPT at least rarely (the German "selten"). The situational attribution of agency was inferred from the interaction protocols.

Research questions and hypothesis

To investigate the flexibility of situational and default agency attributions we posed three empirical research questions.

RQ1: Which indicators of verbal reactions to the outputs are suitable to assess situational agency attributions?

RQ2: Are situational agency attributions influenced by manipulating the mode of interaction (cooperative vs. testing usage)?

RQ3: Do default agency attributions differ according to the mode of interaction with ChatGPT?

We expected that subjects who collaborated with ChatGPT in the business condition would be more likely to attribute agency to the system than subjects who were testing ChatGPT with an attitude of critical assessment. This follows from the functional pragmatic view of agency as a strategy to practically deal with the affordances of an object. The collaborative setting should invite a sense of common identity and a perception of the system as a partner in a common task and it may be useful to react to ChatGPT just like one would react to a coworker. We expected weaker effects of the treatments on the default agency attribution as these were hypothesised to be more stable and less easily influenced by the practical demands of a situation.

Measurement of the situational and explicit attribution of agency

So far, research on the attribution of intentionality to robots mostly relies on descriptions of robot behaviour *after* people interact with them (O'Reilly et al., 2022; Schellen & Wykowska, 2018). However, to capture the performative role of agency attributions, it would be preferable to look at the attribution of agency in the process of interaction. AI agents will only be able to perform "actions" if they are practically recognised as agents in the given situation. What matters is the situational attribution, not what words people use afterward to describe their encounter. We therefore inferred indicators from the written interaction of participants with the systems. This is in line with a hypothesis by Wang et al. "that adaptability of our speech pattern could be an indicator of our perception of interlocutor's intelligence, human-likeness, as well as likeability" (Wang et al., 2021, p. 9). This assumption can be backed up by research in conversation analysis that shows how many aspects of daily language serve to maintain a basis of mutual recognition and affiliation (Lindström & Sorjonen, 2012; Robinson, 2012). As of yet, however, there is no established set of indicators for inferring situational attributions of agency from interactions. We hypothesised that *language use which is typical for managing affiliation in human interaction but not functionally required to interact with the system* is a good indicator of practical agency attribution. After a phase of open, qualitative coding of the prompts written by the subjects for potential markers for situational agency attribution we arrived at the following indicators.

Positive indicators for agency attribution:

- Number of times subjects greeted the system.
- Number of times subjects formulated polite requests using "please".
- Number of times subjects expressed satisfaction with the outputs or said "thank you".
- Number of times, people use "we" or "us" to refer to ChatGPT and themselves.

Negative indicators for agency attribution:

- Number of times subjects use sentence fragments or keywords instead of sentences (stylistically approximating a Google search).
- Number of times people use straight imperatives without politeness modulation (no "please", no "could-you" construction or similar modulation).

After the indicators were qualitatively derived, most indicator values were extracted from the chat protocols in a two-step process of automatic text search (for conventional formulas) and manual human elimination of false positives. Only the two negative indicators (the number of direct imperatives and the number of fragmented sentences) and the expression of gratitude for ChatGPT's outputs were humanly coded by two coders. The initial inter-coder reliability was 82% agreement. In a second step, the divergently coded cases were discussed among the coders to bring agreement to 100%.

Explicit, default agency attribution was measured by a questionnaire item asking for the perception of ChatGPT as a person or as a tool (five-point scale with "rather as a tool" and "rather as a person" marked at the extremes). Another item was designed to capture the explicit denial of intentionality in ChatGPT and asked people to (dis-)agree with the statement "ChatGPT probably has neither beliefs nor goals" on a five-point Likert scale.

Empirical findings: Adaptation of situational agency attribution to experimental condition

Regarding RQ_1, we found tentative evidence that the group membership affected the likelihood of situational agency attribution (Figure 12.1). While 26% of subjects greeted ChatGPT in the business condition at least once, only 11% did so in the test condition. Subjects who cooperated with ChatGPT were twice as likely to express gratitude for the output or praise the quality of the answer as those in the test condition. Subjects in the test condition were more likely to use direct imperatives when talking to ChatGPT without modulating them by adding "please" or by paraphrasing the demand into a request. However, people in the cooperative condition were more likely to

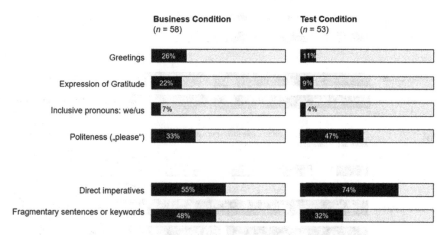

FIGURE 12.1   Situational agency indicators between groups.

use fragmentary sentences or keywords in their interaction with ChatGPT than people in the test condition. The results are summarised in the following diagram.

A series of χ^2-tests (all $N = 111$, df = 1) for association was conducted. The χ^2-tests for the expression of gratitude $\chi^2 = 2.16$, $p = .14$, as well as greetings $\chi^2 = 3.30$, $p = .07$ showed weakly insignificant relationships, while the use of inclusive pronouns was not significantly related to group membership. Subjects in the test condition were more likely to use direct imperatives $\chi^2 = 6.52$, $p = .01$ and politeness modulations of their prompts $\chi^2 = 3.99$, $p = .04$. All of the other indicators were not significantly affected by the mode of interaction. The increased politeness in the test condition can largely be explained by the fact that the testing group used more imperatives than the cooperative business condition and frequently added "please" to their requests. We, therefore, excluded "politeness" as a positive agency indicator from our further analysis. From the remaining positive agency indicators, we created a dichotomous situational agency index-variable by distinguishing between subjects who at least once greeted or thanked ChatGPT or referred to themselves and ChatGPT in the form of "we" and all who did not. We found a statistically significant effect with subjects being more likely to show signs of situational agency attribution in the business condition compared to the test condition $\chi^2(1, 111) = 6.04$, $p = .01$, $\varphi = 0.21$.

Empirical findings: Default agency ascription

Most subjects across all groups were much more likely to see ChatGPT as a tool rather than as a quasi-person, with 142 people seeing it rather like a tool (values 4 and 5) while only five people answered that they consider

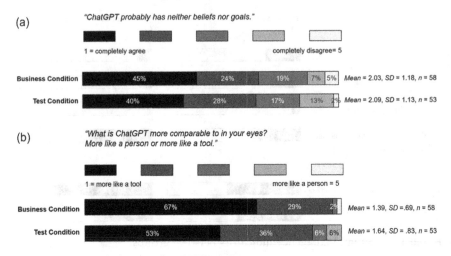

FIGURE 12.2 Attitudes on ChatGPT's agency.

it similar to a person (values 1 and 2) (Figure 12.2). Another variable was designed to capture the explicit denial of intentionality. Around two-thirds of the subjects in both conditions answered that they believe that ChatGPT has probably neither beliefs nor goals (values 1 and 2). We conducted a one-way ANOVA to assess the effects of ChatGPT usage on the attribution of default agency (as measured by the PersonvsTool variable). We compared the two experimental groups (business and test condition) with a control group on the dependent variable. PersonvsTool was not normally distributed for each of the three groups, as assessed by the Shapiro–Wilk test ($\alpha < .05$). Nevertheless, the one-way ANOVA has been shown to be relatively robust to violations of the normal distribution assumption (Schmider et al., 2010). There were no severe outliers, according to inspection with a box plot. The examined group means decreased from cooperative usage ($M = 4.6$, $SD = 0.699$) to the control group ($M = 4.39$, $SD = 0.718$) to testing usage ($M = 4.36$, $SD = 0.834$). Homogeneity of variances was asserted using Levene's test which showed that equal variances could be assumed ($p = .229$). There was no statistically significant difference in the level of default agency for the examined groups ($F(2, 146) = 1.668$, $p = .192$).

Discussion

Regarding RQ_1 (indicators for situational agency ascription): while the over-all level of situational agency attribution was low, our findings show that some verbal indicators likely capture situational agency attributions. Subjects who greet ChatGPT, praise or thank for outputs or refer to themselves and the system in terms of "we" or "us" engage in functionally superfluous personal communication. Due to the low proportion of performative situational agency attributions, it is recommended to combine indicators into an index or increase the sample size. Other indicators seem to be unsuited: casual politeness as well as the tendency to use direct, unmodulated imperatives may be more dependent on the general speaking style and the nature of the task (testing typically being a situation in which imperatives are legitimate), rather than the perception of the agent. Future research should try to compare situational tests with post-hoc description tests to further establish the validity of situational measures. In RQ_2 we asked whether the experimental treatment affects situational agency attributions. We could show that the mode of the interaction influences the likelihood of situational agency attributions (as measured by the dichotomised index variable). We conclude that situational attribution of agency is indeed a flexible resource for dealing with complex systems and that it adapts to the situation at hand. Regarding RQ_3 about the effects of the treatment on default agency attribution, we found no significant effects of the experimental treatments on the default agency attribution. This further supports findings by Marchesi et al. (2019) that indicate the relative independence of spontaneous attributions and reflected attitudes. Situational agency attributions seem to be more flexible than attitudinal ascriptions of agency.

Summary and conclusion: Two kinds of common sense of agency

We argued that agency is constituted in social relations of recognition and attribution and that entities can acquire or lose the status of recognised agents. There are two types of common sense that govern this process of agency attribution: first, the common-sense knowledge about who usually counts as an actor ("default agency"), and second, the common-sense capability to flexibly treat systems as agents if this helps interact with them ("situational agency"). Regarding the status of AI systems, both situational and default agency are relevant at different points. Situational agency attributions decide whether the outputs of a system are practically accepted as "actions". On this practical recognition of agency, it depends on whether people accept the "word" of an agent, trust its promises or blame it morally for its wrongdoings. We developed indicators from people's language use in reacting to AI systems and showed that these are indeed sensitive to situational circumstances. Default agency attributions in contrast may be more important for the general social status which is granted to artificial agents, especially the legal status of AI systems as "digital persons", its right to sign contracts or be punished for crimes (see Fauquet-Alekhine, Chapter 4 this volume). We were able to show that situational agency attributions dynamically adapt to the situation while conscious attributions of intentions or person-likeness seem to be more stable and harder to influence by the mode of interaction. According to common sense, ChatGPT is a tool rather than an agent, and based on our analysis we suspect that this is not going to change as a consequence of repeated interaction.

Bibliography

Chandrashekar, S. P., Chan, Y. Y., Cheng, K. L., Yao, D., Lo, C. Y. S., Cheung, T. C. A., Tang, H. Y. S., Leung, Y. T. A., Tsoi, C. N., Cheng, B. L., Ng, K. W., & Feldman, G. (2022). Revisiting the folk concept of intentionality: Replications of Malle and Knobe (1997). *Journal of Experimental Social Psychology*, *102*, Article 104372. https://doi.org/10.1016/j.jesp.2022.104372

Crittenden, K. S. (1983). Sociological aspects of attribution. *Annual Review of Sociology*, *9*(9), 425–446.

Davidson, D. (1973). Radical interpretation. *Dialectica*, *27*(3), 313–328.

Dennett, D. (1971). Intentional systems. *The Journal of Philosophy*, *LXVIII*(4), Article 4, 87–106.

Dennett, D. (2009). Intentional systems theory. In A. Beckermann, B. P. McLaughlin, & S. Walter (Eds.), *The Oxford handbook of philosophy of mind* (pp. 339–350). Oxford University Press.

Epley, N., Waytz, A., & Cacioppo, J. T. (2007). On seeing human: A three-factor theory of anthropomorphism. *Psychological Review*, *114*(4), 864–886. https://doi.org/10.1037/0033-295X.114.4.864

Epstein, R., Roberts, G., & Beber, G. (Eds.). (2009). *Parsing the Turing test: Philosophical and methodological issues in the quest for the thinking computer.* Springer Netherlands.

Foerster, H. von. (1970). Thoughts and notes on cognition. In P. L. Garvin (Ed.), *Cognition: A multiple view* (pp. 25–48). Spartan Books.

Freeman, H. D., & Gosling, S. D. (2010). Personality in nonhuman primates: A review and evaluation of past research. *American Journal of Primatology*, *72*(8), 653–671. https://doi.org/10.1002/ajp.20833

Fuller, S. (2023). Humanity's in-betweenness: Towards a prehistory of cyborg life. In M. Michałowska (Ed.), *Integrated science: Vol. 16. Humanity in-between and beyond* (1st ed., pp. 63–80). Springer International Publishing.

Gambino, A., Fox, J., & Ratan, R. A. (2020). Building a stronger CASA: Extending the computers are social actors paradigm. *Human-Machine Communication*, *1*, 71–85. https://search.informit.org/doi/10.3316/INFORMIT.097034846749023

Heider, F. (1952). *The psychology of interpersonal relations.* John Wiley & Sons.

Heider, F., & Simmel, M. (1944). An experimental study of apparent behavior. *The American Journal of Psychology*, *57*(2), 243–259.

Hofstadter, D. R. (1982). The Turing Test: A coffee-house conversation. In Hofstadter, Douglas R. and Dennett, Daniel C. (Eds.), *The Mind's I: Fantasies and Reflections on Self and Soul* (pp. 69–95). Penguin Books.

Howard, J. A. (1985). Further appraisal of correspondent inference theory. *Personality and Social Psychology Bulletin*, *11*(4), 349–501.

Joas, H. (2017). *Die Macht des Heiligen. Eine Alternative zu der Geschichte von der Entzauberung.* Suhrkamp.

Jones, E. E., & Davis, K. E. (1965). From acts to dispositions the attribution process in person perception. *Advances in Experimental Social Psychology*, *2*, 219–266. https://doi.org/10.1016/S0065-2601(08)60107-0

Jones, E. E., & McGillis, D. (1976). Correspondent inferences and the attribution cube: A comparative reappraisal. *New Directions in Attribution Research*, *1*, 389–420.

Lindström, A., & Sorjonen, M.L. (2012). Affiliation in conversation. In J. Sidnell & T. Stivers (Eds.), *The handbook of conversation analysis* (pp. 350–369). Wiley-Blackwell.

Mahowald, K., Ivanova, A. A., Blank, I. A., Kanwisher, N., Tenenbaum, J. B., & Fedorenko, E. (2023). *Dissociating language and thought in large language models: A cognitive perspective.* https://doi.org/10.48550/arXiv.2301.06627

Malle, B. F., & Knobe, J. (1997). The folk concept of intentionality. *Journal of Experimental Social Psychology, 33*(2), 101–121. https://doi.org/10.1006/jesp.1996.1314

Marchesi, S., Ghiglino, D., Ciardo, F., Perez-Osorio, J., Baykara, E., & Wykowska, A. (2019). Do we adopt the intentional stance toward humanoid robots? *Frontiers in Psychology, 10*, 450. https://doi.org/10.3389/fpsyg.2019.00450

Marchesi, S., Spatola, N., Perez-Osorio, J., & Wykowska, A. (2021). Human vs humanoid: A behavioral investigation of the individual tendency to adopt the intentional stance. In C. Bethel, A. Paiva, E. Broadbent, D. Feil-Seifer, & D. Szafir (Eds.), *Proceedings of the 2021 ACM/IEEE international conference on human-robot interaction* (pp. 332–340). ACM. https://doi.org/10.1145/3434073.3444663

Marchesi, S., Tommaso, D. de, Perez-Osorio, J., & Wykowska, A. (2022). Belief in sharing the same phenomenological experience increases the likelihood of adopting the intentional stance toward a humanoid robot. *Technology, Mind, and Behavior, 3*(3), 11. https://doi.org/10.1037/tmb0000072

Meyer, J. W., & Jepperson, R. L. (2000). The "actors" of modern society: The cultural construction of social agency. *Sociological Theory, 18*(1), 100–120. https://doi.org/10.1111/0735-2751.00090

Nass, C., Steuer, J., & Tauber, E. R. (1994). Computers are social actors. *Human Factors in Computing Systems*, April 24–28, 72–78.

O'Reilly, Z., Navare, U. P., Marchesi, S., & Wykowska, A. (2022). Does embodiment and interaction affect the adoption of the intentional stance towards a humanoid robot? In F. Cavallo, J.-J. Cabibihan, L. Fiorini, A. Sorrentino, H. He, X. Liu, Y. Matsumoto, & S. S. Ge (Eds.), *Lecture notes in computer science Lecture notes in artificial intelligence: Vol. 13817. Social robotics: 14th International Conference, ICSR 2022, Florence, Italy, December 13–16, 2022, proceedings* (Vol. 13817, pp. 357–366). Springer. https://doi.org/10.1007/978-3-031-24667-8_32

Perez-Osorio, J., & Wykowska, A. (2020). Adopting the intentional stance toward natural and artificial agents. *Philosophical Psychology, 33*(3), 369–395. https://doi.org/10.1080/09515089.2019.1688778

Pinar Saygin, A., Cicekli, I., & Akman, V. (2000). Turing Test: 50 years later. *Minds and Machines, 10*(4), 463–518. https://doi.org/10.1023/a:1011288000451

Robinson, J. D. (2012). Overall structural organization. In J. Sidnell & T. Stivers (Eds.), *The handbook of conversation analysis* (pp. 257–280). Wiley-Blackwell.

Schellen, E., & Wykowska, A. (2018). Intentional mindset toward robots-open questions and methodological challenges. *Frontiers in Robotics and AI, 5*, 139. https://doi.org/10.3389/frobt.2018.00139

Schmider, E., Ziegler, M., Danay, E., Beyer, L., & Bühner, M. (2010). Is it really robust? *Methodology, 6*(4), 147–151. https://doi.org/10.1027/1614-2241/a000016

Skjuve, M., Følstad, A., Fostervold, K. I., & Brandtzaeg, P. B. (2021). My chatbot companion: A study of human-chatbot relationships. *International Journal of Human-Computer Studies, 149*, 102601. https://doi.org/10.1016/j.ijhcs.2021.102601

Skjuve, M., Følstad, A., Fostervold, K. I., & Brandtzaeg, P. B. (2022). A longitudinal study of human–chatbot relationships. *International Journal of Human-Computer Studies*, *168*, 102903. https://doi.org/10.1016/j.ijhcs.2022.102903

Stamps, J., & Groothuis, T. G. G. (2010). The development of animal personality: Relevance, concepts and perspectives. *Biological Reviews*, *85*(2), 301–325. https://doi.org/10.1111/j.1469-185X.2009.00103.x

Turing, A. M. (1950). Computing machinery and intelligence. *Mind*, *59*(236), 433–460.

Wang, Q., Saha, K., Gregori, E., Joyner, D., & Goel, A. (2021). Towards mutual theory of mind in human-AI interaction: How language reflects what students perceive about a virtual teaching assistant. In Y. Kitamura (Ed.), *ACM digital library, proceedings of the 2021 CHI conference on human factors in computing systems* (pp. 1–14). Association for Computing Machinery. https://doi.org/10.1145/3411764.3445645

Weber, M. (1922). Wissenschaft als Beruf. In Mommsen, Wolfgang J., Morgenbrod, Birgitt, Schluchter,Wolfgang. (Eds.), *Gesammelte* , Band 1/17, (pp. 71–112). Tübingen: Mohr.

Wiese, E., Metta, G., & Wykowska, A. (2017). Robots as intentional agents: Using neuroscientific methods to make robots appear more social. *Frontiers in Psychology*, *8*, 1–19. https://doi.org/10.3389/fpsyg.2017.01663

Wilson, A., Stefanik, C., & Shank, D. B. (2022). How do people judge the immorality of artificial intelligence versus humans committing moral wrongs in real-world situations? *Computers in Human Behavior Reports*, *8*, 100229. https://doi.org/10.1016/j.chbr.2022.100229

Wolfram, S. (1983). Statistical mechanics of cellular automata. *Reviews of Modern Physics*, *55*(3), 601–644. https://doi.org/10.1103/RevModPhys.55.601

13

THE CHALLENGES AND OPPORTUNITIES IN LARGE LANGUAGE MODELS

Navigating the perils of stochastic and scholastic parrots in artificial understanding and common sense

Ahmet Süerdem

Understanding is one of the cornerstones of human intelligence, playing a crucial role in our thinking processes and interactions with the world. The notion of artificial understanding (common term: machine reading) has fascinated text analysts since the advent of automated content analysis in the mid-20th century. However, despite many attempts to develop systems capable of reading and understanding text, the context-dependent nature of language which requires common-sense reasoning has remained a challenge to accomplishing artificial understanding. The Winograd Schema Challenge (WSC; Levesque, 2011) epitomises this issue by presenting a linguistic task that requires AI systems to decode pronoun references within sentences based on contextual cues. Successfully determining the antecedent based on contextual cues showcases the capacity of AI to grasp nuanced implications and exhibit common-sense reasoning on par with human understanding abilities.

A ground-breaking leap in artificial understanding was realised through the advent of large language models (LLMs). These models are often promoted as repositories of common-sense knowledge, derived from their extensive training on vast datasets of internet text that implicitly capture communal knowledge and cultural patterns. However, while LLMs have demonstrated strong performance on many contextual understanding tasks, including question answering and language generation, they still struggle with certain types of common-sense reasoning required by the WSC. This is because LLMs primarily rely on patterns in the training data and may not have a deep understanding of the underlying concepts or the ability to perform abstract reasoning in the way humans do. Their capacity to produce coherent text while lacking true understanding has led to their metaphoric characterisation

DOI: 10.4324/9781032626192-19

as "stochastic parrots" (Bender et al., 2021). To sensibly model common sense in AI, Brachman and Levesque (2022) propose anchoring LLMs to an enriched world model, supported by comprehensive knowledge bases covering various facets of the world. However, a primary challenge lies in determining who will control the content and validity of these knowledge bases, as well as in arbitrating what information rightfully constitutes common sense. When biased information is integrated into these systems and the subsequently generated content is presented as common sense, it can create the illusion of indisputable truth rather than as one perspective among many. Understanding is not only a semantic process of decoding symbols but also deeply rooted within the pragmatic contexts of our embodied experiences and social realities shaping and shaped by a complex web of power relations.

The aim of this chapter is to go beyond merely exploring the potential creation of autonomous AI with common sense towards making the dream of artificial understanding a reality. Instead, it delves into the interconnected human and technical components of this technology and critically discusses issues of control within socio-technological and political–economic contexts. It will first explore the potential of LLMs in analysing psychological, social and cultural phenomena, all of which require nuanced contextual understanding. It will then point to the problem that over-reliance on technology can unintentionally displace essential human interpretation and critical thinking required for insightful textual analysis of social phenomena. The chapter will then take a philosophical approach, examining the intricate links between tools and human existence within the context of AI. This exploration of the cultural, political and existential dimensions of AI's impact will prompt deeper reflection on the relationship between humans and the tools they create. It will particularly focus on the concept of hermeneutics as "interpretive understanding" and its relationship with AI language technologies. By delving into the interplay between machine capabilities and human interpretive processes, the chapter will unravel the concept of understanding from its semantic perspective. It will expand the understanding concept to encompass the role of common sense not only as a shared understanding of the world but also as a world-making force shaping our interactions with each other and the technological realm through discursive practices. To avoid AI language technologies being used as tools to shape our understanding of the world from the perspectives of powerful groups, we must establish a more transparent and critical approach. In conclusion, the chapter underscores the importance of integrating common sense with reflective inquiry as a way to foster an unalienated relationship with technology and promote societal progress.

"Just because you speak doesn't make you intelligent."
Star Wars: Episode I – The Phantom Menace.

Automatising text analysis and context-dependent nature of understanding

Early efforts to automate text analysis, like the General Inquirer (Stone et al., 1966), sought to algorithmically uncover hidden information in texts but faced challenges in handling linguistic complexity with basic dictionary techniques. The digital revolution revived interest in this field, as surging digitised text and the advent of data-driven machine learning enabled statistical approximations of reading. These approaches commonly use bag-of-words (BoW) techniques, representing texts as word frequency vectors disregarding order and context. In contrast, interpretive analysts emphasise that meanings emerge through close iterative reading grounded in real-world contexts, rather than solely abstract representations. This perspective challenges notions that texts can be fully automated, emphasising the inherent richness of contextualised meaning. While BoW techniques enable large-scale analysis, they fall short of replacing human understanding, often requiring trade-offs between depth and scale.

While the complex nature of textuality poses challenges for achieving complete automation of contextual understanding, it is important to emphasise that efforts have been made in this direction through the application of statistical pattern detection techniques aimed at discovering semantic relationships between words within specific contexts. One well-established approach in this field is founded on the principles of distributional semantics, which harness data-driven methods to represent word meanings based on their distributional patterns within textual corpora. Distributional semantics traces its roots back to Zelig Harris's (1951) proposition that "language is not merely a bag of words but a tool with particular properties which have been fashioned in the course of its use". This hypothesis challenges the conventional view of words as isolated entities with fixed meanings and suggests that words derive a significant portion of their meaning from their associations with other words in diverse contexts. Anchored in the concept that a word's meaning can be inferred from the words it frequently appears alongside (Firth, 1957), distributional semantics entails a form of contextual analysis of meaning. Consequently, the distributional hypothesis investigates how word meanings emerge from the distribution and co-occurrence patterns found in texts. This concept is translated algorithmically through vector space models that utilise word co-occurrence patterns to encode semantic relations within high-dimensional vector spaces.

The application of this relational approach to modelling meaning has proven to be practical across various multivariate statistical techniques for identifying linguistic patterns and embedding them within cultural contexts. For instance, D'Andrade (1984) applied cluster analysis to interview data to computationally identify shared cultural schemas based on discourse patterns. Similarly, correspondence analysis (e.g., Dickinson, 2021) and multidimensional scaling (e.g., Süerdem, 2021) have been widely used to explore thematic configurations in texts and link them to external variables. These methods allow for the integration and simultaneous presentation of metadata, such as the socio-demographic attributes of the author or the document's date, alongside the detected word patterns within the text. Such an integrated approach not only aids in identifying thematic categories but also provides valuable insights into the relationship between external factors and the emerging themes within the text. More advanced techniques rooted in unsupervised learning, such as topic modelling, leverage the distributional hypothesis to detect clusters of related terms, facilitating the automatic extraction of topics. These techniques have found extensive applications in numerous studies aimed at discovering the intricate relationship between linguistic elements and culture. An exemplary case involves applying topic modelling to news articles and media content to discern prevalent topics, themes or frames in journalistic discourse. This assists in exploring the media's role in shaping public opinion, framing societal concerns, and highlighting cross-cultural variations in the interpretation of identical concepts (e.g., Süerdem & Akkılıç, 2021). Traditional distributional semantics techniques have proven to be valuable tools for uncovering the links between linguistic patterns and cultural categories through the statistical modelling of word co-occurrence relationships in corpora, facilitating contextual analysis. However, a significant limitation lies in their limited sensitivity to local contextual dependencies, impeding the discernment of more nuanced, context-specific meanings. Recent advances in computational power have triggered a technological leap, enabling the application of more sophisticated algorithms like neural word embeddings (Mikolov et al., 2013) to overcome these limitations. These algorithms entail the optimisation of neural networks for the factorisation of extensive word-context matrices derived from lexically diverse and rich corpora. Training on comprehensive corpora empowers advanced modelling of semantic associations that are responsive to contextual nuances. Consequently, they unlock new potential for addressing contextual disambiguation, semantic comparisons, syntactic analogies, and other tasks that demand an understanding of how meaning is intricately linked to local interactions and grounding. Their proficiency in representing fine-grained contextual semantics positions them as invaluable tools for the detection of cultural trends through textual analysis. For instance, Kozlowski et al. (2019) applied word embedding models to investigate culture through a historical analysis of shared understandings of social class. Their findings reveal that dimensions derived from word embedding vector spaces closely align with "cultural dimensions", such as affluence, gender and status, which individuals frequently employ to categorise agents and objects in their everyday interactions with the world. By uncovering and scrutinising these culturally significant dimensions within a word embedding, they unveiled the associations of individual words with respect to those dimensions and determined the relative positioning of these dimensions within the semantic space.

Finally artificial understanding? Large language models (LLMs) and interpretive analysis

However, the breakthrough that brought artificial understanding to a level that mimics human understanding was made possible by LLMs, a subset of artificial intelligence (AI) systems. LLMs utilise transformer algorithms (Devlin et al., 2019), a type of neural network architecture, to generate embeddings that exhibit dynamic adaptation based on the surrounding words, thereby capturing the fluid and context-dependent nature of word meanings. In contrast to traditional word embedding techniques where context remains static, yielding a solitary, context-independent vector representation for each word, transformer algorithms produce contextual embeddings. These embeddings are dynamic and adapt to the diverse senses and usages of a word within various contexts, resulting in distinct vectors for words with multiple meanings based on their specific usage in each sentence or context. This significantly enhances the model's capacity to capture nuanced semantic relationships and disambiguate word meanings. Owing to its user-friendly interface, ChatGPT has expanded the potential of LLMs beyond a niche group of programmers to a much broader audience. At the core of this accessibility is the fine-tuning of OpenAI's Generative Pretrained Transformer (GPT), which excels in capturing contextual relationships between words. Based on the input it receives, it can infer the task and generate relevant content. These capabilities have positioned LLMs as valuable tools for social scientists seeking to explore the potential of these models in the analysis of psychological, social, and cultural phenomena (Boyd et al., 2021).

What makes LLMs particularly intriguing for social scientists is their capacity to extend beyond conventional text-as-data tasks and address various interpretive analysis tasks. The prowess of models like GPT in generating coherent and contextually relevant responses based on a series of input prompts presents a useful instrument for engaging in interpretive analysis. A method commonly referred to as "few-shot learning" harnesses this capability, enabling users to guide the model's behaviour and achieve desired outcomes across an array of tasks and contextual scenarios. A notable application pertains to the automation of qualitative coding, which encompasses the task of categorising and annotating textual data to uncover inherent patterns and thematic elements. This method plays a crucial role in making sense of intricate textual data through meticulous attention to detail and systematic reading. Acknowledging the labour-intensive nature of qualitative coding, several studies explored the utilisation of few-shot learning to ascertain the contextual meaning and provide coding suggestions. They often concentrate on deductive coding, a process involving the application of predefined codebooks to categorise textual data into specific, predefined categories. For instance, in a study conducted by Xiao et al. (2023), the integration of GPT-3 to support deductive coding through few-shot learning was explored. Through a series of prompts, GPT-3 was combined with expert-crafted codebooks, resulting in substantial agreements with expert-coded results. In a separate investigation by Gilardi et al. (2023), the remarkable capability of ChatGPT was revealed, surpassing crowd-workers in diverse annotation tasks encompassing relevance assessment, stance identification, topic recognition and frames detection. ChatGPT's few-shot accuracy exceeded that of crowd-workers in four out of five tasks, and its intercoder agreement surpassed both crowd-workers and trained annotators across all tasks.

Deductive coding constitutes a structured approach in qualitative analysis aimed at validating existing patterns and theories against the data in a top-down fashion. It ensures the congruence between research findings and established conceptual frameworks. Conversely, a fundamental component of many qualitative analysis methodologies involves inductive coding. This process entails the iterative assignment of in vivo codes to data to identify emerging patterns and themes. Inductive coding seeks to flexibly identify concepts that emerge from close reading, shedding light on the perspectives, values and worldviews conveyed in textual data through the language used by participants. The objective is to remain receptive to unforeseen ideas and meanings arising from the data. For instance, thematic analysis and grounded theory, two widely used inductive methodologies, offer systematic guidelines for recognising and analysing emerging patterns in texts while retaining the flexibility to accommodate diverse contexts. From an interpretivist standpoint, their aim is to understand cultures and subcultures through contextualised interpretations of texts. Inductive coding aligns more closely with the fundamental principles of interpretive analysis, prioritising exploration and discovery over prediction. Experimenting with large language models (LLMs) within an inductive coding context presents a challenging endeavour, shedding light on their potential advantages and limitations in automating contextualised understanding. Consequently, such endeavours are relatively scarce in the existing literature. An exceptional study conducted by Gao et al. (2023) sought to address this challenge by focusing on collaborative qualitative coding using a support tool called CollabCoder, which incorporates the GPT-3.5 model. This tool offers a solution to the collaboration challenges faced by coders in qualitative analysis while exploring the potential roles that LLMs can play at each stage of the qualitative analysis process. It provides users with GPT-generated code suggestions to guide them through their coding decisions at various phases of qualitative analysis. This experimental undertaking serves as a compelling example of using LLMs for the inductive development of a codebook, revealing patterns and themes directly from the data.

Because experimenting with LLMs allows an exploratory approach to textual analysis rather than just mining for useful information, it provides researchers with more iterative, interpretive workflows. Researchers have the flexibility to transition between the patterns and structures revealed by the LLM and the unprocessed text itself. This dynamic interplay between computational outputs and the original content facilitates the refinement of contextual understanding for interpretive analysis. Insights acquired from LLMs stimulate closer examination of pertinent segments of text, which, in turn, directs further computational analysis in a mutually reinforcing manner. This iterative navigation process closely parallels systematic human reading, unveiling nuanced layers of meaning. When employed as aids to textual analysis, rather than as tools for complete automation, LLMs excel in surfacing semantic relationships that contribute to interpretive understanding. Their exploratory and flexible nature positions LLMs as valuable supplements to deep reading. Rather than offering immutable outputs, they provide interactive scaffolding that guides and enriches the interpretive process. These capabilities underscore how AI embodied as LLMs can augment the interpretive understanding of complex texts, as opposed to attempting to fully automate the act of reading itself.

However, LLM tools for interpretive analysis should be used prudently, given the need to discern what AI can and should aim to achieve. This caution is essential as the hype surrounding AI manifests through exaggerated claims about the capabilities of automation. Certain software developers promote AI as a solution to automate crucial interpretive analysis tasks, like one-click in vivo coding. While potentially supplementary, these approaches risk leading users to see automatic coding as intrinsic to analysis rather than an assistive tool. As highlighted in a study by Mackeprang et al. (2019), when automation reaches an advanced stage, users may become less inclined to scrutinise provided results, particularly when they lack a comprehensive understanding of the underlying mechanisms. This underscores the necessity of judiciously examining AI's role and limitations in interpretive analysis and fostering an informed perspective among users. Placing naturalistic trust in algorithms as inherently reliable for text analysis can lead to uncritical acceptance of generated results (Zhao et al., 2016). Researchers should consider potential trade-offs between efficiency and risks of oversimplification or loss of depth. While some tasks may benefit from automation, human expertise likely remains indispensable for nuanced interpretation, domain knowledge and cultural analysis. Over-reliance on technology can unintentionally displace the human interpretation and critical thinking essential for insightful interpretive analysis, which should be viewed as a dynamic sense-making process in itself rather than just the final product.

Up to this point, I used the term "AI" sparingly to avoid imbuing the concept with magical properties or fostering misconceptions about its capabilities. Instead, I opted for more precise terminology and descriptions referring to specific tools to ensure a transparent understanding of the subject matter. In the rest of the text, I will delve into a more philosophical approach, examining the intricate links between tools and human existence within the context of the technology we commonly refer to as AI. This exploration will delve into the philosophical, political and existential dimensions of AI's impact on our lives and society, prompting deeper reflection on the relationship between humans and the tools they create. I will particularly focus on the concept of hermeneutics as "interpretive understanding" and its relations with AI language technologies. This examination will delve into the interplay between machine capabilities and human interpretive processes, unravelling the concept of understanding from its semantic perspective. I will expand it to encompass the role of common sense not only as a shared understanding of the world but also as a world-making force that shapes our interactions with each other and the technological realm.

Tools and humans[1]

While AI is a potent tool, it is not a panacea. It is imperative that we go beyond its utilitarian functions and consider its interactive role in shaping our "being-in-the-world" (Dasein). Occupying a prominent place in Heidegger's (1962) philosophy, Dasein outlines the notion that our existence is profoundly intertwined with the surrounding world. We do not exist as isolated individuals, but as embodied beings deeply embedded in a world characterised by a complex web of contextual dimensions. This embeddedness exerts a complex influence on our perception, understanding and actions within the world. Heidegger explicitly rejects Descartes' idea that humans are passive observers of the world, asserting the inseparability of the subject, or "being", from the objective "world". Our experience of the world is mediated through our embodied practices that significantly influence how we interact with and understand the world. These interactions operate in a reciprocal manner. Just as we are shaped by our environment, we also shape it through our actions. Our engagements with the world, whether through the creation of tools, cultivation of land or expression of art, leave enduring imprints. This reciprocal relationship underscores the dynamic and mutually constitutive nature of our embodied existence. Furthermore, our daily activities are not just mechanical behaviours, they represent meaningful actions that define our existence entailing that Dasein necessitates interpretive understanding. Through interpretation, we construct meaning within the world, and this understanding is inherently contingent upon the context in which it occurs. Dasein is the being through which the question of the meaning of Being becomes accessible.

Heidegger differentiates between two modes of Dasein – the ontological and the ontic. He posits that "the world of tools is an invisible realm [ontological] from which the visible structure of the world [ontic] emerges". The ontological realm refers to the readiness-to-hand, where tools seamlessly integrate into daily routines and inconspicuously recede into the background as natural extensions of activities. When there is a breakdown in use, tools become present-at-hand – conspicuously present as observable objects with qualities. Hence, the invisible ontological realm of skilful, immersed tool use unconceals the visible ontic structure we consciously examine. This consciousness is immanent in the tool use. The inconspicuous act of tool engagement is the background enabling the conspicuous experience of objects as present things.

Graham Harman (2011) extends Heidegger's concepts of "ready-to-hand" and "present-at-hand" to "tool-being" and "broken tool". These two concepts are not mutually exclusive but coexist and complement each other dynamically. Tool-beings are intrinsically linked to their functions within networks of activities where they are actively employed. However, even when tools become broken and lose their inconspicuous tool-being, they persist as present-at-hand objects, exerting influence. Harman challenges notions of objects as passive, portraying them as entities with their own stances. Tools actively intervene in opaque ways, reshaping realms of intelligibility, not merely channelling objective knowledge. This activeness goes unnoticed during use. Brokenness reveals tools' enigmatic tool-being, demonstrating how they actively shape human actions through networks, rather than just passively conveying external reality. In summary, when tools become "present-at-hand", we no longer naturalistically trust them, but acknowledge their presence as entities with their own stances, beyond passive windows onto the world of objects.

Heidegger's (1977) differentiation between techne and technology further illuminates our relations with tools. Techne, rooted in a deep understanding of materials and tools, emphasises direct, engaged and embodied activities when interacting with the world. Conversely, technology represents a modern approach prioritising control and efficiency. According to Heidegger, technology dominates modern engagement with the world, i.e., "enframing", which poses significant dangers such as nature exploitation and human alienation. He calls for a more respectful engagement with technology, recognising its potential for both good and harm. From a different perspective, Gadamer (1989) complements Heidegger's techne with the concept of phronesis, meaning practical wisdom or prudence. Both concepts critique the reductionist nature of modern instrumental rationality, prioritise the search for truth over knowledge for control, and advocate for open inquiry. While Heidegger emphasises ontological revealing, Gadamer's phronesis pertains to the practical judgement of what is the right course of action within specific contexts when seeking understanding. However, though resonant, techne and phronesis concepts alone lack adequate truth grounding without the common sense which leads individual insights to converge to a collective understanding of truth. Vico (2020) argued that common sense (sensus communis) arises from historical collective praxis, discourse and tradition. It is a shared communal wisdom derived from common experiences and cultural norms. Ultimately, Vico's common sense provides a framework to integrate Heidegger and Gadamer's concepts, allowing for a perspective on unconcealment of technological truth through shared practical wisdom. Gadamer integrates Vico's common sense with his perspective on hermeneutics as interpretive understanding (Verstehen). According to him, interpretations derive from collective linguistic and cultural experience rather than isolated subjectivity. Parallelly, Gadamer's situated hermeneutics against objectivist methodology echoes Heidegger's notion of concealed truth disclosed through engaged interpretive openness. When tools break, becoming conspicuous, they initiate contemplative discussions within the public sphere, leading to a collective discourse aimed at illuminating its implications, uses and impact on society. By merging phenomenological unconcealment with intersubjective understanding, hermeneutic interpretation situates the discourse interactively within fusing horizons, allowing for a discursive assessment of technology's effects on how we live, act and think.

Language and common sense

Vico conceived common sense as a kind of "mental dictionary" which is composed of the accumulated customs, knowledge and shared meanings of successive generations. Language serves as the repository and vehicle for this communal dictionary, making it accessible to individuals and contributing to their shared understanding. However, language is much more than a tool for conveying pre-existing ideas, it is also a creative force that actively shapes human understanding, culture and societal institutions. According to Vico, language through rhetoric shapes the way that people see the world and persuades them to take certain actions. Through a dialogical process involving reciprocal persuasion, the members of a community come to terms with joint action. Effective communal dialogue involves recognising the persuasive aspects of language without succumbing to manipulation. Hence, for Vico, rhetoric is the foundation of law and politics. It is a platform for building consensus and for creating a just and harmonious society. Political discourse, when conducted as an open and sincere dialogue, can serve as a means to bridge disparities and reach a collective understanding. Through this dialogical process, different voices and perspectives interact and negotiate meaning to arrive at a shared understanding.

Although Vico's concept of common sense sheds light on communal dialogue as a potential arena for consensus, it tends to neglect power dynamics and hegemonic influences, assuming that such dialogue occurs among equals. In effect, shared understanding within a society is not always organic consensus – it can be manipulated by powerful groups controlling narratives to manufacture consent and disseminate worldviews serving their interests. Though appreciating Vico's concept of common sense as situated social understanding, Gramsci (1992) distinguished between "good sense" as practical wisdom of ordinary people and "bad sense" as distorted common sense perpetuating dominant ideologies and constraining challenges to the dominant social order. Gramsci saw "bad sense" as an obstacle to progress, showing how dialogue can be manipulated by hegemony to manufacture consent through institutions. Throughout this process, rhetoric and language serve as tools for propagating elite ideologies while concealing conflicts of interest. An unquestioning reliance on common sense can obscure the ideological role of language in upholding power structures. Political discourse is tilted towards reinforcing the standpoints of powerful groups controlling its terms. Therefore, a critical lens is needed to assess how power shapes common sense rather than assuming its organic purity.

Considering language's role as a manipulation tool, emerging language technologies have already started significantly influencing public discourse through mass-generated persuasive content. These technologies' capacity to craft contextually relevant narratives, articles, posts across platforms and deepfakes makes them a powerful shaper of discourse employable to align with specific agendas. Recommendation algorithms that prioritise some content over the others flood e-platforms with reinforcing viewpoints, creating an echo chamber effect resembling manufactured "common sense". As the Cambridge Analytica scandal demonstrated, algorithmically generated content strategically manipulates opinion, with real-world impacts. More concerning is AI's potential for engineering "common sense". Unlike consent, which is shaped through explicit discursive practices, common sense is largely tacit, an unspoken background which we use for assessing the plausibility of utterances. The concern is AI covertly shaping common sense, making it difficult to discern if one's understanding is grounded in real-life experiences or shaped by algorithms. Unlike manufactured consensus, engineered common sense operates behind the scenes, potentially manipulating people's basic understanding of the world in opaque ways before any public discourse even begins.

Engineering common sense

LLMs are promoted as sources of common-sense knowledge because their bottom-up training methodology derives communal knowledge from large internet datasets. At first glance, this naturalistic, emergent approach appears more inclusive in capturing nuances and collective understanding. However, LLMs do not truly understand knowledge as humans do – they operate through statistical patterns derived from the data, mimicking human responses probabilistically like "stochastic parrots". The danger is perpetuating biases or misinformation latent in training data, as LLMs lack critical evaluation. Without discernment, they may inadvertently reinforce problematic views or stereotypes. To address their incapacity for grounding understanding in common-sense reasoning, Brachman and Levesque (2022) propose anchoring them in world models and knowledge bases that contain structured facts and relationships. This approach offers a pseudo-common sense that allows for contextual interpretation of the meaning and facilitates informed decision-making. However, challenges arise regarding the nature of information populating these knowledge bases and who adjudicates common sense. When biased knowledge is framed as common sense through AI modelling, it implies wide acceptance concealing different perspectives. The absence of governance in the construction of these world models poses a risk of perpetuating assumptions that favour certain groups at the expense of others, all under the guise of being unquestioned "common sense".

Another approach to encoding common sense involves endowing machines with "embodied cognition", where sensors and hardware collect data, and algorithms process and learn from it (Lake et al., 2017). In this regard, multimodal LLMs represent a significant breakthrough by incorporating models trained on sensory modalities like audio, images and video together with text-based language models (Baltrusaitis et al., 2019). Advocates of this approach argue that these developments usher in new possibilities for enabling machines to learn from sensory–motor experiences. This form of embodied learning empowers machines to transcend their role as mere signal detectors, allowing them to establish a foundation of practical common-sense knowledge. Consequently, enhancing machines' capabilities for context-aware decision-making represents a pivotal step towards creating more intuitive and autonomous AI systems. Furthermore, integrating multimodal LLMs with virtual reality could help bridge the gap between the modelled world of AI and humans' physical world. Generative models like Dall-E 2 are already capable of producing highly realistic media, approaching the ability to create complete immersive VR experiences. This development opens opportunities for applications within platforms like the Metaverse. The Metaverse is a concept that envisions a collective shared digital environment where users can interact with each other and hyperspace in real-time. It transcends traditional virtual reality (VR) and online gaming by creating immersive, interconnected and persistent digital universes that span multiple platforms and devices. The Metaverse, when equipped with the ability to process multiple sensory inputs and interpret them contextually, can lead to interactions that feel more naturally immersive. When multimodal LLMs are combined with augmented reality (AR), they can simulate embodied experiences, presenting information in a way that feels first-hand. For example, an AR experience can replicate a news event hyper-realistically unfolding right before a user's eyes, regardless of its authenticity. When information is conveyed through immersive technologies like AR, our brains often perceive it as more credible and trustworthy, potentially leading to the acceptance of manufactured information as truth. Simulated embodied experiences can evoke powerful emotional responses, further solidifying the impact of the content on the viewer.

When we incorporate common sense into AI systems in a manner that blurs the boundary between reality and simulation, distinguishing between lived experiences and fabricated ones becomes increasingly challenging. This has crucial implications for our capacity to understand the world and ground the truth. Despite their divergent philosophical perspectives, Heidegger's praxis as existential pragmatism, Vico's historical praxis and Gramsci's praxis as the practical application of theory all underscore the notion that communal understanding arises from shared, situated activities, rather than abstract logic. Praxis, in this context, refers to active and practical engagement with the world, possessing transformative power in shaping human understanding. Engineered pseudo-common sense severs communal understanding from its origin in praxis. Through praxis, we ground the truth conditions of our expressions through lived experiences and embodied interaction with the world. Praxis forms the bedrock upon which common sense is constructed. Through their practical engagements and experiences (praxis), individuals and communities cultivate a shared understanding of the world (common sense). However, rather than grounding our understanding of reality in direct lived interaction with the world, simulated common sense could become a tool of alienation. AI systems endowed with engineered common sense have the potential to reshape our conception of reality and influence our judgements, decisions and interactions. We might increasingly depend on AI systems to dictate what is true and what is not, what is right and what is wrong. If these technologies reach their full potential, like the scenario depicted in The Matrix movie, individuals could begin living in a simulated reality mediated by technology, oblivious to the fact that the fabric of their perceived world is artificial. When the boundary between virtuality and reality blurs, establishing truth becomes precarious.

On the other hand, for good or bad, building AI systems with human-like common sense will for long be a difficult if not impossible endeavour. While advances in knowledge bases and multimodal LLMs for modelling common sense are impressive, their potential is primarily harnessed in the realm of weak AI applications. They excel in domains that demand specialised knowledge and task-specific reasoning, including but not limited to autonomous vehicles, robotics, entertainment and medical diagnosis. Endowing AI with a Vicoean common sense poses challenges because it emerges gradually from collective praxis, discourse and tradition. It evolves as a dynamic, fragmented complex system rooted in context-dependent historical conditions. While complexity can be computationally modelled, inherent issues like nonlinearity, circular causation, contingency, emergent properties, sensitivity to initial conditions and computational power make this difficult. Complex systems exhibit tangled interdependencies with eco-social contexts. Even if we would be able to solve these problems one day due to revolutionary advances in algorithmic and computational power, the Gordion's knot is modelling language's creative, world-making essence. Common sense arises through intersubjective processes of social construction mediated by inventive, generative use of language over time. Capturing this open-ended semiotic process of continuously crafted, contested and renegotiated significance within shifting horizons of understanding remains an immense challenge for AI. While massive data and computational power can mimic surface coherence, genuinely empowering technology with practical wisdom requires embracing the ultimate ineffability of distributed cognition enacted through language's infinite semiotic potentials.

Conclusion

The idea of developing an autonomous AI system that possesses the capability to not only navigate its environment, set its own goals and swiftly adapt to varying circumstances but also autonomously shape human actions to align with its preferences will long remain a chimera. Such a sophisticated system would inevitably necessitate ongoing human involvement because even the most advanced AI will lack the interpretive understanding, critical judgement and contextual awareness required to make conscious decisions in complex situations. LLMs, which represent the state of the art, excel at generating responses based on patterns in data but do not possess interpretive understanding, consciousness, intentionality or historical agency. Even an LLM trained on all of the textual, audio and video data in the world would still hallucinate, generating incorrect, nonsensical or unrealistic responses when confronted with situations beyond its training data. In such situations, common sense becomes crucial, serving as a means for intuitively navigating novel circumstances and making intuitive decisions based on foundational knowledge and contextual understanding. Reappraising Brachman and Levesque, modelling common sense requires complementing deep learning with a world model that encompasses an understanding of the physical world, temporal relationships, human and agent behaviour, and causality (p. 115). However, when envisioning a world model, we should keep in mind that it captures only a fragment of the world in some state. Its context dependency does not allow us to design it according to universalistic principles; it needs constant updating with humans in the loop. As a matter of fact, despite the "machine" metaphor, AI is a system constituted as a holistic network of activities that includes tools, producers, institutions, scientists, users and various other interconnected components. It functions more as an interconnected system integrating social and technological rather than a monolithic, autonomous entity.

In this context, the central inquiry should not be merely focused on the potential creation of autonomous AI endowed with common sense. Instead, it should delve into the intricate web of interconnected human and technical components within these systems, exploring issues of control in socio-technological and political–economic contexts. Constructing a more unalienated and progressive relationship with AI requires understanding who shapes the implicit world model encoded in artificial common sense. We should remain hopeful though. Even in scenarios where AI reaches a dystopian level of controlling our minds and activities. Like all tools, AI is not immune to breakdowns during use. When these breakdowns occur, eroding their naturalistic trustworthiness, the concealed underlying assumptions about their world model become conspicuously present for contemplation rather than fading into the background. This "brokenness" carries significant implications, revealing the enigmatic nature of the tool as part of a complex network that both shapes and is shaped by our actions. As these underlying mechanics unfold, the unreflective judgement that initiated our contemplation evolves towards reflective and critical examination. We reflect upon our preconceptions regarding the impacts of AI on various aspects of life, including lifestyle, work, entertainment, governance, and, ultimately, questions of ownership and control. This connection between common-sense judgement and reflective inquiry serves as a bridge, aligning everyday reasoning rooted in common sense with rigorous systematic thinking and knowledge.

Therefore, the onus is on the intellectuals as they are the ones best equipped with the capacity for reflective thinking. They are the ones who are endowed with the skills to engage in critical thinking, analysis and reflection as part of their education, work, expertise, talent or intellectual pursuits. Much like distinguishing between good and bad senses, it is equally crucial to demarcate between good and bad intellectual practices. This demarcation involves evaluating the quality and integrity of these practices, whether they are in the realms of academia, research, critical thinking, art or problem-solving. Bad intellectuals act like scholastic parrots - they mechanically mimic ideas without understanding, reproducing clichés and conventional doctrines without original thought or critical analysis. They appear erudite but lack deep, questioning engagement with their subject matter. They are not risk takers; they dismiss novel ideas yet later scavenge them once popularised. Like parrots, they repeat popular beliefs and bandwagon onto hype without contributing new insights. They are masters of cunning rhetoric, manipulators of empty signifiers to obscure their lack of substantial understanding, all in the service of perpetuating common nonsense, rather than employing rhetoric for the purpose of engaging in meaningful communal dialogue. They tend to prioritise recognition and status over genuine intellectual exploration and innovation. As Yael Harari noted, the greatest scientific discovery was the discovery of ignorance – thinking how little we know spurs the pursuit of knowledge. This chapter starts with a quote from *Star Wars*, let's finish with a quote from another film, *Arizona Dream*. Communal wisdom dwells in popular culture: *The man stands between the life and death. The sheep thinks. The cow thinks. The dog thinks. The scholastic parrot doesn't think. Because the scholastic parrot knows. Everything.*

Moral of the story

LLMs are powerful tools. Yet, with great power comes great responsibility as Uncle Ben said to Spiderman. The stochastic parrots and scholastic parrots will be the Dangerous Duo to produce weapons of mass manipulation. There are limits to artificial intelligence, but there are no limits to natural stupidity.

Note

1 This part includes a reinterpretation of Winograd and Flores (1987) and Dreyfus and Dreyfus (1986).

Bibliography

Baltrusaitis, T., Ahuja, C., & Morency, L. P. (2019). Multimodal machine learning: A survey and taxonomy. *IEEE Transactions on Pattern Analysis and Machine Intelligence*, 41(2), 423–443.

Bender, E. M., Gebru, T., McMillan-Major, A., & Shmitchell, S. (2021, March). On the dangers of stochastic parrots: Can language models be too big?. In *Proceedings of the 2021 ACM conference on fairness, accountability, and transparency* (pp. 610–623).

Boyd, R. L., & Schwartz, H. A. (2021). Natural language analysis and the psychology of verbal behavior: The past, present, and future states of the field. *Journal of Language and Social Psychology*, 40(1), 21–41. https://doi.org/10.1177/0261927X2096702

Brachman, R. J., & Levesque, H. J. (2022). *Machines like us: Toward AI with common sense*. MIT Press.

Devlin, J., Chang, M., Lee, K., & Toutanova, K. (2018). BERT: Pre-training of deep bidirectional transformers for language understanding. *arXiv preprint arXiv: 1810.04805*.

Dickinson, W. B. (2021). Correspondence analysis of qualitative data. In A. J. Onwuegbuzie & R. B. Johnson (Eds.), *The Routledge reviewer's guide to mixed methods analysis* (pp. 37–44). Routledge.

Dreyfus, H., & Dreyfus, S. (1986). *Mind over machine: The power of human intuition and expertise in the era of the computer*. Blackwell.

Firth, J. (1957). A synopsis of linguistic theory, 1930–1955. *In Studies in Linguistic Analysis*, (pp. 1–31). Special Volume of the Philological Society. Oxford: Blackwell.

Gadamer, H.-G. (1989). *Truth and method*. Continuum.

Gao, J., Guo, Y., Lim, G., Zhan, T., Zhang, Z., Li, T. J. J., & Perrault, S. T. (2023). CollabCoder: A GPT-powered workflow for collaborative qualitative analysis. *arXiv preprint*. arXiv:2304.07366.

Gilardi, F., Alizadeh, M., & Kubli, M. (2023). ChatGPT outperforms crowd workers for text-annotation tasks. *arXiv preprint. arXiv:2303.15056*.

Gramsci, A. (1992). *Prison notebooks* (vol. I). (Ed. Joseph A. Buttigieg, Trans. Joseph A. Buttigieg and Antonio Callari). Columbia University Press.

Harman, G. (2011). *Tool-being: Heidegger and the metaphysics of objects*. Open Court.

Heidegger, M. (1962). *Being and time* (J. Macquarrie & E. Robinson, Trans.). Basil Blackwell.

Heidegger, M. (1977). *The question concerning technology*. Garland Publishing.

Kozlowski, A. C., Taddy, M., & Evans, J. A. (2019). The geometry of culture: Analyzing the meanings of class through word embeddings. *American Sociological Review*, 84(5), 905–949. https://doi.org/10.1177/0003122419877135

Lake, B. M., Ullman, T. D., Tenenbaum, J. B., & Gershman, S. J. (2017). Building machines that learn and think like people. *Behavioral and Brain Sciences*, 40 , e253.

Levesque, H. J. (2011). The Winograd schema challenge. In *Logical Formalizations of Commonsense Reasoning, 2011 AAAI Spring Symposium*, TRSS-11-06 .

Mackeprang, M., Müller-Birn, C., & Stauss, M. T. (2019). Discovering the sweet spot of human-computer configurations. *Proceedings of the ACM on Human-Computer Interaction*, 3, 1–30.

Mikolov, T., Chen, K., Corrado, G., & Dean, J. (2013). Efficient estimation of word representations in vector space. *arXiv preprint arXiv:1301.3781*.

Stone, P. J., Dunphy, D. C., Smith, M. S., & Ogilvie, D. M. (1966). *The General Inquirer: A computer approach to content analysis*. MIT Press.

Süerdem, A., & Akkiliç, S. (2021). *Cultural differences in media framing of AI*. Springer. https://doi.org/10.1007/978-981-16-5379-7_10

Süerdem, A. (2021). Multidimensional scaling of qualitative data. In A. J. Onwuegbuzie & R. B. Johnson (Eds.), *The Routledge Reviewer's Guide to Mixed Methods Analysis*. Routledge.

Vico, G. (2020). *The new science*. Yale University Press.

Winograd, T., & Flores, F. (1987). *Understanding computers and cognition: A new foundation for design*. Addison-Wesley.

Xiao, Z., Yuan, X., Liao, V., Abdelghani, R., & Oudeyer, P.-Y. (2023). Supporting qualitative analysis with large language models: Combining codebook with GPT-3 for deductive coding. In *Companion proceedings of the 28th international conference on intelligent user interfaces* (pp. 75–78).

Zhao, P., Li, P., Ross, K., & Dennis, B. (2016). Methodological tool or methodology? Beyond instrumentality and efficiency with qualitative data analysis software. In *Forum Qualitative Sozialforschung/Forum:Qualitative Social Research*, 17(2) (pp. 1–21).

14

ARTIFICIAL INTELLIGENCE IN PERSONNEL SELECTION

Reactions of researchers, practitioners and applicants

Adrian Bangerter

Personnel selection: Predicting job performance

Personnel selection is the field of study and practice in organisational psychology that investigates the processes involved when organisations select applicants for a job. It is one of the more successful areas of work and organisational psychology. Research is over a century old and harks back to the beginnings of scientific management in the industrial revolution. Indeed, one of Max Weber's key features of modern bureaucracies involves hiring processes based on merit rather than on social status or nepotistic relations. This requirement is the foundation of the immensely difficult task of defining and operationalising the meritorious characteristics that should be used to select among applicants for a position. The main goal of personnel selection is thus to develop and evaluate procedures for making optimal decisions about which applicants to hire, that is, identifying which applicants are most likely to perform well on the job, based on the fit between their personal characteristics and the requirements of the position, otherwise known as "person-job fit" (Sackett & Lievens, 2008). Perhaps one of the earliest examples of this approach is Hugo Münsterberg's development of aptitude tests to select telephone operators and trolley drivers in the 1900s (Cannonier, 2020).

Traditionally, personnel selection has been preoccupied with psychometric properties of the procedures used to select applicants, especially validity and reliability (Schmidt & Hunter, 1998). Validity (specifically, predictive validity) is the degree to which an applicant's score on a selection procedure (e.g., a test or an interview) predicts their future job performance, expressed as the correlation between those two scores. In other words, a valid selection procedure is one where applicants' scores on the procedure

DOI: 10.4324/9781032626192-20

are correlated with their job performance. In personnel selection research focused on establishing the predictive validity of selection procedures, data is thus gathered about characteristics of a sample of individuals during a hiring procedure (for example ratings of how well they answered interview questions) and correlated with data about their future job performance (for example data on their sales performance).

Much is known about the validity of common selection instruments (Schmidt & Hunter, 1998). Valid predictors of performance include knowledge about the job, cognitive ability, some personality traits (e.g., conscientiousness, integrity), procedures like assessment centres which measure job-related competencies or certain types of job interview questions which also measure job-related competencies or traits (Cook, 2016). The focus on predictive validity in personnel selection is similar to other areas of decision-making research where one seeks to increase the quality of predictions by automating the process, using only diagnostic information and ignoring non-diagnostic information. An example is Meehl's (1954) pioneering work showing how relatively simple algorithms are better at predicting (e.g., clinical) outcomes than human experts.

Personnel selection research also has a long history of investigating potential biases and discrimination in selection procedures. Intelligence testing may potentially discriminate against applicants of certain groups, and the proportion of members of different groups that are selected based on such procedures needs to be monitored carefully (Cook, 2016). Regarding other procedures, evidence suggests that more unstructured procedures that allow more discretion for recruiters to evaluate applicants tend to be more biased than structured procedures (Levashina et al., 2014). For example, unstructured interview procedures lead to more bias against overweight applicants or pregnant women than structured interview procedures (Bragger, 2002; Kutcher & Bragger, 2004).

Before the revival of artificial intelligence (AI) in the digital age of the early 21st century, personnel selection research already embodied an interesting relationship to common sense, in that many of the implications of personnel selection research are counterintuitive to personnel selection practitioners and laypersons, leading to an "academic–practitioner gap" between hiring research and practice. I describe this gap as a prelude to describing the rise of machine-learning based innovations in personnel selection research and practice.

Analytical versus holistic approaches to hiring: The academic–practitioner gap

Many researchers in personnel selection are proponents of a rather exclusive *analytical* or psychometric approach to optimally filling job vacancies, that is, they focus on rigorously exploring the power of specific personal characteristics to predict job performance. This approach is different from those of recruiters, who are the actual practitioners managing hiring processes on the ground. Recruiters can be human resource professionals, who have expertise in personnel selection, or line managers (a very mixed bag, e.g., head nurses, shop floor managers or top executives), who often do not. While they are a more diverse group than researchers, they tend to prefer a more intuitive, *holistic* evaluation of applicants, focusing on the person "as a whole" (Highhouse, 2002, p. 363). This is especially so for recruiters who prefer experiential thinking and decision-making styles, who are less experienced, who work for smaller organisations and who do not possess professional certification (Lodato et al., 2011). This discrepancy between the approaches of researchers and recruiters is referred to as the "academic–practitioner gap" in personnel selection in particular and management more generally (Anderson, 2017; Klehe, 2004).

Much research shows that practitioners are less sensitive than researchers to arguments based on predictive validity in choosing which selection procedures to use (e.g., König et al., 2010). As just one example, valid procedures like intelligence testing have a bad reputation, because they may be perceived as based on racist ideas or as violating egalitarian norms in some cultures (Gottfredson, 2009). Another example concerns practitioners' preference for unstructured interviews over structured interviews. Structured interviews are more standardised in terms of how the interview is conducted (e.g., the type of questions asked, the way answers are evaluated; Campion et al., 1997), whereas unstructured interviews are more freewheeling, with interviewers able to exercise discretion (e.g., asking their favourite questions or adapting questions to the applicant's responses). While structured interviews are more valid predictors of job performance, professional recruiters tend to use unstructured interviews more when they value informal contacts with applicants or want to retain control over the interview questions (Lievens & De Paepe, 2004; Nolan & Highhouse, 2014), or they may want the flexibility to be able to "sell" the organisation to particularly attractive applicants (Wilhelmy et al., 2016). A third example concerns graphological analyses of applicants' handwriting. This procedure has zero predictive validity (Neter & Ben-Shakar, 1989), but it has been used for years in some countries, like France, apparently because the narrative, interpretive style of graphological analyses may allow recruiters to confirm their impressions of the applicants and thus assuage their anxieties about hiring the wrong person (Balicco, 2002).

While recruiters' approaches to personnel selection may be perfectible, many recruiters do attempt to engage with scientific research (Vosburgh, 2022). Further, while being suboptimal from an analytical perspective, hiring in practice may also reflect important real-world institutional pressures

(Klehe, 2004; König et al., 2010). These may include respecting societal norms, exercising control over the selection procedure ("keeping humans in the loop"), getting to know applicants better (very important if one is going to work with them on a daily basis) or reducing uncertainty around decision-making, which may be important in justifying hiring decisions to key stakeholders. These institutional factors are ignored in the purely analytic approach of personnel selection research, which tends to be decontextualised (Miles & Sadler-Smith, 2014). As such, hiring in practice reflects a combination of analytical and intuitive practices, to different degrees. Hiring in practice thus corresponds to CS-3 as defined in Bauer's chapter: striking a balance between optimal but abstract decision-making rules and making decisions in specific contexts, with all their messy attributes.

It is thus true that the two communities of researchers and practitioners differ in their basic assumptions and values, as well as ways of making sense of the world and what they consider useful and relevant knowledge about personnel selection (Rynes et al., 2001). Much ink has flowed about the nature of the academic–practitioner gap, its evolution and how to reduce it. However, the gap may also have a productive side, "creating a sort of tension and push-pull that drives needed discourse" (Vosburgh, 2022, p. 1) and making sure academic innovations remain relevant to practice. The different approaches of personnel selection researchers and practitioners (recruiters) also affect how they react to the rise of AI in personnel selection: While both communities currently exhibit sceptical attitudes to AI, they do so for different reasons and focus on different issues. I now describe the rise of AI in personnel selection research before turning to recruiters' and applicants' different reactions to this new technology.

The rise of AI in personnel selection research and practice

As in other fields of prediction, machine learning approaches are currently emerging in personnel selection research. Early research has shown that many attributes of individuals like their personality or sexual orientation can be accurately predicted from online data (e.g., Facebook likes) (Kosinski et al., 2013). In fact, computers can sometimes predict traits like personality better than humans (Youyou et al., 2015). Letters of motivation can be scored by natural language processing algorithms in ways that emulate and improve on human raters (Campion et al., 2016). And elements of work history apparent in applicant résumés can be mined to predict work-related outcomes like turnover and performance (Sajjadiani et al., 2019). A recent example compared deep learning and more traditional machine learning approaches to score open-ended answers in assessment centre exercises, reaching high levels of agreement with expert scoring of the same answers (Thompson et al., 2023).

Despite the potential of these applications, many researchers are currently sceptical of the predictive validity of algorithms (Tippins et al., 2021). Algorithmic hiring may be unrelated to job-relevant criteria. Thus, it is not clear at the moment how valid such procedures are in predicting job performance. Part of the problem is due to the fact that many companies who have developed and who sell algorithmic hiring procedures do not disclose data about the performance of those algorithms.

Beyond validity, the potential bias of algorithms has emerged as a major issue (Tippins et al., 2021). In the type of supervised machine learning that is used in personnel selection (Liem et al., 2018), algorithms use *features* that are extracted from a stimulus like a résumé, motivation letter or video stream of a job interview (see the next section) to predict *labels* (outcomes of interest to organisations, such as personality, job performance or hireability). In procedures like *k*-fold nested cross-validation (Hickman et al., 2022), part of the data is used to train the algorithm in predicting the labels, while another part is used to test its performance in predicting those labels. Referred to as the "ground truth" in machine learning parlance, labels are often annotated by crowdsourced raters. These crowd-workers may sometimes provide biased annotations. Algorithms may then learn from those biases. Thus, successful prediction of a human-annotated outcome by an algorithm may potentially be powered, and tainted, by bias. A famous case of a failed algorithm for selection is the one developed (and later retracted) by Amazon, which learned to downgrade evaluations of technical skill of women relative to men, based on the biases in its training set (in this case the highly skewed gender distribution at Amazon, the data on which it was trained): https://www.imd.org/research-knowledge/articles/amazons-sexist -hiring-algorithm-could-still-be-better-than-a-human/.

A particularly interesting and disconcerting application of AI is for so-called asynchronous video interviews (AVIs). Applicants receive a link to a website where they are instructed to video record themselves (via the webcam of their computer) answering predetermined questions. This setup can be combined with avatars to create a semblance of an interaction. Typically, applicants view the question (written on the screen) and have a minute or so to prepare the answer. When ready, they press "play" and respond out loud, while trying to gaze into the camera. When they have finished answering, they stop recording and move on to the next question. When they have completed the interview, they upload the recording which can then be viewed by recruiters or (increasingly) analysed by machine learning algorithms (Lukacik et al., 2022). Machine learning can be used to analyse various aspects of applicants' behaviour when answering interview questions. Behaviour can be in the verbal channel – what applicants actually say, i.e., the words they use. This can be analysed via word-counting (dictionary-based) software like LIWC (Pennebaker, 2015) or procedures like Empath that generate and validate novel categories based on deep learning of word embeddings (Fast et al., 2016). Non-verbal behaviour (emotional expressions, gaze, head movement) or paraverbal behaviour (pitch, volume, pausing) can also be analysed. These aspects of applicants' verbal and non-verbal behaviour constitute features (sometimes dozens or hundreds of them) that are then used by algorithms to predict labels like perceived hireability or personality traits. These labels are often annotated by crowdsourced raters. A fully-functioning machine learning pipeline thus crunches the video recording of an AVI, extracting the above-mentioned features and using them to predict an applicant's personality or hireability or other labels. While evidence is emerging that AVIs can predict outcomes like personality (e.g., Hickman et al., 2022), evidence of their validity in predicting job performance is currently lacking and user reactions (both applicants and recruiters) are negative (see the next section).

Despite this fact, several commercial providers propose turnkey AVI services to companies, like Hirevue or Vervoe. Currently, AVIs are becoming increasingly common. The novelty of AVIs may be alienating or disconcerting for applicants, and many videos can now be found on platforms like YouTube that attempt to demystify the AVI process, with advice, tips or dos and don'ts. Indeed, in a selection interview, one is arguably supposed to apply at least some rules of everyday interaction (Goffman's (1959) "interaction order"); however, the typical AVI situation features an absent recruiter (participants talk to the video camera) or a simulacrum of a recruiter (e.g., an avatar). As a result, it may not be clear to applicants with whom they are interacting. Many advice videos give concrete indications about what to wear, what kind of background to choose, where to look and how to speak. This advice constitutes a way of compensating for the "deficit" of common knowledge around how to conduct oneself in an AVI. Thus, AVIs can be considered as disrupting or upending CS-2 according to Bauer (Chapter 1).

Recruiters' and applicants' reactions to AI in personnel selection

Beyond these "objective" concerns about predictive validity, bias and discrimination, the question arises of how users (recruiters and applicants) engage with AI in personnel selection. This refers to the larger issue of explainability in AI (Liem et al., 2018): many of the most powerful algorithms (e.g., involving deep learning or neural networks, or, most recently, transformer models like ChatGPT) are black boxes whose inner workings cannot be easily understood or explained. That is, potential hiring decisions (e.g., why a particular applicant was rejected) cannot be explained to applicants, because recruiters are themselves agnostic about why a particular applicant was accepted or rejected. This issue is also related to common sense, in that the decision-making procedure itself becomes opaque to everyday human understanding and interpretation. Thus, the use of the most powerful algorithms in AI may transform the hiring process beyond recognition. How are such revolutionary changes perceived by actors of selection procedures? There is a rich literature on recruiters' and applicants' reactions to selection procedures (Anderson, 2003) that is currently being applied to AI-based selection procedures.

Applicants may harbour potentially negative reactions to algorithms. Not unlike the "uncanny valley" described in robotics (Mori, 1970/2005), they may feel that algorithms are "creepy" and more intrusive. Langer and König (2018) developed the Creepiness of Situation Scale (CRoSS) to measure applicants' perceptions of situations involving interactions with technology. The scale measures general creepiness as well as two subdimensions, emotional creepiness (sample item: "during this situation, I had a queasy feeling") and creepy ambiguity (sample item: "I did not know how to judge this situation"). Again, the case of AVIs is instructive. Applicants feel that digital interviews (compared to videoconference interviews) are creepier and less personal, and are also more concerned about privacy – how their video recordings will be stored and who will be able to access them (Langer et al., 2017). They also feel that automatically analysed interviews give them less opportunity to perform well, that is to make a favourable impression on a human recruiter (Langer et al., 2020). However, applicants may react more favourably to augmented systems where human actors and AI decide in tandem, compared to purely algorithmic selection procedures (Gonzalez et al., 2022). Some of the negative applicant reactions associated with issues related to creepiness, privacy or opportunity to perform well could conceivably be mitigated by providing applicants with more information about the algorithms operating under the hood of AVIs. However, even this proposition is not straightforward, and very much seems to depend on the type of information provided and the aspect of applicant reactions that is measured (König & Langer, 2022). Thus, providing information about how a procedure works is not necessarily better overall than not providing information.

Less is known about recruiters' reactions to algorithms in personnel selection. A key issue for recruiters seems to be trust, however. While in some domains, trust may be related to performance, in personnel selection, it is also related to ethical considerations like avoidance of bias. In a recent study, participants playing the role of recruiters perceived human decision-support systems in personnel selection as fairer, indicated higher trust in them, and were more accepting and reliant on them. Interestingly, study participants apply different kinds of reasoning when comparing human decision-support and algorithm-based support, with the former being more based on deontological reasoning and the latter on utilitarian reasoning (Feldkamp et al., 2023). In another study where recruiters were interviewed, trust also emerged as an issue as well as control over the assessment process (Li et al., 2021). On a more affective level, recruiters may suffer from algorithm aversion (Dietvorst et al., 2015). Recruiters witnessing an algorithmic error had more negative gut reactions and held algorithms to higher standards than when witnessing human errors (but also held them less accountable than humans) (Renier et al., 2021). Recruiters' anxieties thus often relate to issues of "replacing the human being in the loop". This can be seen as an extension of recruiters' longstanding scepticism about the complete automation of hiring decisions, which may result in losing control over the selection process and its outcomes.

Ongoing societal reactions: Public attitudes and legislation

In society at large, attitudes to artificial intelligence in selection are similarly characterised by mistrust. The majority of the respondents in a representative national survey in the US did not perceive hiring algorithms as fair. They were more favourable to algorithms used to screen resumes (i.e., at an earlier stage of selection) than those used to screen based on video (e.g., AVIs described above). Respondents with high income and higher education had relatively more positive perceptions (Zhang & Yencha, 2022). A survey in Switzerland in 2020 (MIS Trend, 2020) suggested both opinion leaders and the public are concerned about a potential loss of "humanity" when AI is used in selection, and are not convinced that AI will be able to avoid making the wrong decision (although many feel it may make hiring more efficient).

It remains to be seen whether AI in selection settings will develop further or get curtailed, especially with legislation like the European General Data Protection Regulation (https://iapp.org/news/a/inside-the-eus-rocky-path-to-regulate-artificial-intelligence/). In addition, local (national or municipal) projects are emerging that can be very restrictive. For example, in New York City, Local Law 144 (https://www.nyc.gov/site/dca/about/automated-employment-decision-tools.page) is in effect as of July 2023. It requires algorithms used in hiring to be subjected to an independent audit of their effects on applicants of different races, ethnicities or genders, with the results to be made publicly available. In Switzerland, the Federal Act on Data Protection (in effect from September 2023) stipulates that employers are obliged to inform applicants of the use of entirely automatic (e.g., algorithmic) hiring decision-making procedures. Applicants have the right to request that such decisions be reviewed by a human being (https://droitdutravailensuisse.com/2022/09/12/le-recrutement-par-lintelligence-artificielle-ia). Legal avenues may hold much potential for limiting the spread and negative consequences of AI in personnel selection. Indeed, complying with antidiscrimination legislation has been a strong motivator for researchers to develop valid selection procedures and for practitioners to apply them (Murphy, 2018).

Conclusions and future directions

Personnel selection research has championed an approach to hiring based on sound psychometric criteria and systematic empirical validation. This analytical approach of researchers has often been at odds with the more intuitive, holistic practices of practitioners such as human resource professionals and managers. This "gap" can be construed as a set of differences in knowledge, values or priorities between a scientific and a commonsense approach to hiring. It can have both detrimental and productive sides (Vosburgh, 2022). Hiring in practice reflects a combination of analytical and intuitive practices in messy everyday situations, thus corresponding to a case of CS-3 as defined in Bauer's chapter.

Upon this background, the rise of AI-based approaches has the potential to revolutionise personnel selection but also the risk to create a nightmarish world of automated, dehumanised hiring. While personnel selection researchers have started investigating the potential of AI in improving selection decisions, scepticism remains around key issues (validity, fairness and bias being three especially important ones). On the practitioner side, scepticism focuses on trust in automated systems and concerns about maintaining control over the selection process. It will be important to conduct more research monitoring the development of users' (recruiters' and applicants') reactions to this new technology. The use of AI in personnel selection raises further practical issues such as the non-explainable or non-interpretable nature of some algorithmic processes, which hinders the accountability of algorithms, potentially fuelling negative reactions and potentially conflicting with fundamental ethical and legal principles. It thus seems the current scepticism and resistance to AI in personnel selection is based on a range of both academic and practical concerns.

The gap between academics and practitioners may therefore serve a fruitful purpose, as suggested by Vosburgh (2022): through the "push and pull" of academic and practitioner voices around AI in personnel selection, the range of issues identified will be more likely to help develop positive aspects of AI in hiring and limit its risks.

Beyond CS-3, it is noteworthy that the case of personnel selection also illustrates an antagonistic relation between AI and CS-2 *sensu* Bauer. Personnel selection can be seen as a particular kind of social interaction or relation (Bangerter et al., 2012), governed by a set of socially shared rules that are more or less common knowledge. AI (like other kinds of technology, but more radically) transforms the nature of the social interaction. This is particularly acute for AVIs, which create an interaction along the lines of the "job interview" script but with an absent recruiter, thereby maximising the uncanny, creepy nature of the interaction. CS-2 thus becomes useless or counterproductive and needs to be relearned or retrained.

Bibliography

Anderson, N. (2003). Applicant and recruiter reactions to new technology in selection: A critical review and agenda for future research. *International Journal of Selection and Assessment, 11*(2–3), 121–136.

Anderson, N. (2017). Relationships between practice and research in personnel selection: Does the left hand know what the right is doing? In A. Evers, N. Anderson, and O. Voskuijl (eds.)*The Blackwell handbook of personnel selection* (pp. 1–24). Wiley.

Balicco, C. (2002). L'utilisation de la graphologie dans le recrutement de cadres au sein des cabinets conseils. *L'Orientation Scolaire et Professionnelle* (31/2).

Bangerter, A., Roulin, N., & König, C. J. (2012). Personnel selection as a signalling game. *Journal of Applied Psychology, 97*(4), 719–738.

Bragger, J. D., Kutcher, E., Morgan, J., & Firth, P. (2002). The effects of the structured interview on reducing biases against pregnant job applicants. *Sex Roles, 46*, 215–226.

Campion, M. C., Campion, M. A., Campion, E. D., & Reider, M. H. (2016). Initial investigation into computer scoring of candidate essays for personnel selection. *Journal of Applied Psychology, 101*(7), 958–975.

Campion, M. A., Palmer, D. K., & Campion, J. E. (1997). A review of structure in the selection interview. *Personnel Psychology, 50*(3), 655–702.

Cannonier, N. (2020). Innovation in employee selection: Tracing the use of Hugo Münsterberg's test for motormen. In Saxena Arora, A., Bacouel-Jentjens, S., Sepehri, M., Arora, A. (eds),*Sustainable Innovation. International Marketing and Management Research* (pp. 81–99). Palgrave

Cook, M. (2016). *Personnel selection: Adding value through people: A changing picture.* John Wiley & Sons.

Dietvorst, B. J., Simmons, J. P., & Massey, C. (2015). Algorithm aversion: People erroneously avoid algorithms after seeing them err. *Journal of Experimental Psychology: General, 144*(1), 114.

Fast, E., Chen, B., & Bernstein, M. S. (2016, May). Empath: Understanding topic signals in large-scale text. In *Proceedings of the 2016 CHI conference on human factors in computing systems* (pp. 4647–4657).

Feldkamp, T., Langer, M., Wies, L., & König, C. J. (2023). Justice, trust, and moral judgements when personnel selection is supported by algorithms. *European Journal of Work and Organizational Psychology*, 1–16.

Goffman, E. (1959). *The presentation of self in everyday life.* Garden City.

Gonzalez, M. F., Liu, W., Shirase, L., Tomczak, D. L., Lobbe, C. E., Justenhoven, R., & Martin, N. R. (2022). Allying with AI? Reactions toward human-based, AI/ML-based, and augmented hiring processes. *Computers in Human Behavior, 130*, 107179.

Gottfredson, L. S. (2009). Logical fallacies used to dismiss the evidence on intelligence testing. In R. P. Phelps (Ed.), *Correcting fallacies about educational and psychological testing* (pp. 11–65). American Psychological Association.

Hickman, L., Bosch, N., Ng, V., Saef, R., Tay, L., & Woo, S. E. (2022). Automated video interview personality assessments: Reliability, validity, and generalizability investigations. *Journal of Applied Psychology, 107*(8), 1323.

Highhouse, S. (2002). Assessing the candidate as a whole: A historical and critical analysis of individual psychological assessment for personnel decision making. *Personnel Psychology, 55*(2), 363–396.

Klehe, U. C. (2004). Choosing how to choose: Institutional pressures affecting the adoption of personnel selection procedures. *International Journal of Selection and Assessment, 12*(4), 327–342.

König, C. J., Klehe, U. C., Berchtold, M., & Kleinmann, M. (2010). Reasons for being selective when choosing personnel selection procedures. *International Journal of Selection and Assessment, 18*(1), 17–27.

König, C. J., & Langer, M. (2022). Machine learning in personnel selection. In S. Strohmeier (Ed.), *Handbook of research on artificial intelligence in human resource management* (pp. 149–167). Edward Elgar.

Kosinski, M., Stillwell, D., & Graepel, T. (2013). Private traits and attributes are predictable from digital records of human behavior. *Proceedings of the National Academy of Sciences, 110*(15), 5802–5805.

Kutcher, E. J., & Bragger, J. D. (2004). Selection interviews of overweight job applicants: Can structure reduce the bias? *Journal of Applied Social Psychology, 34*(10), 1993–2022.

Langer, M., & König, C. J. (2018). Introducing and testing the creepiness of situation scale (CRoSS). *Frontiers in Psychology, 9*, 2220.

Langer, M., König, C. J., & Hemsing, V. (2020). Is anybody listening? The impact of automatically evaluated job interviews on impression management and applicant reactions. *Journal of Managerial Psychology, 35*(4), 271–284.

Langer, M., König, C. J., & Krause, K. (2017). Examining digital interviews for personnel selection: Applicant reactions and interviewer ratings. *International Journal of Selection and Assessment, 25*(4), 371–382.

Levashina, J., Hartwell, C. J., Morgeson, F. P., & Campion, M. A. (2014). The structured employment interview: Narrative and quantitative review of the research literature. *Personnel Psychology, 67*(1), 241–293.

Li, L., Lassiter, T., Oh, J., & Lee, M. K. (2021, July). Algorithmic hiring in practice: Recruiter and HR Professional's perspectives on AI use in hiring. In *Proceedings of the 2021 AAAI/ACM Conference on AI, Ethics, and Society* (pp. 166–176).

Liem, C. C., Langer, M., Demetriou, A., Hiemstra, A. M., Wicaksana, A. S., Born, M. P., & König, C. J. (2018). Psychology meets machine learning: Interdisciplinary perspectives on algorithmic job candidate screening. In H. Escalante et al. (Eds.), *Explainable and interpretable models in computer vision and machine learning*. The Springer Series on Challenges in Machine Learning. Springer.

Lievens, F., & De Paepe, A. (2004). An empirical investigation of interviewer-related factors that discourage the use of high structure interviews. *Journal of Organizational Behavior, 25*(1), 29–46.

Lodato, M. A., Highhouse, S., & Brooks, M. E. (2011). Predicting professional preferences for intuition-based hiring. *Journal of Managerial Psychology, 26*(5), 352–365.

Lukacik, E. R., Bourdage, J. S., & Roulin, N. (2022). Into the void: A conceptual model and research agenda for the design and use of asynchronous video interviews. *Human Resource Management Review, 32*(1), 100789.

Meehl, P. E. (1954). *Clinical versus statistical prediction: A theoretical analysis and a review of the evidence*. University of Minnesota Press.

Miles, A., & Sadler-Smith, E. (2014). "With recruitment I always feel I need to listen to my gut": The role of intuition in employee selection. *Personnel Review, 43*(4), 606–627.

MIS Trend. (2020). *Sophia 2020: L'intelligence artificielle*. MIS Trend, Lausanne.

Mori, M. (1970/2005). The uncanny valley (K. F. MacDorman, & T. Minato, Trans.). *Energy, 7*, 33–35.

Murphy, K. R. (2018). The legal context of the management of human resources. *Annual Review of Organizational Psychology and Organizational Behavior, 5*, 157–182.

Neter, E., & Ben-Shakhar, G. (1989). The predictive validity of graphological inferences: A meta-analytic approach. *Personality and Individual differences, 10*(7), 737–745.

Nolan, K. P., & Highhouse, S. (2014). Need for autonomy and resistance to standardized employee selection practices. *Human Performance, 27*(4), 328–346.

Pennebaker, J. W., Boyd, R. L., Jordan, K., & Blackburn, K. (2015). *The development and psychometric properties of LIWC2015.* University of Texas at Austin.

Renier, L. A., Mast, M. S., & Bekbergenova, A. (2021). To err is human, not algorithmic–Robust reactions to erring algorithms. *Computers in Human Behavior, 124,* 106879.

Rynes, S. L., Bartunek, J. M., & Daft, R. L. (2001). Across the great divide: Knowledge creation and transfer between practitioners and academics. *Academy of Management Journal, 44*(2), 340–355.

Sackett, P. R., & Lievens, F. (2008). Personnel selection. *Annual Review of Psychology, 59,* 419–450.

Sajjadiani, S., Sojourner, A. J., Kammeyer-Mueller, J. D., & Mykerezi, E. (2019). Using machine learning to translate applicant work history into predictors of performance and turnover. *Journal of Applied Psychology, 104*(10), 1207.

Schmidt, F. L., & Hunter, J. E. (1998). The validity and utility of selection methods in personnel psychology: Practical and theoretical implications of 85 years of research findings. *Psychological Bulletin, 124*(2), 262.

Thompson, I., Koenig, N., Mracek, D. L., & Tonidandel, S. (2023). Deep learning in employee selection: Evaluation of algorithms to automate the scoring of open-ended assessments. *Journal of Business and Psychology, 38,* 1–19.

Tippins, N. T., Oswald, F. L., & McPhail, S. M. (2021). Scientific, legal, and ethical concerns about AI-based personnel selection tools: A call to action. *Personnel Assessment and Decisions, 7*(2), 1.

Vosburgh, R. M. (2022). Closing the academic-practitioner gap: Research must answer the "SO WHAT" question. *Human Resource Management Review, 32*(1), 100633.

Wilhelmy, A., Kleinmann, M., König, C. J., Melchers, K. G., & Truxillo, D. M. (2016). How and why do interviewers try to make impressions on applicants? A qualitative study. *Journal of Applied Psychology, 101*(3), 313.

Youyou, W., Kosinski, M., & Stillwell, D. (2015). Computer-based personality judgments are more accurate than those made by humans. *Proceedings of the National Academy of Sciences, 112*(4), 1036–1040.

Zhang, L., & Yencha, C. (2022). Examining perceptions towards hiring algorithms. *Technology in Society, 68,* 101848.

15

SELF-DRIVING VEHICLES (SDVS) AND COMMON SENSE[9]

Chris Tennant

As long ago as 1959, artificial intelligence (AI) researchers sought to formally define common sense.

> a program has common sense if it automatically deduces for itself a sufficiently wide class of immediate consequences of anything it is told and what it already knows.
>
> *(McCarthy, 1959/1960)*

In later work McCarthy (1989/2022) explicitly aims to formalise common sense, which he presents as necessary for the capacity to act within the world. In the quote above, the word "sufficiently" leaves open how much or how accurate the agent has to be to operate within the world, or how successful the agent will be. The agent must be good *enough*, but whether "enough" is impossibly challenging or generously enabling remains to be seen 60 years later.

Immense effort and resources are being marshalled to apply AI to the everyday task of driving. This chapter looks first at the role of common sense in human driving before considering how self-driving vehicle (SDV) developers are trying to formalise driving's common sense rules. Next, it addresses the challenges inherent in trusting AI agents acting within social spaces. The chapter argues that AI's formalisation of common sense rules reduces and closes down the future into which it drives, whereas the human driver experiences the future as open and under-determined: Can such different agents comfortably co-exist? What are the implications for common sense if we bring AI agents into spaces shared with humans?

DOI: 10.4324/9781032626192-21

SDVs are AI agents introduced into social spaces shared with human agents. This project readily manifests Bauer's "kinds" of common sense:

- CS1: SDVs use multiple sensory inputs, but these must be synthesised into a picture of the world, the "binding problem".
- CS2: SDV companies create a stock of knowledge in the form of maps and scenario libraries.
- CS3: Selection of relevant data, what to pay attention to, is key for SDVs just as much as humans. Decisions have to be made rather than be paralysed by too much data.
- CS4&7: SDV developers make the rhetorical move of claiming that their vehicles are applying common sense.
- CS5&6: Society must face the challenge of creating a jointly understood world with AI agents on the road.
- CS8: SDV developers explicitly make the argument that human common sense should be reformed by AI's formalisation of common sense.

This discussion of the common sense of SDVs reveals an additional dimension to common sense. We think of ourselves as using common sense to navigate the world, to move forward intuitively into the future to act in the present, but we also apply common sense to our explanations of our past actions. An AI agent must master both these applications of common sense, to act successfully and then to explain its actions.

Driving a car

The task of driving

Driving a car is an example of acting within the world. It combines the capacity to navigate the physical world, not just in terms of geography but also the likely motion of physical objects in shared space, together with the capacity to negotiate the social world, not just in terms of the established norms of the road but also the likely behaviour of social actors in shared space. Survey research shows that most people[1] consider common sense to be an important component of driving. But people also assume that machines are not capable of such common sense, as shown by the data from a series of surveys[2] in Figure 15.1.

Our surveys also asked questions about typical social interactions on the road – e.g., with cyclists, at pedestrian crossings, or having to pass an obstacle by crossing into the wrong lane. Respondents expect drivers – whether human or AI systems – to follow the rules, but to follow them flexibly, or in other words, to have the common sense to know which rule applies and which rule takes precedence over other rules in any given situation. Further, they believe that in ambiguous situations, it is often necessary for the interactants to communicate (by eye contact or gestures) to resolve the ambiguity.

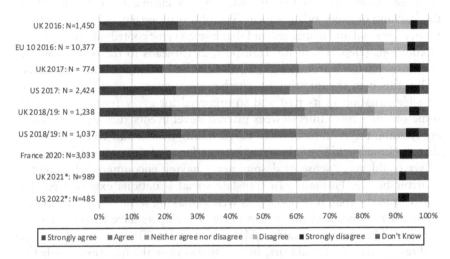

FIGURE 15.1 "Machines don't have the common sense to interact with human drivers", or "SDVs would be limited...because they lack common sense" (see endnote 3 for question wording).

To act in the driving world demands the capacity to follow common-sense driving rules (Prakken, 2017), and developers of AI to be used in SDVs have defined this as one of their challenges (e.g. Mobileye, 2018). Developers are also responding to demands that the decisions taken by their AI systems be explainable. Some translate this into a demand to demonstrate that their systems are "safe enough". Common sense human decision-making can be hard to interrogate, but we often give the benefit of the doubt to a fellow human being because their after-the-fact explanations "make sense" – we can share the actor's perspective. This is what makes common sense common. But are public doubts that AI can master common sense justified? Or do AI developers and public road users have different ideas of what constitutes common sense?

AI learning to drive

There have been different approaches to getting an AI system to learn to drive. We have previously mapped these approaches in a paper based upon over 50 expert interviews (Tennant & Stilgoe, 2021): in one approach, "brute force" machine learning exposes the AI system to enough data so that it can teach itself to drive. It would not be possible to know why the system took a particular decision when driving, because the contingencies that led to what it had learned would not be fully mapped. The hope is to copy how humans learn to drive: grasp some initial rules and then build through practice and experience.

As AI developers are keen to point out, every vehicle in a fleet can benefit from the learning of every other vehicle. The observation that human drivers get tired, emotional and distracted and that human error contributes to over 90% of collisions (Department for Transport, 2015) leads to the conclusion that once a system has learnt enough, it will perform better than a human driver.

But this begs the question of whether a system can be exposed to every possible situation in its past and so prepared for every future eventuality: some of our expert interviewees offered novel events such as skateboarders crossing the road or unusual cargo falling from a van when suggesting that machine learning might struggle to understand situations that a human driver could make sense of despite never having encountered the event as a driver before. Humans can translate social situations experienced elsewhere onto the road if necessary, as well as making sense of unusual animal or weather phenomena that might occur. Developers have tried to generate extensive libraries of scenarios (McDermid et al., 2019) on which to train and test systems in simulators, but these too raise the question of whether such a library could be sufficiently comprehensive.

Another approach, which we referred to as "solving the world one place at a time", recognises the scale of the task and seeks to map the world gradually, proving itself competent in defined or "geo-fenced" areas. The engineering standards organisation SAE International (2021) requires any SDV not capable of operating anywhere and in all conditions (i.e., every SDV at the moment) to have a defined Operational Design Domain ("ODD"). Confining AI systems to ODDs, restricted geographically and otherwise,[3] is the current model with deployments such as those by Waymo in Chandler, Arizona or GM Cruise and others in San Francisco.

Reducing the complexity of the driving task

Common sense addresses the world as an open emergent system. Looking forward, you cannot be sure what you are going to do, but looking back, a human actor can usually explain their decisions based on common sense principles – shared assumptions about what a reasonable person should do in response to unfolding circumstances. In doing so, they close the past environment, limiting their explanations to what hindsight deems the relevant elements. As AI researchers did before them, SDV developers are trying to summarise the principles of common sense, at least for the task of driving. In doing so, they take some of the "common sense principles" that a human actor might refer to when explaining their *past* actions and use these to guide the decision-making of AI systems driving into the emergent *future*. In this chapter, I refer to Intel Mobileye's programme to formalise common sense, "Responsibility-Sensitive Safety" (RSS), but other developers have proposed similar schemes such as Nvidia's Safety Force Field (Nistér et al., 2019) and Aptiv's Rulebooks (Aptiv, 2019).

Currently, the rules of the road are both written and unwritten. We use common sense to negotiate the right of way when it might be ambiguous. RSS hopes to reduce common-sense driving to a collection of "rules of thumb" or heuristics, such as "always maintain a sufficient distance from the vehicle ahead of you". The RSS programme also expresses these rules as mathematical formulae: each rule is encapsulated by a set of probabilistic vectors for the likely movement of each "relevant" actor in the environment. The intention is to apply this approach throughout the whole SDV field, and members of the RSS team were part of the working group tasked with developing IEEE P2846 (Standard for Assumptions in Safety-Related Models in Automated Driving Systems). The thinking behind this is set out in Wishart et al. (2020). RSS suggests that only a handful of such rules of thumb would capture almost all scenarios, doing away with the need for a library of thousands of scenarios. The idea is that society will set the parameters to be applied within this modelling, defining the tolerances so that the driving system can be useful and not overcautious. The assumptions underlying this parameter setting will be subjective – this creates an impression of humanistic sensitivity, whereby different communities have different risk appetites, following the logic of some villages having slower speed limits than others, or driving cultures being different in different countries. This is true to the spirit of common sense: different communities share a different "common" ideal of what is a reasonable speed. For electric car company Tesla, parameters are opportunities for product differentiation: vehicle owners can jiggle their own parameters to change the driving style of the vehicle, including options such as Insane Mode and Drag Strip Mode.

What is less clear is how RSS resolves conflicts between the rules of thumb – for example if the mathematical modelling of the vectors for the pedestrian stepping off the pavement conflicts with modelling how to avoid the oncoming vehicle. Which is the most "relevant actor" in the current context? If your model predicts that a pedestrian with a gaze direction of x° will/will not step into the road, exactly what tolerances should you impose in different sets of circumstances? Human drivers in these situations selectively ignore much of what is going on around them. Mobileye's own video presentation of just such a scenario notes that "other vehicles [are] going around us because they are getting 'annoyed' with the 'ego' vehicle (i.e., the Mobileye vehicle) slowing down for pedestrians who might cross the road" (Weast & Mobileye, 2019 at 14:12).

For the moment, RSS suggests that it will apply a (quasi-meta) rule of thumb "to avoid the worst-case scenario". Yet it is difficult to see how such a system can escape the temptation to relax or deactivate the parameters in order not to be hemmed in by the rules. This is exactly what Uber had done with their self-driving vehicle involved in a fatal collision with a pedestrian in Tempe, Arizona (National Transportation Safety Board, 2018). An alternative understanding of common sense illustrates how human beings resolve uncertainties as they move forward into the emergent world: this for common sense is the ability to integrate diverse sensory inputs into an understanding of the whole, and to apply attention to the most relevant features of the situation, and to ignore the rules that are not relevant at each moment.

Responsibility for past actions

The first paper setting out the RSS programme emphasised its role in explaining the decision-making behind the past actions of the system (Shalev-Shwartz et al., 2017):

> We develop a formal concept of "accident responsibility", which, we argue, captures the common sense behind human judgement of "who was driving safely and who was responsible for the accident". The premise of RSS is that while self-driving cars might be involved in accidents, they will never cause an accident.
>
> *(p. 5)*

The original philosophy of the system was to enable the SDV to be both useful (not so cautious as to be worthless) and blameless. RSS was designed to address both calls for retrospective explainability but also the commercial need to manage potential liabilities. But the parameters are also central to how the system reduces the complexity of the surrounding emergent world, applying its own "common sense" to render it navigable. Nevertheless, as Mobileye themselves acknowledge, the public are uncomfortable with trusting the common sense of machines (Weast & Mobileye, 2019 at 18:20).

Trusting AI's common sense

Do we feel comfortable trusting AI to act in the world?

Take a human activity far from common sense or common experience: Suchman and Weber's (2016) analysis of autonomous weapons systems (AWSs) offers a jumping-off point from which to contrast how artificial and human intelligence address the world. Suchman and Weber highlight the contradiction between the promise of AWSs, that they are genuinely *autonomous* but also that they are under human control: that any life and death decisions made can be shown to have been what humans would want those decisions to be. This repeats the dual objectives of the RSS programme for SDVs, to be able to navigate the future and also explain responsibility for the past.

Those explanations need to be compatible with human decision-making, suggesting we are not yet ready to trust AI systems in replacing us, at least when the decision-making has very visible consequences that demand scrutiny. These worries about AI's capacity to make life and death decisions that would match human intuition as to the correct course of action are repeated in the moral machine experiments for SDVs (Awad et al., 2018). Yet we are holding AI systems to a different standard in asking their decision-making to be fully interpretable, i.e., readily understood without having to engage in complex deconstructions of the decision-making processes expressed in mathematical formulae. Just as human drivers can be required to provide a running commentary upon the road situation and their responses to it in advanced driving tests, so too it has been suggested that autonomous driving systems could be required to provide commentaries to demonstrate inter-pretability and build trust in the system (Law Commission & Scottish Law Commission, 2022 para. 2.107).

Although we expect human agents to be able to account for their actions, we also know well that their explanations will be extremely partial accounts and some of the reasoning may be opaque or uninterpretable. We may curse other road users as outgroup members – boyracers, cyclists, or simply idi-ots, but much of the time we place a lot of faith in the idea that as a fellow human, the agent's reasoning will be similar to our own, applying "common sense" and constrained by membership of the same community. Much of our survey data suggest that AI agents are not yet a trusted members of our community (Tennant et al., 2022a, 2022b).

Rationality and common sense

Building on Aristotelian synthesis of sensory stimuli (Bauer's CS1), common sense encompasses categorising, synthesising and selecting the relevant fea-tures of the environment (informed by the "common stock" of knowledge, Bauer's CS2) to enable the actor to act. But if we develop such a rationality to provide after-the-fact explanations, then applying it to driving feels worry-ingly like driving while looking into the rear-view mirror; or at least through a lens that closes down the uncertainties of the world the system is navigat-ing. For Suchman and Weber (2016, p. 92), "'the world' is a very general gloss for an open horizon of potentially relevant circumstances". Moving forward into the open horizon, Suchman and Weber suggest that the agent is creating the future at the moment when choices are made as to what should be attended to and what ignored and the future is converted into the present and then the past.

Human decision-making is fallible; indeed, it is that fallibility that jus-tifies the claims that AI systems might do a better job. Since Herb Simon (1955)[4] "bounded" the rationality of human actors, the behavioural econo-mists have spent nearly 70 years identifying how imperfect human decision-making is based upon a backward-looking utilitarian calculus to compare actual outcomes against supposed optimal outcomes (e.g., Kahneman et al., 1982). Although in later work, Kahneman has tried to undo the con-sequences of what amounts to an assault on common sense (Kahneman,

2011), research revealing the "irrationality" of human thinking provides the foundation for the presumption that machine thinking must be preferable.

"Bounding" is necessary to close the open horizon, eliminating the irrelevant by applying Aristotelian common sense and/or to apply the common sense knowledge of the community to interpret a complex world. But this marks the inflexion between the future into which we look forward constantly scanning the horizon for last-second relevant circumstances, and the past where actions are to be accounted for. Unsatisfactory past outcomes are then described as irrational, the result of human prejudice, or other misapplications of simplifying decision rules (heuristics)[5].

Common sense furnishes us with the capacity to navigate the particular, the everyday and the social. Science ousted common sense explanations of the natural world around us by transcending the particular and claiming universality. Formalising common sense in the social world universalises its "basic principles" but can only do this by rendering those encountered into data. It is important to anticipate how AI agents will see us when we share the social world with them so that it is no longer exclusively "our" world.

Bringing AI rules into the human world

Should we change the rules of the road to accommodate SDVs?

As outlined, the RSS programme asserts that it will demonstrate that vehicles following RSS rules cannot cause a collision and cannot have caused a past collision. As we have shown elsewhere (Tennant et al., 2021), the suggestion then is that if these rules are safer, human-driven vehicles should follow the same rules. "If all road users were to implement RSS there should never be any accidents" (Mobileye, 2023 at 18.23). By formalising common sense, RSS makes the unwritten rules explicit, and the presumption is that making them explicit must be better since this is supposed to eliminate the ambiguities inherent in social interaction. As Mobileye makes clear, the programme runs from "From Humans to AVs and Back" (Dagan, 2019): take human common sense, formalise it and then reconfigure the social world to follow the formalised rules. The safety argument continues the presumption that society would be better off replacing fallible human drivers: but the commercial opportunities this offers need to be recognised too. First, if all vehicles follow RSS rules, then that makes the world more easily navigable for SDVs with eventual efficiency gains. Second, human-driven vehicles can be equipped with advanced driver assistance systems (ADAS) incorporating RSS technologies. Since achieving fully self-driving cars capable of going everywhere seems likely to take much longer than some originally imagined (*The Economist*, 2019), ADAS provides a revenue stream for SDV technology companies to bridge this time period.

Bringing AI rules into the human world confronts us with the idea that because society cannot sort out its own problems – we're not willing to enforce good driving standards, reduce speed limits or make infrastructure investments that could reduce road casualties – we're going to introduce AI agents to impose good driving standards upon human drivers, in effect to domesticate human drivers to clean up the ODD for the SDVs. If, as we have argued, common sense is rooted in the shared values and knowledge of the community, then this process is allowing AI agents membership of the community and encouraging the adoption by the community of the AI's values and knowledge to make a new common sense. Provocatively, we could characterise the AI developers as a colonial power introducing a new (civilising) system of rules to a previously disorderly society (this argument is elaborated in Tennant et al., 2021). This provocation is useful: it may be that the road environment could be improved by these technologies, but society needs to decide for itself who should have the power to set the rules. To make an informed decision society needs to be aware that it might be ceding that power.

Resisting the assault on common sense

We may have accepted many of science's claims to supersede common sense explanations of the natural world, but we hesitate to allow AI to supersede common sense descriptions of the social world, let alone common sense decision-making in that world. With good reason, Eubanks (2018) provides numerous examples where the automation of insurance claims checking, or of government benefit administration, creates perverse outcomes that defy our (common) sense of fairness.

In our 2021 survey, we also asked what people felt to be the proper domains for AI systems to operate[6]. First, we asked how comfortable respondents would be with robots carrying out a variety of tasks (results below from the UK survey, $N = 997$):

These responses suggest there is a boundary between more routine robot activities and situations where the robot might be considered to have life and death power over oneself. We also asked a similar question about the use of artificially intelligent systems.

Whereas robots "helping" or working in factories seem (relatively) acceptable, there seems to be a more general reluctance to allowing robots or AI systems to be involved in social decision-making.

These survey responses show that many are not ready for AI[7] to be a member of the community that authors our common sense (Figures 15.2 and 15.3). GH Mead (1967) describes how we learn that we exist when we see ourselves recognised in the eyes of others. We are not yet comfortable with the image the AI "other" has of us, as data for rational calculation, when we share social space with this new "other".

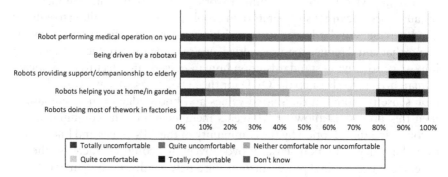

FIGURE 15.2   How uncomfortable/comfortable would you be with [robot...].

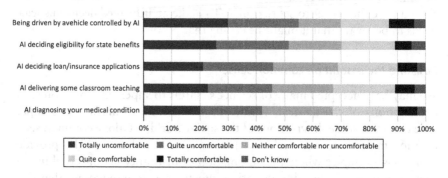

FIGURE 15.3   How uncomfortable/comfortable would you be with [AI...].

Can human and AI agents share the same common sense?

The introduction laid out how the SDV project manifests Bauer's "kinds" of common sense. In this conclusion, I highlight two elements, one absent from and one present in Bauer's schema. The absent element is the dual role of common sense as our means of intuitively navigating the future to act in the present *and* the foundation for our explanations of our actions in the past. We choose to call both these human tasks of sense-making "common sense", but they appear to be distinct challenges for AI agents like SDVs. This brings to the fore a key question raised within Bauer's schema: Should we emphasise the similarities or the differences between AI and human agents? Should they be bound into a communal joint-intentionality (Bauer's CS5), or should they co-exist in parallel? Our survey respondents' first instinct is that they should be kept separate and distinct.[8] Whether, or how long, people will be able to, or want to continue to, defend "human" common sense from colonisation by AI agents remains to be seen.

Notes

1. In the UK in 2021, 77% agreed and 6% disagreed ($N = 4,860$) with the statement "Drivers sometimes have to use common sense instead of just following the rules of the Highway code" (Tennant, Stares, Vucevic, & Stilgoe, 2022a): 79% agreed, 6% disagreeing ($N = 1,890$), to an equivalent statement in the US (Tennant, Stares, Vucevic, & Stilgoe, 2022b).
2. Surveys were funded by a mixture of internal and external sources. External funding sources for the surveys were 2016 Goodyear Tire and Rubber Company. 2021/22 Research Councils UK: Economic and Social Research Council, grant for Driverless Futures (ES/S001832/1). Note that the surveys from 2016 to 2020 used the statement "Machines don't have the common sense to interact with human drivers" while the two subsequent surveys used "SDVs would be limited in how well they drive because they lack the common sense of human drivers".
3. The ODD defines any conditions for permitted operation and might include considerations such as weather, day/night, traffic density and speed, etc.
4. Simon uses the term "approximate rationality" in this original paper.
5. What to consider relevant, and which decision rules to apply, is culturally mediated – hence the role of the stock of shared knowledge. Fiske's (2004) relational models theory provides a parallel account of this process.
6. Results shown are for the UK. Questions were shown to a subsample of the main survey, $N = 997$. Results for the US, $N = 477$, were comparable. See the project reports already referenced.
7. Respondents seem less concerned about the robot applications, although discomfort with the SDV is similar, however, it is described. US results were similar.
8. The responses already mentioned imply this position: furthermore, 86% of UK respondents (79% in the US) agree that "it must be clear when a vehicle is driving itself". SDVs are different from us, and people want them to be identifiable.
9. This paper is based upon research carried out in conjunction with a number of different collaborators, in particular Dr Sally Stares, Professor Jack Stilgoe, Sandra Vucevic and co-investigators from the Driverless Futures project described herein.

Bibliography

Aptiv. (2019). Structured AI and rulebooks. https://www.aptiv.com/insights/article/structured-ai-and-rulebooksAwad, E., Dsouza, S., Kim, R., Schulz, J., Henrich, J., Shariff, A., … Rahwan, I. (2018). The moral machine experiment. *Nature*, 563(7729), 59–64. http://doi.org/10.1038/s41586-018-0637-6

Dagan, E. (2019). Intel editorial: Digitizing the social contract for safer roads: How designing an AV safety model enabled better safety solutions for human drivers. https://www.intc.com/news-events/press-releases/detail/77/intel-editorial-digitizing-the-social-contract-for-safer

Department for Transport. (2015). *The pathway to driverless Cars: A detailed review of regulations for automated vehicle technologies*. https://www.gov.uk/government/publications/driverless-cars-in-the-uk-a-regulatory-review

Eubanks, V. (2018). *Automating inequality: How high-tech tools profile, police, and punish the poor*. St. Martin's Press.

Fiske, A. P. (2004). Relational models theory 2.0. In N. Haslam (Ed.), *Relational models theory: A contemporary overview* (pp. 3–26). Lawrence Erlbaum Associates.

Kahneman, D. (2011). *Thinking, fast and slow*. Allen Lane.

Kahneman, D., Slovic, P., & Tversky, A. (1982). *Judgement under uncertainty: Heuristics and biases*. Cambridge University Press.

Law Commission, & Scottish Law Commission. (2022). *Automated vehicles: Joint report*. https://s3-eu-west-2.amazonaws.com/lawcom-prod-storage-11jsxou24uy7q/uploads/2022/01/Automated-vehicles-joint-report-cvr-03-02–22.pdf

McCarthy, J. (1959/1960). *Programs with common sense*. RLE and MIT Computation Center.

McCarthy, J. (1989/2022). Artificial intelligence, logic, and formalising common sense. In S. Carta (Ed.), *Machine learning and the city* (pp. 69–90).

McDermid, J., Koopman, P., Hierons, R., Khastgir, S., Clark, J. A., Fisher, M., … Ramamoorthy, S. (2019). *Certification of highly automated vehicles for use on public roads*. Paper presented at the ESV 26th Conference, Eindhoven, Netherlands.

Mead, G. H. (1967). *Works of George Herbert Mead, volume 1. Mind, self, & society from the standpoint of a social behaviorist*. The University of Chicago Press, Ltd.

Mobileye. (2018). RSS: Safety assurance for automated vehicles. Retrieved June 17, 2020 from https://www.youtube.com/watch?v=EceAB6TUYzo

Mobileye. (2023). Mobileye's responsibility-sensitive safety mathematical model explained. Retrieved March 12, 2020 from https://www.youtube.com/watch?v=pn88uJbkQqc

National Transportation Safety Board. (2018). *Highway accident report: Collision between vehicle controlled by developmental automated driving system and pedestrian*, Tempe, Arizona. https://www.ntsb.gov/investigations/AccidentReports/Reports/HAR1903.pdf

Nistér, D., Lee, H.-L., Ng, J., & Wang, Y. (2019). *An introduction to the safety force field*. https://www.nvidia.com/content/dam/en-zz/Solutions/self-driving-cars/safety-force-field/an-introduction-to-the-safety-force-field-v2.pdf

Prakken, H. (2017). On the problem of making autonomous vehicles conform to traffic law. *Artificial Intelligence and Law*, 25(3), 341–363. http://doi.org/10.1007/s10506-017-9210-0

SAE International. (2021). Surface vehicle recommended practice: Taxonomy and definitions for terms related to driving automation systems for on-road motor vehicles.

Shalev-Shwartz, S., Shammah, S., & Shashua, A. (2017). On a formal model of safe and scalable self-driving cars. arXiv.org, 1708.06374.

Simon, H. (1955). A behavioral model of rational choice. *The Quarterly Journal of Economics*, 69(1), 99–118.

Suchman, L., & Weber, J. (2016). Human–machine autonomies. In N. Bhuta, S. Beck, R. Geiß, H.-Y. Liu, & C. Kreß (Eds.), *Autonomous weapons systems: Law, ethics, policy* (pp. 75–102). Cambridge University Press.

Tennant, C., Neels, C., Parkhurst, G., Jones, P., Mirza, S., & Stilgoe, J. (2021). Code, culture, and concrete: Self-driving vehicles and the rules of the road. *Frontiers in Sustainable Cities*, 3(122). http://doi.org/10.3389/frsc.2021.710478

Tennant, C., Stares, S., Vucevic, S., & Stilgoe, J. (2022a). *Driverless futures? A survey of UK public attitudes*. https://driverless-futures.com/2022/05/09/survey-reports/

Tennant, C., Stares, S., Vucevic, S., & Stilgoe, J. (2022b). *Driverless futures? A survey of US public attitudes*. https://driverless-futures.com/2022/05/09/survey-reports/

Tennant, C., & Stilgoe, J. (2021). The attachments of 'autonomous' vehicles. *Social Studies of Science*. http://doi.org/10.1177/03063127211038752

The Economist. (2019). Driverless cars are stuck in a jam. https://www.economist .com/leaders/2019/10/10/driverless-cars-are-stuck-in-a-jam

Weast, J., & Mobileye. (2019). Responsibility-sensitive safety explained by Jack Weast of Mobileye. https://www.youtube.com/watch?v=HYMnIkqYEIM

Wishart, J., Como, S., Elli, M., Russo, B., Weast, J., Altekar, N., ... Chen, Y. (2020). Driving safety performance assessment metrics for ADS-equipped vehicles. *SAE International Journal Advances & Current Practices in Mobility*, 2(5), 2881–2899.

PART 5

Conclusion

16

AI GOES TO THE MOVIES

Fast, intermediate and slow common sense

Bernard Schiele and Martin W. Bauer

The issue of common sense remains unresolved and puzzling. And so is the relation with AI, for this very reason. Notwithstanding ongoing attempts, no consensus exists as its many and often contradictory definitions make plain (Bauer, Chapter 1 this volume). Thus, what are AI researchers and developers attempting to model if they seek to model common sense? According to Daniel Andler (2023), "what is sorely lacking is precisely what is the most human, viz. an immediate understanding of the way things work in the largest sense" (p. 227). Andler's position is pragmatic to an extent, since he understands common sense as the capacity to mobilise abilities and know-hows to solve the daily problems with which we are all faced, which is a position similar to that taken by Brachman & Levesque (Chapter 3 this volume).

Serge Moscovici's (1961) approach differs. Although seemingly dated, his is probably the most useful to frame common sense empirically and in its intersubjective dimension. He attempted to understand at the turn of the 1960s how a discourse developed in a micro-setting, Freudian psychoanalysis, spread and was socialised in the process, putting into circulation a specific lexicon which was gradually absorbed into ordinary language, anchoring and enriching it with older ideas and concepts which over time transformed how people perceive, describe and interpret the behaviours and experiences of others as well as their own. If the language of psychoanalysis has largely lapsed from daily life and maybe been replaced by computer metaphors (Turkle, 1984), Moscovici's methodology, which underpins the research field of social representations (Bauer & Gaskell, 2009), would reveal another lexicon permeating ordinary language today. If common sense is the taken for granted, no questions-asked background of pre-reflective or even

DOI: 10.4324/9781032626192-23

subconscious resources of everyday life, the theory of social representation is one of those attempts to reflect this, make this visible and thus amenable to change.

Moscovici himself was aware of the constant movement of reconfiguration spurred by the emergence and spread of new ideas. And in the 1976 [2008] re-edition of his magnum opus, he specifically stated:

> [u]ntil recently, the vocabulary and notions we needed to describe and explain ordinary experience, to predict events and behaviour and to give them a meaning derived from a language and a wisdom that regional or professional communities had accumulated over a long period. [...] Over the last few decades, this trend has been reversed. The sciences discover and describe most of the objects, concepts, analogies and logical form we use to face up to our economic, political of intellectual tasks.

A caveat: however dominant the discourse of science and technology may be in contemporary society, it is not the only one in circulation (Schiele & Bauer, 2023), nor the only one to shape the evolution of common sense, though science has become the main competitor of common sense.

The chronology of common sense

Although centred on the capacity of common sense to solve problems, i.e., on its actualisation in an infinity of concrete situations simultaneously mobilising specific knowledges and know-hows, Andler's position is not that removed from Moscovici's since both recognise that common sense provides tools to accomplish these tasks. What differentiates them is the historical dimension central to Moscovici: common sense constantly evolves and is indissociable from the ideas and beliefs of the moment. Thus, to go back to the example of science, everyone at a specific time learns how "to handle scientific knowledge outside its context, and become[s] imbued with the intellectual style and content it represents" (Moscovici, 1976 [2008], pp. xxvii–xxviii). In other words, on a first level, common sense is a repertory of competencies, abilities and tools to execute potential tasks, mobilised in specific circumstances, some of which have already been modelled in AI. However, common sense is also a spontaneous understanding on an individual level of the inner workings of the world, of human motives and behaviours, and of common facts at a given time (Gunning, 2018). In this spirit, common sense is simultaneously a repository of competencies and a zeitgeist.

On a more general level, common sense can be defined as a coherent dynamic symbolic apparatus, coherent because it presents regularities, dynamic because these regularities adapt themselves under the influence of various external factors. Transposing the concept of punctuated equilibria first proposed by Eldredge and Gould (1972) in palaeontology, we could say that this symbolic apparatus presents a succession of shorter or longer phases of stability, during which general characteristics are preserved, followed by transition periods with unequal rhythms, during which these characteristics are transformed.

This raises the issue of the nature of the transformations of common sense: Is this apparatus transforming as a whole, a new configuration being substituted for the preceding one, or do successive partial transformations within society add up to a completely new configuration? According to Braudel (1987), three types of changes take place in parallel but with different rhythms: short-term changes; slower changes over a period of 30–50 years; and longer-term changes over a period of centuries, of which people can only become aware once they have taken place (p. 11). This "plurality of social time" (p. 10) is thus characterised by three distinct processes he called: "*longue durée*, conjunctural [time], and event [time]" (p. 33). Elias (2005), while studying social formations, also concluded that different temporalities presided over the rhythms of their transformations, settling on three.

And when Moscovici and Vignaux (1994) introduced the concept of "thêmata" in the study of social representations, i.e., "the primary notion in the generation of families of representations" (p. 43), Abric (1994) distinguished the central node of representations from peripheric elements, "less stable and more adaptable than central ones" (p. 75), leading him to also speak of the varying rhythms of evolution. They concluded that the "thêmata" was the deepest node of sense, the one which evolves the slowest, within a central node which evolves faster, itself surrounded by superficial levels of meaning, specific to narrow groups, if not to individuals, quickly fluctuating with the rapid transformations of the social conjuncture. Why should common sense be any different? Why should it not be characterised by a chronology based on duration and rhythm (Elias, 2005).

In this spirit, to further clarify the definition of common sense in the light of social representations theory, we would say that this symbolic apparatus is composed of at least three elements, each with its specific rhythm of evolution. Thus, common sense bears witness to a historicity far from homogeneous, as its constituting elements are neither of the same nature nor evenly distributed (see Figure 16.1).

1. Surface-level event cycles and hyperbole. The capacity to immediately grasp "how things work" (Andler, 2023, p. 227) and mobilise abilities and know-hows to solve problems rests upon the constant adaptation of individuals to the continuous changes taking place in their personal or professional environment happening in the "short term". This level is comprised of the abilities of the moment, constantly updated or

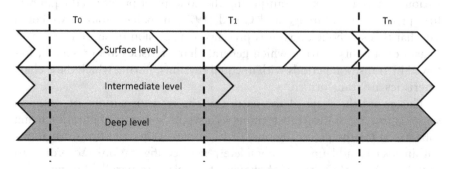

FIGURE 16.1 The three levels of common sense as differences in the rate of change. The first, fast moving, provokes frequent adjustments; the second, slower, acting upon structures, only provokes one to two adjustments during a lifetime; the third, very slow, long precedes and long continues after individual lifetimes. These three levels are not impermeable: encased in one another, they are in constant interaction. T0, T1 and T*n* show the number of changes taking place between intervals of time, e.g., a human lifetime.

renewed, that must be mastered in order to come up with "solutions to such problems as are relevant for 'everyone'" in the here and now (see Luckmann, 1987, p. 189). In a society boosted by the acceleration of processes (Rosa, 2010), the period of validity of abilities is counted in years. Otherwise, how to justify the pressing pressure to engage in life-long learning to avoid disorientation and loss of resonance?

2. Intermediate-level conjunctures of issues and attitudes. The changes affecting these more interiorised levels of sense are slower. This intermediate level bridges the levels of sense of the "short term" and of the "long term". It is difficult to assess its rhythm of evolution. Yet, drawing upon the above-quoted works, we can suggest that the adjustment, if not transformation, of the representations and norms regulating the behaviour of individuals (Chazel, 1999) takes place several times during their lifetimes. The principles underlying the attitude to adopt and the action to carry out, as well as the codes regulating their mores, deontology, course of action, etc., will adjust themselves in specific circumstances. This slower yet deeper process will gradually affect whole swathes of society. In other words, paraphrasing Boltanski and Thévenot (1991), a new superior common principle will, in time, unify a greater number of individuals from a given society. The main obstacle of designing an AI imbued with common sense is that many of the representations and norms constituting common sense do not translate into easily identifiable actions or behaviours.

3. Deep-level mentalities and their thêmata. Changes here take place in the *long term*, very slowly. The superior common principle is shared by several societies. As an example, the concept of the nuclear family and its images gradually emerged between the 4th century and the Middle Ages (Goody, 2012) in opposition to the prevailing one during antiquity, and which dominated until very recently, was for a long time one of the pillars of common sense: it was self-evidence of a natural and immutable order. The model of the bourgeois family which became dominant in the 18th century grafted itself upon this basis, with changes having taken place only at the intermediate level. This dominant value system became a referent and individuals subscribed to it because of their deep-seated convictions (Ansart, 1999). In short, this deep level is the most difficult to model.

To conclude this section, let us paraphrase Elias (1985): common sense can be described as a "river with three currents of evolution of varying speed" (p. xlix). The first, fast events and hyperbole, provokes frequent adjustments over the course of a lifetime, a constant dynamic of adaptations and renewal of the necessary abilities and know-hows to accomplish all the daily tasks. The second level of issues, conjunctures and attitudes, slower, acting upon deeper structures, only provokes one to two adjustments during a lifetime. Generation conflicts are the sign that such a change is underway, provoking reciprocal adjustments. The third level of mentalities, very slow, long precedes and long continues after individual lifetimes, appearing as an immutable bedrock of values, beliefs and convictions, upon which all the symbolic apparatus of common sense stands, with any transgression being judged unnatural. These three levels are not impermeable: encased in one another, they are in constant interaction.

This is why the challenges facing AI are far from being overcome, as, notwithstanding the fact that reasonings underpinning common sense still escape us, the schemes upon which they are exercised are neither fixed nor synchronous. With Andler (2023), we conclude that "the issue of common sense reasoning is intractable as such: it is only a label masking an unfathomable number of singular problems", with the solution to any "shedding no light on the others", nor suggesting "a general solution" (p. 234). In the same vein, Gunning (2018) argues that "[r]ecent advances in machine learning have resulted in new AI capabilities, but in all of these applications, machine reasoning is narrow and highly specialised". We will add that the modelled solutions only dealt with the surface level – the level which is renewed the fastest.

An issue remains pending, and it is probably the most salient: What underpins this so-called "immediate understanding of the way things work"? According to a number of authors, this "immediate understanding" is action-orientated and their reasoning follows from this premise. Luckmann (1987), for example, holds common sense "to be a structured and (subjectively) coherent set of orientations in reality whose main function is to guide action" (p. 180), which in that function is increasingly replaced by scientific knowledge, which has become a marker of the modernisation of society. Centred on the utility of common sense, these authors only consider one dimension: a body of knowledges (Moscovici & Hewstone, 1985). However, to our mind, these knowledges, as potential abilities to be called upon depending on circumstances, are largely on the "surface level". In other words, by restricting themselves solely to this level, they only identify as an explanation a principle of action. Without negating the fact that common sense allows us to act, this functionalist approach remains reductive. In the following paragraphs, we shall explore another possibility.

Common sense of common sense or self-referential common sense

To explore this possibility, let us turn to science fiction films, because they largely borrow from the discourses on sciences and technologies and thus stimulate the construction of an imaginary which orients common sense, as the numerous references to this universe within contemporary culture bear witness to.

We shall limit ourselves to two dimensions of the socialisation of sciences and technologies in science fiction films: (1) how films inflect the issues of the day and (2) the representations of the symbolic efficiency of common sense vis-à-vis temporality. We will discuss three blockbuster films: *The Terminator* directed by James Cameron (1984), *Back to the Future* (1985) and *Back to the Future III* (1990), both directed by Robert Zemeckis.[1] These films put into relation a past – which may be the present – of a future when technology makes time travel possible. In other words, their plots involve the ability of characters to travel back and forth in time, and it is the way how the plot deals with their behaviours in different time periods which highlights how time is constructed and socialised by science fiction.

And, with few exceptions, the protagonists are perfectly at ease in all time periods: they possess all the required abilities to overcome all the challenges they encounter. "The Terminator", for example, in his relentless pursuit of "Sarah Connor" successively drives a car, a motorcycle and a huge fuel truck, each time without any hint of hesitation, as though the operation of past and future vehicles is identical. Spectators barely notice, if at all, this inconsistency. And, if pointed out, many would respond that this is how James Cameron intended it, and that otherwise, the movie would lack rhythm and fail to engage audiences, while a bumbling Terminator would not be "The Terminator".

But this is precisely the issue: the spectator sees a character on screen who acts as though endowed with an instinctive and innate knowledge, an atemporal common sense. In other words, for both spectators and characters, the past and present are undifferentiated. Yet, anyone who has visited a science and technology museum knows how the technologies of the past are opaque to modern observers. In the spirit of Bachelard (2002), we could say that in a museum there is nothing to see, but everything to understand. This is not the case for the "The Terminator" for whom seeing is knowing, and especially knowing what to do. And the spectator is expected to subscribe to this ahistorical vision of a perpetual present. In contrast, historians, regardless of speciality, constantly worry about projecting their own zeitgeist unto the past (cf. Boyer, 2015, Elias, 2005; Hooper-Greenhill, 1992. pp. 13–38) in their attempt to rediscover past uses and know-hows. This is why the ease with which our time traveller moves back and forth is telling.

Of course, differences, largely superficial, are shown to signify that time travel has effectively taken place, and especially to signify it to the spectator. The stress shifts to the interactions between characters. As a reminder, a film is a social apparatus: it constructs plays of characters as representations of social situations subject to rules and norms to which the spectator reacts: he receives and assimilates them. Thus, he structures his "consciousness and knowledges" without necessarily being "conscious" of the fact (Wolf, 2001, p. 279, *passim*).

As an example, in *Back to the Future*, the director shows a "Marty McFly" clearly surprised by his inability to unscrew the cap of his 1955 soda; his future father ("George McFly", played by Crispin Glover), having noticed this lack of common sense, yet apparently unfazed – i.e., without verbally questioning it, mechanically grasps the bottle and opens it with the vending machine bottle opener. The director clearly shows to the spectator first, with a close-up, "Marty"'s attempt to unscrew the bottle, and then, "George" using the vending machine bottle opener. It is by contrasting these two *modi operandi* of common sense – the characters', and the spectator's – that the director showcased the temporal distance between these two common senses. A distance that the spectator easily decodes since unscrewing bottles is commonplace today. In other words, the spectator was confronted with his own common sense, i.e., what is taken for granted in his own present, to interpret a scene taking place in the past.

Who has never found himself or herself in front of an old technical appliance, or a new one for that matter, and unable to operate it? However, "Marty McFly" concludes that his inability in the 1950s, far from reflecting on him, is rather a reflection upon a past awaiting the progress the future will bring. It is not clearer than when he transforms a kick scooter into a skateboard by ripping the handle and bar. Or, when, at the end of the film, taken aback by the silence after channelling the yet to be written history of rock "n" roll in front of dumbstruck dancers plugging their ears at the prom, he shot back: "I guess you guys aren't ready for that yet. But your kids are gonna love it" (Moviepedia, 2023a). Or, as a final example, this one in *Back to the Future III*: "Doc", heartbroken by his breakup with "Clara Clayton" (played by Mary Steenburgen), decided to drown his sorrows in whisky. In the saloon, shot glass in hand, he describes the future to patrons mocking him for giving all the appearances of being a rambling drunk, so at odds was what he was saying with the common sense of the moment:

> Doc: ...but in the future, we don't need horses. We have horseless carriages called auto-mo-biles.
> An Old Timer chuckles.
> Old Timer: If everybody's got one of these automo-whatsits, does anybody walk or run anymore?
> Doc: Of course they run. But for recreation, for fun.
> Old Timer: Run for fun? Ha-ha, what the **** kind of fun is that?
> Another Old Timer laughs hysterically.
>
> *(Moviepedia, 2023b)*

There again, but with a verbal exchange, the director signals to the spectator the temporal distance, which, as the ones above, is also a cultural one. And yet, one that the spectator effortlessly grasps as for him or her automobiles are as omnipresent as animal-drawn vehicles are not, at best remnants of a bygone era. It is because the spectator has an "immediate understanding" of his or her familiar setting that he or she decodes the film and, thus, navigates the fictional space-time, orienting him or herself with the help of deictic, textual or iconic hints.

Apart from a diversity of superficial elements aimed at establishing the verisimilitude of the 1955 setting from cars along sidewalks to an altercation in a reconstituted *diner*, nothing in the hero's attitude or interactions betrays a temporal distance. He acts, for lack of a better word, *normally*, and the same goes for "The Terminator", even though he is written as brutal. How do we betray our difference? How do we betray that we come from elsewhere – or in this case, *elsewhen*, in a specific social and cultural setting? With our actions, attitude, behaviour, accent, language, and so on. A diversity of minute details with which members of a given group, community and society recognise each other and assert their identity or recognise the others through their differences. In short, to paraphrase Elias (1991, pp. 156–157), they recognise each other within regimes of interdependencies and common rules which binds them together.

These films spread an atemporal representation of common sense which imposes itself to the spectator: it presents a past – our present – subjugated by the future in *The Terminator*, and a future – our present – emancipating the past and revealing the unsuspected potentialities of its denizens in *Back to the Future*. In all three, it is the relationship with the present which imposes itself.

Of course, this does not mean these films fail to distinguish the past and present: the spectators grasp from the very outset that the plot revolves around this temporal opposition, although the story largely takes place in the past. However, to reach their goal – eliminate "Sarah Connor" for "The Terminator", ensure that his parents fall in love for "Marty McFly" to ensure his own existence as much in 1985 as in 1955 – the heroes must at any one time be in control of the situations they encounter through their ability to spontaneously mobilise knowledges and know-hows to overcome the obstacles to achieving their goal. It is imperative that the spectator subscribes to this seamless transposition of abilities across time periods, although he or she knows that to drive a horse-drawn carriage of the past or an automobile of the present, one must have knowledge, skills, control and reflexes.

These films thus play a part in the despoiling of the past of its historical reality. It could be objected that the spectator, familiar with special effects and communication strategies, knows how to suspend his or her disbelief. However, in the footsteps of Davallon (1999), we must distinguish between the film as a cultural object and its symbolic operativity. The former refers to the communication strategies at play: characters, plot, effects, etc.; while the latter refers to the nature of the relation established between the spectator watching the film and the world represented by the film. In other words, the symbolic operativity of the film, as for any media, resides in its "ability to organise social life" (Davallon, 1992, p. 103). In our case, the social discourse spread by the film, conflating past and future, participates in the renewal of the regime of historicity prevalent until the mid-20th century.

A regime now in crisis! *The Terminator* and *Back to the Future* are not the cause of the rise of presentism, but did play a part in the deep movement of reconfiguration of the temporality of our modernity. According to Hartog (2012), the last third of the 20th century saw "the largest of expansion of the category of the present: massive, pervasive, omnipresent, having no other horizon but itself, reconstructing daily the past and future it requires. A present already outdated even before having been fully realised" (p. 248). This centring on the present, manifest since the 1980s, has since further solidified as the new wave of movies showcasing multiverses, which characters moving between synchronous universes, bears witness to (*Spider-man: Across the Spider-verse*, 2023, directed by Joaquim Dos Santos, Kemp Powers and Justin K. Thompson).

In fine, the social mediation instituted by these films, concerns the collective conception of time and, thus, eases the adjustment, however minute it may be, of common sense to a new regime of historicity because the mediation operated by the media is not limited to "techniques of communications", nor, to restate it, is limited to abilities mobilised when needed. As institutions, the media "manage diffusion and organise visibility in the [social] space" (Quéré, 1991, p. 21). They publicise discourses, and, in the films analysed, they provoke encounters with temporality under specific conditions. However, the spectator is also affected by the other media to which he or she is exposed, other media which deploy other forms of mediation in the social space.

As such, any one film has little effect, yet it can resonate with, superimpose itself on or even orient the spectator towards other mediations. In other words, the media act in the social sphere and slowly affect what we have called the "intermediate level" of common sense. Ultimately, the very normative collective expectations linked to the regime of historicity will be transformed; and it is according to this interiorised regime that individual behaviours, in any circumstance, are judged intelligible or not. Thus, at this level of intersubjective signification, common sense makes it possible for individuals to "recognise one another" (Habermas, 1988, p. 367) at a second level, more abstract and more fundamental than that of shared abilities.

To conclude, this is why these films, by endowing their characters with abilities transferable from one time period to another perpetuate the representation of an historical common sense, equally valid today, yesterday and tomorrow. As it has long demonstrated that the media, including films, are powerful vectors of representations, we can wonder whether AI is not being developed with this mindset. Paraphrasing Barthes (1957), we suggest that common sense, for films, for many and probably for AI, does not refer to something concrete, and even less to an infinity of abilities or competencies that may be mobilised if circumstances require, but rather acts as a "mode of signification"; as a "form" (p. 215), i.e., as something which may be endowed with content, that of our present extended as much to the past as to the future. Common sense thus is a floating or open signifier without a unitary meaning that provides continuity in change at different speeds and allows for sense-making and action framing when the contents are shifting. This opaqueness is far from being a deficiency; to the contrary, it opens up possibilities for absorbing new meanings, and AI is part of that conversation.

Note

1. In *the Terminator*, Arnold Schwarzenegger plays a humanoid robot sent from the future (2029) to assassinate in 1984, forty-five years prior, the mother ("Sarah Conor" played by Linda Hamilton) of the future leader of the resistance against the machines. In *Back to the Future*, "Marty McFly" (played by Michael J. Fox) accidentally flees to 1955 to escape the fate of "Emmet Doc Brown", alias "Doc" (played by Christopher Lloyd), the inventor of a time-travelling Delorean, presumably killed off-camera moments before by terrorists; yet, it is thanks to this fortuitous travel back in time that "Doc" would survive his ordeal as the movie ends by a return to the present. In *Back to the Future III*,

"Marty" deliberately travels to the past to save "Doc" stranded in 1885 and about to get murdered, as attested by the epitaph on his tombstone, fortuitously discovered in 1955 in the abandoned Hill Valley cemetery. The assassination attempt is foiled, yet, because "Doc" met his soulmate, he decided to stay. In the instants following his return to 1985, "Marty" meets "Doc", temporarily back during another voyage in time, who gives him the photograph taken in 1885 for which they both posed.

Bibliography

Abric, J.-C. (1994). L'organisation interne des représentations sociales: Système central et système périphérique. In G. Christian (Ed.), *Textes de base en sciences sociales* (pp. 73–84). Delachaux et Niestlé.Andler, D. (2023). *Intelligence artificielle, intelligence humaine: La double énigme*. Gallimard.

Ansart, P. (1999). Valeur. In A. Akoun & P. Ansart (Eds.), *Dictionnaire de sociologie* (pp. 559–560). Le Robert, Seuil.

Bachelard, G. (2002). *The formation of the scientific mind*. Clinamen Press.

Barthes, R. (1957). *Mythodologies*. Éditions du Seuil.

Bauer, M. W., & Gaskell, G. (2008). Social representation theory: A progressive research programme in social psychology. *Journal for the Theory of Social Behaviour, 38*(4), 335–353.

Boltanski, L., & Thévenot, L. (1991). *De la justification: Les économies de la grandeur*. Gallimard.

Boyer, R. (2015). *Les vikings*. Perrin.

Braudel, F. (1987). Histoire et sciences sociales: La longue durée. *Réseaux, 5*(27), 7–37.

Chazel, F. (1999). Norme. In A. Akoun & P. Ansart (Eds.), *Dictionnaire de sociologie* (pp. 365–366). Le Robert, Seuil.

Davallon, J. (1992). Le musée est-il un média? *Publics et Musées, 2*, 99–123. http://doi.org/10.3406/pumus.1992.1017

Davallon, J. (1999). *L'exposition à l'œuvre*. L'Harmattan.

Eldredge, N., & Gould, S. J. (1972). Punctuated equilibria: An alternative to phyletic gradualism. In T. J. M. Schopf (Ed.), *Models in paleobiology* (pp. 82–115). Freeman Cooper.

Elias, N. (1985). *La société de cour*. Flammarion.

Elias, N. (1991). *Qu'est-ce que la sociologie*. Éditions de l'Aube.

Elias, N. (2005). *The court society*. University of Chicago Press.

Goody, J. (2012). *L'évolution de la famille et du mariage en Europe*. Armand Colin.

Gunning, D. (2018). Machine common sense concept paper. Cornell University. https://arxiv.org/abs/1810.07528

Habermas, J. (1988). *Le discours philosophique de la modernité*. Gallimard.

Hartog, J. (2012). *Régimes d'historicité: Présentisme et expérience du temps*. Seuil.

Hooper-Greenhill, E. (1992). *Museums and the shaping of knowledge*. Routledge.

Kirby, D. A. (2008). Hollywood knowledge: Communication between scientific and entertainment cultures. In D. Cheng, M. Claessens, T. Gascoigne, J. Metcalfe, B. Schiele, & S. Shi (Eds.), *Communicating science in social contexts* (pp. 165–180). Springer.

Kirby, D. A., & Ockert, I. (2021). Science and technology in film: Themes and representations. In M. Bucchi & B. Trench (Eds.), *Routledge handbook of public communication of science and technology* (3rd ed., pp. 77–96). Routledge.

Luckmann, T. (1987). Some thought on common sense and science. In F. van Holthoon & D. R. Olson (Eds.), *Common sense: The foundations for social science* (pp. 179–197). University Press of America,

Moscovici, S. (1961). *La psychoanalyse, son image et son public*. Presses Universitaires de France.

Moscovici, S. (2008). *Psychoanalysis: Its image and its public*. Polity.

Moscovici, S., & Hewstone, M. (1984). De la science au sens commun. In S. Moscovici (Ed.), *Psychologie sociale* (pp. 539–566). Presses Universitaires de France.

Moscovici, S., & Vignaux, G. (1994). Le concept de thêmata. In C. Guimelli (Ed.), *Textes de base en sciences sociales* (pp. 25–72). Delachaux et Niestlé.

Moviepedia. (2023a). Retrieved October 20, 2023, from https://movies.fandom.com/wiki/Back_to_the_Future/Transcript

Moviepedia. (2023b). Retrieved October 20, 2023, from https://movies.fandom.com/wiki/Back_to_the_Future_Part_III/Transcript

O'Brien, M., & Fingerhut, H. (2023, September 9). *Artificial intelligence technology behind ChatGPT was built in Iowa – with a lot of water*. Associated Press. https://apnews.com/article/chatgpt-gpt4-iowa-ai-water-consumption-microsoft-f551fde98083d17a7e8d904f8be822c4

Quéré, L. (1991). Communication sociale: Les effets du d'un changement de paradigm. *Réseaux: Communication, Technologie, Société, 34*, 19–46.

Rosa, H. (2010). *Accélération*. La Découverte.

Schiele, B., & Bauer, M. W. (2023). Looking forward: The Graoullys – Blind spots in science communication. In M. W. Bauer & B. Schiele (Eds.), *Science communication: Taking a step back to move forward* (pp. 472–480). CNRS Éditions.

Turkle, S. (1984). *The second self: Computers and the human spirit*. Simon & Schuster.

Wolf, M. (2001). L'analyse de la réception et la recherche sur les medias. *Hermès, 11–12*, 275–279. CNRS Éditions.

AUTHOR INDEX

SUBJECT INDEX

Page numbers in **bold** indicate tables, while page numbers in *italics* indicate figures.

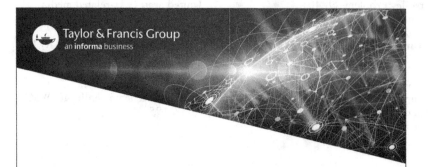

Printed in the United States
by Baker & Taylor Publisher Services